SCHOOL LEADERSHIP *that works*

FROM RESEARCH TO RESULTS

ROBERT J.
MARZANO

TIMOTHY
WATERS

BRIAN A.
MCNULTY

Association for Supervision and
Curriculum Development
Alexandria, Virginia USA

Mid-continent Research for
Education and Learning
Aurora, Colorado USA

ASCD®

Association for Supervision and Curriculum Development
1703 N. Beauregard St. • Alexandria, VA 22311-1714 USA
Telephone: 800-933-2723 or 703-578-9600 • Fax: 703-575-5400
Web site: www.ascd.org • E-mail: member@ascd.org
Author guidelines: www.ascd.org/write

Mid-continent Research for Education and Learning
2550 S. Parker Road, Suite 500 • Aurora, CO 80014-1678 USA
Telephone: 303-337-0990 • Fax: 303-337-3005
Web site: www.mcrel.org • E-mail: info@mcrel.org

ASCD Staff: Gene R. Carter, *Executive Director;* Nancy Modrak, *Director of Publishing;* Julie Houtz, *Director of Book Editing & Production;* Darcie Russell, *Project Manager;* Reece Quiñones, *Senior Graphic Designer;* Barton Matheson Willse & Worthington, *Typesetter;* Eric Coyle, *Production Specialist*

Copyright © 2005 by Mid-continent Research for Education and Learning (McREL). All rights reserved. No part of this publication may be reproduced or transmitted in any form or by any means, electronic or mechanical, including photocopy, recording, or any information storage and retrieval system, without permission from McREL.

Printed in the United States of America. Cover art copyright © 2005 by ASCD. ASCD publications present a variety of viewpoints. The views expressed or implied in this book should not be interpreted as official positions of the Association.

All Web links in this book are correct as of the publication date below but may have become inactive or otherwise modified since that time. If you notice a deactivated or changed link, please e-mail books@ascd.org with the words "Link Update" in the subject line. In your message, please specify the Web link, the book title, and the page number on which the link appears.

ASCD Member Book, No. FY06-01 (Sept. 2005, PCR). ASCD Member Books mail to Premium (P), Comprehensive (C), and Regular (R) members on this schedule: Jan., PC; Feb., P; Apr., PCR; May, P; July, PC; Aug., P; Sept., PCR; Nov., PC; Dec., P.

Paperback ISBN: 1-4166-0227-5 • ASCD product #105125
e-books: retail PDF ISBN: 1-4166-0314-X • netLibrary ISBN 1-4166-0312-3 • ebrary ISBN 1-4166-0313-1

Quantity discounts for the paperback book: 10–49 copies, 10%; 50+ copies, 15%; for 500 or more copies, call 800-933-2723, ext. 5634, or 703-575-5634.

Library of Congress Cataloging-in-Publication Data
Marzano, Robert J.
   School leadership that works : from research to results / Robert J. Marzano, Timothy
      Waters, Brian A. McNulty.
      p. cm.
   Includes bibliographical references and index.
   ISBN 1-4166-0227-5 (alk. paper)
   1. School management and organization.   2. Educational leadership.   I. Waters, Timothy,
1948–   II. McNulty, Brian A., 1948–   III. Title.

LB2805.M2845 2005
371.2—dc22   2005011789

12 11 10 09 08 07 06 05   12 11 10 9 8 7 6 5 4 3 2 1

School Leadership That Works

From Research to Results

Preface v

Part 1: The Research Base

1 In Search of School Leadership 3
2 Some Theories and Theorists on Leadership 13
3 The Meta-Analysis 28

Part 2: Practical Applications

4 The 21 Responsibilities of the School Leader 41
5 Two Types of Change 65
6 Doing the Right Work 76
7 A Plan for Effective School Leadership 98

Epilogue 123
Technical Notes 124
Appendix A: Reports Used in the Meta-Analysis 171
Appendix B: Cotton's 25 Leadership Practices and the 21 Responsibilities 178
References 180
Index 188
About the Authors 193

Preface

Unlike many other books about school leadership, this one blends practical advice and research. Most books on the topic address one or the other, but not both. We believe that, at this particular time in the history of K–12 education in the United States, a book like this one is not only useful but also necessary because calls for research-based practices have never been as strong as they are now. Similarly, calls for school leadership that translates into enhanced student achievement have never been as strong. To answer both calls we conducted a meta-analysis of the research on school leadership spanning 35 years and found studies from 1978 to 2001 that met our selection criteria. Additionally, we conducted a factor analysis of a survey derived from our meta-analysis and administered to more than 650 building principals.

To answer those who rightfully will want to know the specifics of our methodology and the assumptions underlying our conclusions, we provide what we consider to be all requisite technical information in a series of notes beginning on page 124. To provide practical guidance for those who face the daily challenges of leading a school, we translate all of our findings into specific recommendations for practice. We believe that our advice will help those interested in our research methodology better understand our purpose and focus. Alternatively, we believe that our discussion of the research will help those interested in our practical advice understand the solid research base underlying our recommendations.

For those who want to more closely examine their own leadership challenges, we offer McREL's Balanced Leadership Profile 360™, a subscription-based online survey and professional development tool based on the 21 principal leadership responsibilities described in this book. You may access the principal self-assessment version of the survey and receive immediate feedback on your fulfillment of the 21 leadership responsibilities as they apply to a specific school or districtwide improvement initiative that you identify. The Balanced Leadership Profile 360™ also provides principals with a variety of online professional development resources and tools associated with the 21 leadership responsibilities and change leadership.

McREL is pleased to offer you a discount subscription to the survey. To access the discount, please visit www.mcrel.org, click Balanced Leadership Profile 360™, and enter the registration code **reader.** Then follow the directions. If you have questions concerning the survey, please call McREL at 800-781-0156.

Part 1

The Research Base

1

In Search of School Leadership

Each school day more than 53.6 million students (National Center for Education Statistics, 2002b) walk into more than 94,000 K–12 schools (National Center for Education Statistics, 2002a) in the hopes that the 13 years of schooling they will experience will dramatically enhance their chances of success in the modern world. Indeed, evidence of income in 2001 supports these hopes. According to the U.S. Census Bureau (March 2002), the earning potential (that is, the median income) of a student who graduates from high school is $19,900, compared with $11,864 for a student who does not. If the high school graduate completes college, that earning potential increases to $37,203. A master's degree increases the figure to $49,324. A doctorate raises annual income to $63,952, and with a professional licensure, it reaches $71,606. School, then, can be the door to advancement—at least financial advancement—in our complex society. For a particular school to be the launchpad to the levels of success sought by students, however, it must operate effectively.

Whether a school operates effectively or not increases or decreases a student's chances of academic success. Marzano (2003) has shown that students in effective schools as opposed to ineffective schools have a 44 percent difference in their expected passing rate on a test that has a typical passing rate of 50 percent. To illustrate, consider two schools—School A and School B. In terms of how they are run, School A is effective and School B is ineffective. (In Chapter 6 we consider the specific characteristics of effective versus ineffective schools.) Now assume that the two schools have a typical population of students—some with many advantages in their home environment and background experiences; some with few if any advantages; most somewhere in the middle. If students in both schools take a test that has a typical passing rate of 50 percent, we would expect 72 percent of the students in the effective school to pass the test and only 28 percent in the ineffective school to pass—a difference of 44 percent. This is depicted in Figure 1.1. (For an explanation of this scenario, see Technical Note 1 on p. 124.)

Although the difference in expected student achievement in "effective" versus "ineffective" schools is dramatic, the difference is even greater when we contrast "highly effective" schools with "highly ineffective" schools—more specifically, the top 1 percent of schools with the bottom 1 percent. This scenario produces a difference in passing rates of 70 percent. In the top 1 percent of schools we would expect 85 percent of students to pass a test that has a typical passing rate of 50 percent; in the bottom 1 percent of schools we would expect only 15 percent to pass that same test. (See Technical Note 2 on p. 129 for a more detailed explanation.)

FIGURE 1.1
Percentage of Students Expected to Pass or Fail a Test in Effective Versus Ineffective Schools

	Expected Pass Rate	Expected Fail Rate
Effective School (A)	72%	28%
Ineffective School (B)	28%	72%

The central question addressed in this book is this: To what extent does leadership play a role in whether a school is effective or ineffective? That is, How much of a school's impact on student achievement is due to the leadership displayed in that school? We begin with some past and current beliefs about leadership.

Past and Current Beliefs About Leadership

If we consider the traditions and beliefs surrounding leadership, we can easily make a case that leadership is vital to the effectiveness of a school. In fact, for centuries people have assumed that leadership is critical to the success of any institution or endeavor.

The concept of leadership dates back to antiquity. According to Bass (1981), the study of leadership is an ancient art. Discussions of leadership appear in the works of Plato, Caesar, and Plutarch. Additionally, leadership is a robust concept that "occurs universally among all people regardless of culture, whether they are isolated Indian villagers, Eurasian steppe nomads, or Polynesian fisher folk" (p. 5).

Theories of leadership abound. They include approaches such as the "great-man" theory, which suggests that, for example, without Moses the Jewish nation would have remained in Egypt and without Churchill the British would have acquiesced to the Germans in 1940; trait theories, which contend that leaders are endowed with superior qualities that differentiate them from followers; and environmental theories, which assert that leaders emerge as a result of time, place, and circumstance. Regardless of the theory used to explain it, leadership has been intimately linked to the effective functioning of complex organizations throughout the centuries.

The traditions and beliefs about leadership in schools are no different from those regarding leadership in other institutions. Leadership is considered to be vital to the successful functioning of many aspects of a school. To illustrate, the list below depicts only a few of the aspects of schooling that have been linked to leadership in a school building:

- Whether a school has a clear mission and goals (Bamburg & Andrews, 1990; Duke, 1982)
- The overall climate of the school and the climate in individual classrooms (Brookover, Beady, Flood, Schweitzer, & Wisenbaker, 1979; Brookover et al., 1978; Brookover & Lezotte, 1979; Griffith, 2000; Villani, 1996)
- The attitudes of teachers (Brookover & Lezotte, 1979; Oakes, 1989; Purkey & Smith, 1983; Rutter, Maughan, Mortimore, Ouston, & Smith, 1979)
- The classroom practices of teachers (Brookover et al., 1978; Brookover & Lezotte, 1979; McDill, Rigsby, & Meyers, 1969; Miller & Sayre, 1986)
- The organization of curriculum and instruction (Bossert, Dwyer, Rowan, & Lee, 1982; Cohen & Miller, 1980; Eberts & Stone, 1988; Glasman & Binianimov, 1981; Oakes, 1989)
- Students' opportunity to learn (Duke & Canady, 1991; Dwyer, 1986; Murphy & Hallinger, 1989)

Given the perceived importance of leadership, it is no wonder that an effective principal is thought to be a necessary precondition for an effective school. To illustrate, a 1977 U.S. Senate Committee Report on Equal Educational Opportunity (U.S. Congress, 1970) identified the principal as the single most influential person in a school:

> In many ways the school principal is the most important and influential individual in any school. He or she is the person responsible for all activities that occur in and around the school building. It is the principal's leadership that sets the tone of the school, the climate for teaching, the level of professionalism and morale of teachers, and the degree of concern for what students may or may not become. The principal

is the main link between the community and the school, and the way he or she performs in this capacity largely determines the attitudes of parents and students about the school. If a school is a vibrant, innovative, child-centered place, if it has a reputation for excellence in teaching, if students are performing to the best of their ability, one can almost always point to the principal's leadership as the key to success. (p. 56)

Given the perceived importance of leadership in schools and the central role of the principal in that leadership, one might assume that suggestions regarding leadership practice in schools are based on a clear, well-articulated body of research spanning decades. Unfortunately, this assumption is incorrect for at least two reasons. First, far less research on school leadership has been done than one might expect. To illustrate, in a review of the quantitative research from 1980 to 1995, Hallinger and Heck (1996) identified only 40 studies that address the relationship between school leadership and student academic achievement. In our analysis of the research over the last 35 years, we found more than 5,000 articles and studies that address the topic of leadership in schools, but only 69 that actually examine the quantitative relationship between building leadership and the academic achievement of students. (We discuss our study in depth in Chapter 3.) In spite of the relative paucity of empirical studies on school leadership, books recommending leadership practices for educational administrators abound.

Second, the research that has been done on school leadership is quite equivocal, or at least is perceived as such. For example, some assert that it provides little specific guidance as to effective practices in school leadership. As Donmoyer (1985) explains:

> Recent studies of schools invariably identify the principal's leadership as a significant factor in a school's success. Unfortunately these studies provide only limited insight into how principals contribute to their school's achievements. (p. 31)

Others assert that the research does not even support the notion that school leadership has an identifiable effect on student achievement. For example, a recent synthesis of the research on school leadership concluded that statistically there is almost no relationship between school leadership and student achievement. Specifically, as a result of their analyses of 37 studies conducted internationally on the impact of building leadership on student achievement, Witziers, Bosker, and Kruger (2003) report almost no direct relationship. We deal with this particular study in Chapters 2 and 3. However, taken at face value, the findings from this study would lead one to conclude that little effort should be put into developing leaders at the school building level.

A Different Perspective

The conclusions we offer in this book stand in sharp contrast to those suggesting that the research on school leadership provides no guidance as to specific leadership behaviors and to those suggesting that school leadership has no discernable direct effect on student achievement. Our basic claim is that the research over the last 35 years provides strong guidance on specific leadership behaviors for school administrators and that those behaviors have well-documented effects on student achievement. A logical question is, How can we make such claims in light of the previous statements regarding the research (or lack thereof) on school leadership? The answer lies partially in the research process we employed—a methodology referred to as meta-analysis—which is specifically designed for synthesis efforts such as ours.

The Nature and Function of Meta-Analysis

There have been a number of calls for a new paradigm of research in educational leadership (see Heck & Hallinger, 1999; Hill & Guthrie, 1999). These calls come at a time when the methodology of meta-analysis has provided impressive advances in the art and science of synthesizing studies within a given domain.

The term *meta-analysis* refers to an array of techniques for synthesizing a vast amount of research quantitatively. The technique was formally developed and made popular by Gene Glass and his colleagues in the early 1970s (see Glass, 1976; Glass, McGaw, & Smith, 1981). Since then, individuals in a variety of fields have used meta-analysis to construct generalizations that were previously unavailable (see Hunt, 1997). For example, in his book *How Science Takes Stock: The Story of Meta-Analysis,* Hunt provides compelling illustrations of the successful use of meta-analysis in medicine, psychology, criminology, and other fields.

In simple terms, meta-analysis allows researchers to form statistically based generalizations regarding the research within a given field. We discuss some of the more technical aspects of meta-analysis in Technical Note 3 (see p. 130). Here we briefly consider some aspects of meta-analysis that are particularly important to our assertions about the research on school leadership and our reasons for using this particular methodology.

At least two questions might come to mind about our decision to use meta-analysis. First, why did we choose to synthesize the research of others as opposed to conducting a study of our own? That is, why didn't we study the relationship between school leadership and student achievement by examining a number of high- and low-performing schools and the leadership in those schools instead of examining the research of others? The answer is that any study we would have conducted, no matter how well constructed, would have contained "uncontrolled error" influencing its outcome.

As an example, assume we had been able to identify 10 principals who were strong leaders and 10 principals who were weak leaders and randomly assign them to serve for three years in 20 schools with about the same average academic achievement. In educational circles, this type of study would be considered strong. In fact, the No Child Left Behind Act of 2001, passed by an overwhelming margin in both houses of Congress in December 2001 and signed into law on Jan. 8, 2002, recommends the use of research designs (like our hypothetical example) that employ random assignment to experimental and control groups as a form of what it refers to as "scientifically based research" (see Goodwin, Arens, Barley, & Williams, 2002). However, educators quickly note that using a design like our hypothetical example is not only impractical from a resource perspective (for example, how can you find 20 principals willing to work for three years in a school to which they have been assigned?), but unacceptable from an ethical perspective (how can you in good conscience assign 10 principals to schools knowing that they are weak leaders?). Nevertheless, for illustrative purposes, let's assume that we employed this rather "tight" empirical design. Even with this tight level of control, the findings from the study might be strongly influenced by uncontrolled factors, such as substantive differences in the background and experience of the teachers and in the family circumstances of the students in the various schools. Such factors are sometimes referred to as "sampling error."

In practice, it is impossible to control all the error that might creep into a study. This is precisely why researchers assign a probability statement to their findings. That is, when a researcher reports that her findings are significant at the .05 level, she is saying that her findings could occur 5 times in 100 or less if they are a function of some type of uncontrolled error. If she reports that her findings are significant at the .01 level, she is saying that there is even less of a chance—1 in 100 or less—that her findings are a function of this uncontrolled error. Meta-analysis helps control for this error by examining findings across many studies. Doing this tends to cancel out much of that uncontrolled error. Whereas the findings in one study might be influenced positively by the background of the teachers, let's say, another study might be influenced negatively by this same factor. Across many studies the effect of this factor tends to cancel out.

The second question our use of meta-analysis might prompt is, Why did we use a quantitative approach to synthesis research as opposed to the more traditional approach others have used (for example, Cotton, 2003)? Indeed, every doctoral dissertation and every master's thesis in education attempts to include a comprehensive review of the research relative to its specific research topic. However, these reviews typically use what is referred to as a narrative approach (see Glass, 1976; Glass, McGaw, & Smith, 1981; Rosenthal, 1991; Rosenthal & Rubin, 1982). With a narrative approach, a researcher attempts to logically summarize the findings from a collection of studies on a topic by looking for patterns in those studies. Unfortunately, the narrative approach is highly susceptible to erroneous conclusions. To illustrate, in a study of the quality of narrative reviews, Jackson (1978, 1980) found the following:

- Reviewers tended to focus on only part of the full set of studies they reviewed.
- Reviewers commonly used crude and misleading representations of the findings of the studies.
- Reviewers usually reported so little about their method of analysis that no judgment could be made about the validity of their conclusions.
- Reviewers commonly failed to consider the methods used in the studies they reviewed.

To examine the difference between reviewing research using a narrative approach versus a meta-analytic approach, Cooper and Rosenthal (1980) conducted a study in which 40 graduate students were randomly split into two groups. Both groups were asked to examine the same seven studies on gender differences in persistence. Their basic task was to determine whether the seven studies supported the hypothesis that gender is related to persistence. One group used the narrative approach and the other used a rudimentary form of meta-analysis. What the two groups were not told was that, statistically, the seven studies considered as a set supported the hypothesis that gender and persistence are related. The vast majority of graduate students in the narrative group incorrectly concluded that the studies did not support this hypothesis, whereas the vast majority of graduate students in the meta-analysis group correctly concluded that the studies did support the hypothesis. Discussing this study, Glass, McGaw, and Smith (1981) note that these are "strikingly different conclusions for equivalent groups trying to integrate only seven studies" (p. 17). They go on to hypothesize that conclusions based on narrative reviews of vast amounts of research are probably strongly biased by the conventional wisdom to which the synthesizer subscribes.

In summary, we chose to synthesize the research on leadership using a quantitative, meta-analytic approach because it provided the most objective means to answer the question, What does the research tell us about school leadership?

Our Basic Findings

After examining 69 studies involving 2,802 schools, approximately 1.4 million students, and 14,000 teachers, we computed the correlation between the leadership behavior of the principal in the school and the average academic achievement of students in the school to be .25. We discuss the meaning of this correlation in depth in Chapter 3; however, we briefly consider it here. We should first caution that reducing the findings of a meta-analysis, particularly one that claims to be as comprehensive as ours, to a single correlation is at best an oversimplification of the findings. In fact, Glass, commonly considered to be the founder of modern-day meta-analysis, warns against this practice (Robinson, 2004). With this caution noted, we consider the average correlation found in our meta-analysis because it is still the most commonly used currency for discussing meta-analytic findings in educational research.

To interpret the .25 correlation, assume that a principal is hired into a district and assigned to a school that is at the 50th percentile in the average achievement of its students. (See Technical Note 1, p. 124, for further explanation.) Also assume that the principal is at the 50th percentile in leadership ability. We might say that we have an average principal in an average school.

Now assume that the principal stays in the school for a few years. Our .25 correlation tells us that over time we would predict the average achievement of the school to remain at the 50th percentile. But now let's increase the principal's leadership ability by one standard deviation—from the 50th percentile to the 84th percentile. This increase might have occurred as a result of the principal's attendance at an extended set of courses or seminars on leadership offered in the district. Our correlation of .25 indicates that over time we would predict the average achievement of the school to rise to the 60th percentile. This increase is depicted in Figure 1.2. In terms of the average achievement of students in the school, this is substantial.

To further examine the interpretation of the .25 correlation, let's increase the principal's leadership ability even more—from the 50th percentile to the 99th percentile. In other words, the leadership training the principal attends is so powerful that it places the principal at the top percentile in leadership behavior. Our correlation of .25 indicates that over time we would predict the average student achievement of the school to rise to the 72nd percentile. This is depicted in Figure 1.3.

Taken at face value, these findings are compelling. A highly effective school leader can have a dramatic influence on the overall academic achievement of students. Most teachers, parents, and students would be thrilled to see the average performance of their school increase 22 percentile points—even 10 percentile points.

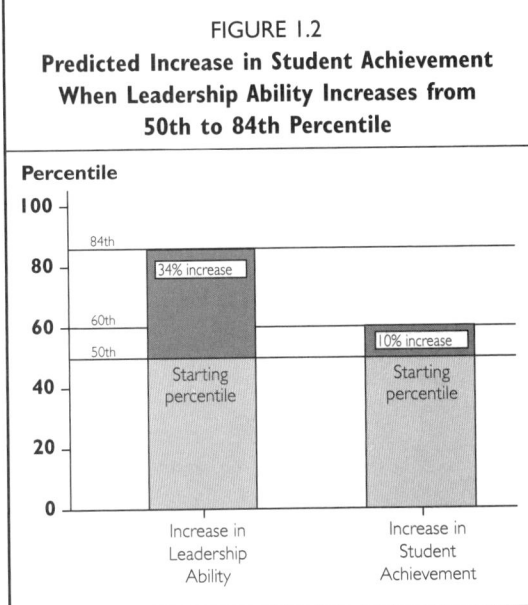

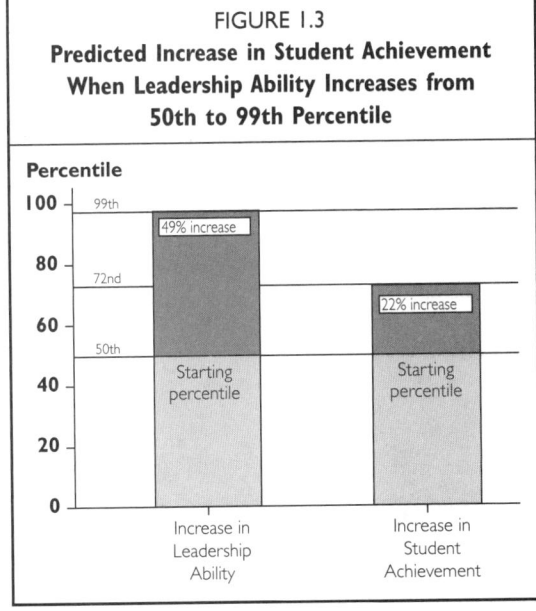

Toward Research-Based Principles of School Leadership

Our meta-analysis was designed to determine what 35 years of research tells us about school leadership. We report our findings in Chapter 3. However, we didn't stop with the findings. Rather, we wove those findings into what we consider to be perhaps the most rigorous and comprehensive set of principles regarding school leadership to date. The reader should note that we purposely avoid the use of the word *theory* in describing our conclusions. Anderson (1983) explains that a theory is a precise deductive system that allows one to accurately predict behavior given knowledge of the variables within the theory. Principles are general rules for behavior but do not constitute a precise predictive system. We offer principles as opposed to a theory in accordance with the most current thinking in educational research. Again, to quote Glass in his article marking the 25th anniversary of meta-analysis, "We need to stop thinking of ourselves as scientists listing grand theories, and face the fact that we are technicians collecting and collating information" (2000, p. 12). Glass credits Meehl (1978) as first pointing out that the "soft social sciences" such as education simply cannot conceive, test, and advance theories in the same manner as the hard sciences such as physics, chemistry, medicine, and the like. This is not to say that educators should not use the results of studies to develop general rules or principles of behavior to guide them in specific situations. This is precisely what we have attempted to do.

Summary and Conclusions

Leadership has long been perceived to be important to the effective functioning of organizations in general and, more recently, of schools in particular. However, some researchers and theorists assert that at best the research on school leadership is equivocal and at worst demonstrates that leadership has no effect on student achievement. In contrast, our meta-analysis of 35 years of research indicates that school leadership has a substantial effect on student achievement and provides guidance for experienced and aspiring administrators alike.

2
Some Theories and Theorists on Leadership

Organizing the research on school leadership into a set of principles that current and future school leaders can use to guide their behavior obviously requires that we stand on the shoulders of those who have made similar efforts. In this chapter we briefly review some of the more prominent theories and theorists on leadership. In subsequent chapters you will find that much of what we found in our meta-analysis strongly supports the major elements of these theories and theorists.

Some Prominent Theories

Many theories of leadership have been influential in guiding school leaders. Here we examine a few of the theories that were foundational to our analysis of the research.

Transformational and Transactional Leadership

Two terms that are bandied about in discussions of leadership in business and education are *transformational leadership* and *transactional leadership*. Both terms have their roots in the work of James Burns, who is generally considered the founder of modern leadership theory. Working primarily in the area of politics, Burns (1978) first drafted a robust and compelling definition of leadership in general:

> I define leadership as leaders inducing followers to act for certain goals that represent the values and the motivation—the wants and the needs, the aspirations and expectations—of both leaders and followers. And the genius of leadership lies in the manner in which leaders see and act on their own and their followers' values and motivations. (p. 19)

Within his general definition, Burns made a fundamental distinction between two types of leadership: *transactional* and *transformational* (which he referred to as "transforming"). In general terms, transactional leadership is defined as trading one thing for another (quid pro quo), whereas transformational leadership is more focused on change.

In more specific terms, Bass and Avolio (1994) describe three forms of transactional leadership: *management-by-exception-passive, management-by-exception-active,* and *constructive transactional.* Sosik and Dionne (1997) explain that management-by-exception-passive involves setting standards but waiting for major problems to occur before exerting leadership behavior. Followers of this leadership style typically believe that their job is to maintain the status quo. Leaders who demonstrate management-by-exception-active pay attention to issues that arise, set standards, and carefully monitor behavior. In fact, they are so aggressive in their management behavior that followers of this leadership style believe that they should not take risks or demonstrate initiative. Constructive transactional leadership is the most effective and active of the transactional leadership styles. This type of transactional leader sets goals, clarifies desired outcomes, exchanges rewards and recognition for accomplishments, suggests or consults, provides feedback, and gives employees praise when it is deserved. The distinguishing feature of this transactional leadership style is that followers are invited into the management process more than is the case with the other two styles. Followers generally react by focusing on and achieving expected performance goals.

Transformational leadership is the favored style of leadership given that it is assumed to produce results beyond expectations (Bass, 1985; Burns, 1978). According to Burns (1978), transformational leaders form "a relationship of mutual stimulation and elevation that converts followers into leaders and may convert leaders into moral agents" (p. 4). As articulated by Bass (1985), four factors characterize the behavior of transformational leaders: individual consideration, intellectual stimulation, inspirational motivation, and idealized influence. These are referred to as the "Four I's" of transformational leadership (Sosik & Dionne, 1997). Individual consideration is characterized by giving "personal attention to members who seem neglected" (Bass, 1990, p. 218). Intellectual stimulation is characterized by enabling "followers to think of old problems in new ways" (Bass, 1990, p. 218). Inspirational motivation is characterized by communicating "high performance expectations" (Bass, 1990, p. 218) through the projection of a powerful, confident, dynamic presence that invigorates followers. Finally, idealized influence is characterized by modeling behavior through exemplary personal achievements, character, and behavior.

Transformational Leadership in Education

Building on the work of Burns (1978), Bass (1985), and Bass and Avolio (1994), Kenneth Leithwood (1994) developed the transformational model of school leadership. He notes that the Four I's of transformational leadership identified by Bass and Avolio (1994) are necessary skills for school principals if they are to meet the challenges of the 21st century. For example, the school leader must attend to the needs of and provide personal attention to individual staff members, particularly those who seem left out (individual consideration). The effective school administrator must help staff members think of old problems in new ways (intellectual stimulation). Through a powerful and dynamic presence the effective school administrator must communicate high expectations for teachers and students alike (inspirational motivation). Finally, through personal accomplishments and demonstrated character, the effective principal must provide a model for the behavior of teachers (idealized influence).

Total Quality Management

Edward Deming (1986) is generally considered the founder of total quality management (TQM), largely because he provided the framework for post–World War II Japan to restore its manufacturing base and for U.S. firms such as Ford and Xerox to improve the quality of their products and services (Sosik & Dionne, 1997). Although TQM was created for the world of business, it has had a strong influence on leadership practices in education. Central to Deming's conception of TQM are 14 principles that pertain to organizations of all types. Waldman (1993) proposed that Deming's 14 points can be organized into five basic factors that more specifically define the actions of an effective leader: change agency, teamwork, continuous improvement, trust building, and eradication of short-term goals.

Change Agency. Sosik and Dionne (1997) define change agency as the leader's ability to stimulate change in an organization. The leader does so by analyzing the organization's need for change, isolating and eliminating structures and routines that work against change, creating a shared vision and sense of urgency, implanting plans and structures that enable change, and fostering open communication.

Teamwork. One of the distinguishing features of TQM is the importance of teams within an organization. Sosik and Dionne (1997) define teams in the following way:

> Teams consist of two or more individuals with complementary skills who interact with each other toward a common task-oriented purpose. Team members consider themselves to be collectively accountable for the attainment of their goals. Teams are

formed to serve organizational interests within departments, and across departments and divisions. (p. 449)

The effective leader is not only involved in establishing teams, but also sees to their viability by providing necessary resources and support.

Continuous Improvement. This is a concept that is derived from the Japanese term *kaizen,* which means (roughly) the continual and incremental improvement of the critical aspects of the organization by all members of the organization (see Masaaki, 1986). According to Deming (1986), a leader must "invite" continuous improvement into the organization and keep it alive by keeping the goals of the organization up front in the minds of employees and judging the effectiveness of the organization in terms of these goals.

Trust Building. As the term implies, trust building involves creating a climate in which employer and employees perceive the organization as a "win-win" environment (Covey, 1991). Sosik and Dionne (1997) describe trust building as "the process of establishing respect and instilling faith into followers based on leader integrity, honesty, and openness" (p. 450). Leaders establish an atmosphere of trust by their daily actions. Specific actions leaders must exhibit include knowing the concerns of employees, knowing what motivates employees, and knowing the necessary conditions for employees to operate at levels of maximum effectiveness.

Eradication of Short-Term Goals. Deming uses this term to refer to the eradication of the types of goals traditionally set within an MBO (management by objectives) model as articulated by Peter Drucker (1974). Specifically, this means the elimination of goals that are based on quotas, are highly numerical, and are short-term. According to Sosik and Dionne (1997), Deming had a particular disdain for such goals and their emphasis on short-term quantitative results. This is not to say that Deming was averse to specific goals. However, the goals he advocated were focused more on process and the long-term perspective. The effective leader not only helps establish the criteria around which goals are established, but also participates in the goals' design and implementation.

Servant Leadership

The term *servant leadership* first appeared in the leadership literature in the 1970s. It is attributed to Robert Greenleaf (1970, 1977), who believed that effective leadership emerges from a desire to help others. This perspective stands in sharp contrast to those theories (such as transactional leadership) that emphasize control or "overseeing" those within the organization.

Servant leadership also has a unique perspective on the position of the leader within the organization. Instead of occupying a position at the top of a hierarchy, the servant leader is positioned at the center of the organization. This implies that the servant leader is in contact with all aspects of the organization and the individuals within it as opposed to interacting with a few high-level managers who also occupy positions in the upper strata of the hierarchy.

The central dynamic of servant leadership is nurturing those within the organization. Consequently, critical skills of servant leadership include the following:

- Understanding the personal needs of those within the organization
- Healing wounds caused by conflict within the organization
- Being a steward of the resources of the organization
- Developing the skills of those within the organization
- Being an effective listener

Although servant leadership is typically not embraced as a comprehensive theory of leadership as are some other theories (such as TQM), it has become a key component of the thinking of many leadership theorists (see, for example, Covey, 1992; Elmore, 2000; Spillane, Halverson, & Diamond, 2001).

Situational Leadership

The theory of situational leadership is typically associated with the work of Paul Hersey and Kenneth Blanchard (Blanchard, Carew, & Parisi-Carew, 1991; Blanchard & Hersey, 1996; Blanchard, Zigarmi, & Zigarmi, 1985; Hersey, Blanchard, & Johnson, 2001). The basic principle underlying situational leadership is that the leader adapts her leadership behavior to followers' "maturity," based on their willingness and ability to perform a specific task. Four leadership styles match high and low willingness and ability to perform a task:

• When followers are unable and unwilling to perform a given task, the leader directs the followers' actions without much concern for personal relationships. This style is referred to as high task–low relationship focus, or the *"telling" style*.

• When followers are unable but willing to perform the task, the leader interacts with followers in a friendly manner but still provides concrete direction and guidance. This style is referred to as high task–high relationship focus, or the *"participating" style*.

• When followers are able but unwilling to perform the task, the leader does not have to provide much direction or guidance but must persuade followers to engage in the task. This style is referred to as low task–low relationship focus, or the *"selling" style*.

- When followers are able and willing to perform the task, the leader leaves the execution of the task to the followers with little or no interference, basically trusting followers to accomplish the task on their own. This style is referred to as low task–high relationship focus, or the *"delegating" style.*

The effective leader is skilled in all four styles and knows the ability level of followers along with their willingness to perform specific tasks. The effective leader realizes that no one leadership style is appropriate for all followers and all situations and accurately discerns which styles are appropriate for which followers in which situations.

Instructional Leadership

Perhaps the most popular theme in educational leadership over the last two decades has been instructional leadership. In their review of contemporary literature on leadership, Leithwood, Jantzi, and Steinbach (1999) note that instructional leadership is one of the most frequently mentioned educational leadership concepts in North America. Yet, despite its popularity, the concept is not well defined.

The description of instructional leadership that has attained the highest level of visibility over the years is that by Wilma Smith and Richard Andrews (1989). They identify four dimensions, or roles, of an instructional leader: resource provider, instructional resource, communicator, and visible presence. As a resource provider the principal ensures that teachers have the materials, facilities, and budget necessary to adequately perform their duties. As an instructional resource the principal actively supports day-to-day instructional activities and programs by modeling desired behaviors, participating in inservice training, and consistently giving priority to instructional concerns. As a communicator the principal has clear goals for the school and articulates those goals to faculty and staff. As a visible presence the principal engages in frequent classroom observations and is highly accessible to faculty and staff.

Others have proposed slightly different lists of the defining characteristics of instructional leadership. For example, in their Reflection-Growth (RG) model, Blase and Blase (1999) identify the following characteristics: encouraging and facilitating the study of teaching and learning, facilitating collaborative efforts among teachers, establishing coaching relationships among teachers, using instructional research to make decisions, and using the principles of adult learning when dealing with teachers. Glickman, Gordon, and Ross-Gordon (1995) identify the following: direct assistance to teachers in their day-to-day activities, development of collaborative groups among staff, design and procurement of effective staff development activities, curriculum development, and use of action research. Hallinger, Murphy, Weil, Mesa, and Mitman (1983) identify three general functions of the instructional leader: defining the school's mission, managing curriculum and instruction, and promoting a positive school climate. Finally, instructional leadership has also been linked with transformational leadership. According to Leithwood, Jantzi, and Steinbach (1999), transformational leadership is an expansion of instructional leadership because it "aspires, more generally, to increase members' efforts on behalf of the organization, as well as develop more skilled practice" (p. 20).

Some Prominent Theorists

A number of theorists have greatly influenced leadership practice in K–12 education. Again, we consider only a few whose work was foundational to our analysis of the research literature.

Warren Bennis

Warren Bennis (2003) focuses on the future. In his book *On Becoming a Leader,* he forecasts the behaviors necessary for leadership in the 21st century. He emphasizes the fact that modern leaders must not rely on their personal skills or charisma to produce change. He identifies four critical characteristics of effective leadership. First, leaders must be able to engage others through the creation of a shared vision. Second, leaders must have a clear voice that is distinctive to constituents. This voice should be characterized by a sense of purpose, a sense of self, and self-confidence. Third, leaders must operate from a strong moral code and a belief in a higher good that fuels their efforts. Finally, leaders must have the ability to adapt to relentless pressure to change. In *Leaders: Strategies for Taking Charge,* Bennis and Nanus (2003) relate this characteristic to Burns's notion of transformational leadership.

Peter Block

In the book *The Answer to How Is Yes: Acting on What Matters,* Peter Block (2003) frames leadership as the act of effective questioning. Specifically, he suggests that asking "how" questions too early in the change process undermines the power of dialogue. Block suggests that effective leaders are social architects who create a "social space" that enhances or inhibits the effectiveness of an organization.

The ideal social space is one conducive to solving even the most perplexing of organizational problems. For Block, critical leadership skills include convening critical discussions, naming the question, focusing discussion on learning as opposed to premature closure on solutions, and using strategies for participative design of solutions.

Marcus Buckingham and Donald Clifton

Through their work with the Gallup Corporation, Marcus Buckingham and Donald Clifton (2001) identified 34 signature "talents" or "strengths" that individuals within an organization might possess. Each individual is strong in a few of these talents and weak in some. Buckingham and Clifton suggest that to build a "strengths-based" organization, a leader should spend a great deal of time selecting the right people up front, legislate outcomes as opposed to the style or manner in which outcomes are accomplished, focus training on building identified strengths, and avoid promoting people to positions where their strengths are not an asset, or, stated differently, avoid promoting people out of their areas of strength.

James Collins

James Collins's (2001) highly influential work on the nature of businesses that have gone from "good to great" has made its mark in education as well as the business world. Collins's research indicates that the difference between "good" companies and "great" companies is the presence of what he refers to as Level 5 leaders. Collins explains that Level 5 leaders are more interested in building a great company than they are in drawing attention to themselves. They blend personal humility with intense personal will. They exhibit intense commitment to doing what matters most in their companies regardless of the difficulties. When things go wrong, they tend to look inward for the reasons as opposed to ascribing blame to external factors. Other characteristics of Level 5 leaders include the following:

- Relying on high standards as the primary vehicle for attaining goals, as opposed to personal charisma
  - Surrounding themselves with the right people to do the job
  - Creating a culture of discipline
  - Honestly looking at the facts regarding their companies
  - Entertaining difficult questions regarding the future of their companies

Stephen Covey

The work of Stephen Covey, like that of Collins, has been highly influential in education even though it is not directed toward educators per se. Best known for the book *The 7 Habits of Highly Effective People,* Covey (1989) posits seven behaviors that generate positive results in a variety of situations. He frames these habits as directives. *Be proactive* refers to controlling your environment as opposed to letting it control you. The effective leader must control his environment by responding to key situations and circumstances. *Begin with the end in mind* means that an effective leader always keeps the goals of the organization in mind. *Put first things first* refers to focusing on those behaviors that are directly related to the goals of the organization. Actions to this end have priority over all other actions. *Think win-win* involves ensuring that all members of an organization benefit when the goals of the organization are realized. *Seek first to understand and then to be understood* involves establishing strong lines of communication by listening to and understanding the needs of those within the organization. *Synergize* refers to the principle that cooperation and collaboration will produce more than can be expected from the isolated efforts of individuals. *Sharpen the saw* involves learning from previous mistakes and developing skills to ensure that they are not repeated.

Covey's book *Principle-Centered Leadership* (1992) builds on the seven habits as the basic operating principles of effective leadership. However, this second work emphasizes the need for leaders to have a strong sense of purpose in their own lives and principles that guide their actions day-to-day. For Covey, effective leaders communicate by their actions a clear sense of purpose and what their lives stand for.

The third book by Covey commonly used in education is *First Things First* (Covey, Merrill, & Merrill, 1994). Although he addresses the concept of time management, Covey expands on traditional treatments of this topic by emphasizing the highest and best use of a person's time. For Covey the selection of a next step is guided as much by a person's purpose in life as it is by the demands of the task at hand. Thus for Covey, the highest and best use of a person's time is that action that most effectively addresses the problems at hand and is most consistent with the individual's identified purposes in life.

Richard Elmore

Richard Elmore (2000) provides a unique perspective on the role of leadership. He agrees with those who promote instructional leadership in that he emphasizes the importance of understanding effective practices in curriculum, instruction, and assessment and the ability to work with teachers on the day-to-day problems related to these topics. He warns, however, that the knowledge base one must have to provide guidance on curriculum, instruction, and assessment is vast. Elmore's solution is an organization that distributes the responsibility for leadership. Although the principal might not have the time, energy, or disposition to master the extant knowledge base regarding curriculum, instruction, and assessment, others within a school might. In short, Elmore calls for the use of distributed models of leadership as opposed to models that look to the principal to provide all leadership functions for the school.

Michael Fullan

Michael Fullan's contribution to the theory on leadership is expansive but also focused on the process of change and leadership for change. In *Change Forces: Probing the Depths of Educational Reform* (1993), he argues that educational reformers are fighting a battle that is not "winnable" given that the system has a propensity to continually seek change but is inherently averse to it. Although he offers no simple solution to this dilemma, he suggests new ways of thinking about change that include seeing problems as opportunities, realizing that change cannot be mandated, ensuring that individualism and collectivism have equal power, and designing schools to be learning communities. In *Leading in a Culture of Change* (2001), Fullan offers a blueprint for leading change. Based on the premise that the knowledge base regarding effective leadership has reached a point that provides clear guidance to school leaders and the premise that all leaders can become effective, he identifies five characteristics of effective leadership for change: moral purpose; understanding the change process; strong relationships; knowledge sharing; and coherence, or connecting new knowledge with existing knowledge.

Ronald Heifetz and Marty Linsky

Ronald Heifetz (1994) and Marty Linsky (Heifetz & Linsky, 2002a, 2002b) emphasize the need to adapt leadership behavior to the requirements of the situation. They make a fundamental distinction between three types of situations an organization might encounter. Type I situations are those for which traditional solutions will typically suffice. They involve those problems that are part of the normal day-to-day life of an organization. Leadership behaviors that are most appropriate for these situations include establishing routines and operating procedures and protecting staff from problems that might distract them from their work. Type II situations are those for which traditional solutions will not suffice. Leadership behavior that is most appropriate in these situations includes providing resources that help those in the organization identify new ways of addressing problems. Finally, Type III situations are those that cannot be adequately addressed within the context of an organization's current beliefs and values. These situations often require the leader to orchestrate conflict to facilitate the evolution of new beliefs and values that allow for actions not possible within the context of the old system. In Type III situations, leaders use their authority to shift responsibility for the success of the organization to stakeholders.

James Spillane

James Spillane and his colleagues (Spillane & Sherer, 2004; Spillane, Halverson, & Diamond, 2001, 2003) focus their attention on the concept of distributed leadership. Rather than defining distributed leadership as the mere distribution of tasks, they characterize it as an interactive web of leaders and followers who periodically change roles as the situation warrants. Critical to their concept of distributed leadership are three ways that leadership functions can be distributed or "stretched out" over multiple leaders: *collaborative distribution* occurs when the actions of one leader become the basis for the actions of another leader; *collective distribution* occurs when leaders act separately and independently but for a shared goal; and *coordinated distribution* occurs when sequential tasks are led by different individuals.

Other Synthesis Efforts

Like the research that forms the basis for this book, other prominent synthesis efforts have examined the research of others in an attempt to identify some broad principles about school leadership. Here we consider some of those other efforts.

We went back 35 years in our examination of the research literature—back to the early 1970s, the heyday of the school effectiveness movement. A general conclusion from the school effectiveness literature of the 1970s was that educational leadership was an important characteristic of effective schools (Brookover et al., 1979; Brookover et al., 1979; Edmonds, 1979a, 1979b; Rutter et al., 1979). Specific behaviors associated with effective leadership included monitoring student progress on specific learning goals, supervising teachers, promoting high expectations for student achievement and teacher performance, focusing on basic skills, and monitoring the curriculum. Many of the studies on which these conclusions were based used research designs comparing "high-achieving" and "low-achieving" schools, examining the characteristics of both groups to find critical differences. Such studies are called "outlier studies." Since the 1970s, many articles and books have described the characteristics of effective schools, but there have been only a few efforts to synthesize the research on school leadership that may be compared with ours.

In their article entitled "Exploring the Principal's Contribution to School Effectiveness: 1980–1995," Philip Hallinger and Ronald Heck (1998) synthesized the findings from 40 empirical studies that were conducted between 1980 and 1995. They organized those studies into three broad categories: studies that used "direct effect" models, studies that used "mediated effect" models, and studies that used "reciprocal effect" models. Direct effect models are those that posit a direct link between principal behavior and student achievement. This was basically the approach taken in the school effectiveness studies of the 1970s—if the principal engages in certain behaviors, student achievement is enhanced; if the principal doesn't engage in these behaviors, achievement is not enhanced. Mediated effect models assume that the principal influences student achievement only through others—specifically teachers. In more technical terms, mediated effect models assume that a principal affects student achievement through a number of indirect paths that involve factors such as events, people, culture, and structures. Finally, models based on reciprocal effects assume that the principal and the teachers affect each other. The actions of the principal affect the actions of the teachers, which, in turn, affect the actions of the principal. These models involve multiple paths between variables.

Kathleen Cotton (2003) published the findings of her narrative review of the literature in the book *Principals and Student Achievement: What the Research Says*. Recall from the discussion in Chapter 1 that a narrative review is one in which the reviewer conducts a strictly logical (as opposed to quantitative) analysis of the research, looking for patterns and trends. Focusing on studies from 1985 until the present, Cotton reviewed 81 reports in all, some of which dealt with more than one topic. Fifty-six of those reports dealt with the influence of principal leadership on student achievement, 10 dealt with the effect of principal leadership on student attitudes, 8 with student behavior, 15 with teacher attitudes, 4 with teacher behavior, and 3 with dropout rates. Cotton identified 25 categories of principal behavior that positively affect the dependent variables of student achievement, student attitudes, student behavior, teacher attitudes, teacher behaviors, and dropout rates. Here are the 25 categories:

1. Safe and orderly environment
2. Vision and goals focused on high levels of student learning
3. High expectations for student learning
4. Self-confidence, responsibility, and perseverance
5. Visibility and accessibility
6. Positive and supportive climate
7. Communication and interaction
8. Emotional and interpersonal support

9. Parent and community outreach and involvement
10. Rituals, ceremonies, and other symbolic actions
11. Shared leadership, decision making, and staff empowerment
12. Collaboration
13. Instructional leadership
14. Ongoing pursuit of high levels of student learning
15. Norm of continuous improvement
16. Discussion of instructional issues
17. Classroom observation and feedback to teachers
18. Support of teachers' autonomy
19. Support of risk taking
20. Professional development opportunities and resources
21. Protecting instructional time
22. Monitoring student progress and sharing findings
23. Use of student progress for program improvement
24. Recognition of student and staff achievement
25. Role modeling

We list all 25 categories because they are quite similar to the list we identified in our quantitative synthesis of the research (see Chapter 4). Given that she performed a narrative review of the literature, Cotton did not quantitatively estimate the effect of principal leadership on student achievement. However, her conclusions were fairly straightforward: She noted that principal leadership does have an effect on student outcomes, albeit an indirect one. Citing the work of others, she explains:

> In general, these researchers find that, while a small portion of the effect may be direct—that is, principals' direct interactions with students in or out of the classroom may be motivating, inspiring, instructive, or otherwise influential—most of it is indirect, that is, mediated through teachers and others. (p. 58)

The synthesis study that is most similar to our efforts is that conducted by Bob Witziers, Roel Bosker, and Meta Kruger (2003), entitled "Educational Leadership and Student Achievement: The Elusive Search for an Association." The purpose of their study was to examine the quantitative relationship between school leadership and student academic achievement. Like us, they used meta-analysis as their research methodology. Additionally, like us, they used the correlation coefficient as the measure of the relationship between leadership and student achievement. They examined studies from 1986 to 1996 across a variety of countries. As mentioned in Chapter 1, their primary finding was that the overall leadership of the principal has almost no correlation with student achievement. The correlation they found was .02—substantially smaller than our finding of a correlation of .25.

To illustrate, contrast the implication of our findings with that of Witziers and his colleagues in terms of expected gain in student achievement associated with an increase in leadership behavior. Based on our correlation of .25, an increase in leadership behavior from the 50th percentile to the 84th is associated with an increase in student achievement from the 50th percentile to the 60th percentile. If the Witziers correlation represents the true relationship between leadership and student achievement, then an increase in leadership behavior from the 50th percentile to the 84th is associated with an increase in student achievement from the 50th percentile to the 51st percentile. Obviously, their meta-analysis implies that school leadership has almost no effect on student achievement. Indeed, one of their basic conclusions is that the "tie between leadership and student achievement is weak" (p. 418). However, they do qualify this generalization, noting that the findings for studies that assume an indirect effect are more promising. The contrast between the Witziers study and ours is important to understanding the conclusions one can draw from research over the last 35 years. We consider this contrast in some depth in Chapter 3 and in Technical Note 6 (see p. 147).

The final synthesis study that might be likened to ours is that by Kenneth Leithwood, Karen Seashore Louis, Stephen Anderson, and Kyla Wahlstrom (2004). Like Cotton's (2003) study, it employs a narrative approach. One finding of note is that they estimate that the correlation between leadership and student achievement is between .17 and .22 (Leithwood, Seashore Louis, Anderson, & Wahlstrom, 2004, p. 21). The high end of this estimate is, of course, quite close to our estimate of .25. In fact, one of their major conclusions is that leadership is second only to classroom instruction among all school-related factors that contribute to what students learn in school. Where Cotton (2003) identified 25 categories of leadership behavior and we identify 21 (see Chapter 4), Leithwood and colleagues identify three basic practices as the "core of successful leadership" (p. 8). *Setting direction* accounts for the largest proportion of a leader's impact. This set of practices is aimed at helping staff members establish and understand the goals of the school and is the foundation of a shared vision for the school. *Developing people* involves building the capacity of those within the school and using their strengths. Specific behaviors associated with this category include "offering intellectual stimulation, providing individualized support and providing appropriate models of best practice and beliefs considered fundamental to the organization" (p. 9). *Redesigning the organization* involves changing those organizational characteristics that might "blunt or wear down educators' good intentions and actually prevent the use of effective practices" (p. 9). Specific practices associated with this category include strengthening the school culture and building collaborative processes.

Summary and Conclusions

Selected theories, theorists, and synthesis studies have provided the foundation and reference points for many of our conclusions. Theories such as transactional leadership, transformational leadership, and instructional leadership, as well as the work of theorists including Collins, Elmore, and Heifetz, provided a knowledge base that allowed us to review the research from a broad framework. Other synthesis efforts provide points of contrasts to our findings.

3

The Meta-Analysis

Meta-analysis, our primary research methodology, uses quantitative techniques to synthesize studies in a given domain. Our domain of interest was school leadership as practiced by principals. When conducting our meta-analysis, we considered any and all available studies from 1970 to the present that met the following conditions:

- The study involved K–12 students.
- The study involved schools in the United States or situations that closely mirrored the culture of U.S. schools.
- The study directly or indirectly examined the relationship between the leadership of the building principal and student academic achievement.
- Academic achievement was measured by a standardized achievement test or a state test, or a composite index based on one or both of these.
- Effect sizes in correlation form were reported or could be computed.

We should note that one type of study met these criteria but was sometimes excluded from our analysis. Those studies dealt with leadership "styles"—general categories of leadership behavior based on some predetermined theory. For example, Evans and Teddlie (1995) examined the relationship between *initiator, manager,* and *responder* styles of leadership and overall achievement in schools. Similarly, High and Achilles (1986) examined the relationship between the following styles and school achievement: *referent, expert, enabler, coercer, legal authority, norm setter,* and *involver.* Such studies provide useful perspectives. In general, however, we excluded them from our meta-analysis because they represented very broad categories of behavior that were in themselves summaries of more specific behaviors. Because one of our primary goals was to identify specific leadership behaviors, we dealt with only those studies that addressed specific behaviors that had not been collapsed into broad categories.

The Studies in Our Meta-Analysis

To begin our meta-analysis we conducted searches of entries on leadership in three standard databases: ERIC, Psych Lit, and Dissertation Abstracts. In all, we retrieved more than 5,000 titles. Of those, 300 contained descriptions that appeared to meet our criteria. We also reviewed synthesis studies such as those by Cotton (2003), Hallinger and Heck (1998, 1996), and Leithwood, Begley, and Cousins (1990). Finally, to identify other potential studies, we reviewed the reference sections for the studies included in our meta-analysis. In all, we found 69 studies that met our criteria. They are listed in Appendix A.

For the most part, the 69 studies in our meta-analysis used either a convenience sample or a purposeful sample. Convenience samples occurred when a study included all the schools in a given district. Purposeful samples occurred when a study used schools that were singled out as high performing within a district or state and compared with schools that were identified as low performing using some criterion related to student achievement. Figure 3.1 reports some defining characteristics of the 69 studies we analyzed.

FIGURE 3.1
Characteristics of Studies Used in the Meta-Analysis

Number of studies: 69
Years in which studies were completed or published:
   1978–2001
Total number of schools involved: 2,802
Number of studies and schools at various levels:

- Elementary school: 39 studies, 1,319 schools
- Middle school/junior high: 6 studies, 323 schools
- High school: 10 studies, 371 schools
- K–8: 8 studies, 290 schools
- K–12: 6 studies, 499 schools

Estimated number of teachers involved: 14,000*
Estimated number of students involved: 1,400,000**

* This estimate was based on the fact that the average number of teachers completing questionnaires in a study was about 5.

** This estimate was based on the fact that the average number of students in the schools studied was about 500.

As Figure 3.1 indicates, the 69 studies spanned 23 years—1978 to 2001. We found no available studies that met our criteria prior to 1978 nor after 2001. In all, 2,802 schools were represented in the studies. Note that in some discussions of our findings, we refer to 64 studies and 2,599 schools. These lower figures are used when we excluded extreme scores or "outliers" in our analysis (see Notes on figures 3.5 and 3.6). The largest number of studies (39) focused on elementary schools, which numbered 1,319. A much smaller number of studies (8) focused on K–8 samples, which involved the smallest number of schools—290.

The typical study in the meta-analysis used some type of questionnaire asking teachers about their perceptions of the principal's leadership behaviors. We used teacher ratings of principal leadership instead of ratings by the principals themselves or their supervisors. It has been demonstrated that different respondents provide different ratings regarding principal leadership (Heck, 1992). Teachers are thought to provide the most valid information because they are closest to the day-to-day operations of the school and the behaviors of the principal (Ebmeier, 1991; Heck, Larsen, & Marcoulides, 1990).

The average score for the teachers' responses within each school was then correlated with the average achievement of students in that school. The unit of analysis in our study, then, was the school; each school had a single summary score representing the average achievement of the students and one or more summary scores representing the average perception of teachers regarding general leadership behavior and one or more specific leadership behaviors of the principal.

The Overall Impact of Leadership

For each study we analyzed, a correlation between general leadership and student achievement was either computed or extracted directly from the study. (See Technical Note 4 on p. 133 for a description of how we computed correlations for the various studies.) In all, we extracted or computed 69 correlations representing the relationship between general leadership behavior and student academic achievement. As explained in Chapter 1, the average correlation was .25. In Chapter 1 we further explained that this correlation indicates that an increase in principal leadership behavior from the 50th percentile to the 84th percentile is associated with a gain in the overall achievement of the school from the 50th percentile to the 60th percentile. Additionally, an increase in leadership behavior from the 50th percentile to the 99th percentile is associated with an increase in student achievement from the 50th percentile to the 72nd percentile.

Another interpretation of the .25 correlation provides a different perspective on the potential impact of school leadership. (See Technical Note 5 on p. 147 for a discussion of this technique.) Consider Figure 3.2, which presents a situation that is hypothetical but accurate in its interpretation of the average correlation between principal leadership and student academic achievement. To understand the meaning of the row labels referring to schools with the top half and the bottom half of principals, let's go back to Chapter 1. We began that chapter by noting that there are more than 94,000 K–12 schools in the United States.

FIGURE 3.2
Interpretation of a Correlation of .25 in Terms of Expected Passing Rates for Schools, Depending on Leadership Effectiveness

	Percentage of Schools Passing the Test	Percentage of Schools Failing the Test
Schools with Principals Rated in the Top Half of All Principals Based on Leadership Effectiveness	62.5%	37.5%
Schools with Principals Rated in the Bottom Half of All Principals Based on Leadership Effectiveness	37.5%	62.5%

Therefore, there are probably more than 94,000 principals in the United States. Imagine that we listed those principals in order of their effectiveness as school leaders. It is reasonable to assume that they would form a normal distribution like that depicted in Figure 3.3 on p. 32. The top half of the distribution would contain the top 50 percent of the principals in terms of their leadership behavior; the bottom half of the distribution would contain the bottom 50 percent of the principals in terms of their leadership behavior.

Now let's go back to Figure 3.2 and the column headings referring to percentage of schools passing or failing the test. To interpret these headings, assume that a test is given to all the students in those 94,000 schools. For a school to pass the test, the average score for that school's students must surpass a certain "cut score." Additionally, the test is designed so that the general expectation is that normally 50 percent of schools will pass the test and 50 percent will fail. Figure 3.2 shows how this expected passing rate changes based on whether a school has a principal in the top or bottom half of the distribution for leadership. As Figure 3.2 indicates, among schools with principals in the top half of the distribution, 62.5 percent would pass the test and 37.5 percent would fail. For schools with principals in the bottom half of the distribution, the expectation is the opposite—only 37.5 percent of the schools would pass the test and 62.5 percent would fail. In other words, the schools with principals in the top half of the distribution in terms of their leadership would have a 25 percent higher passing rate.

Whether we use this example based on expected passing rates or the previous example based on expected percentile change in the average achievement of students, the message is clear—the leadership behavior of the principal can have a

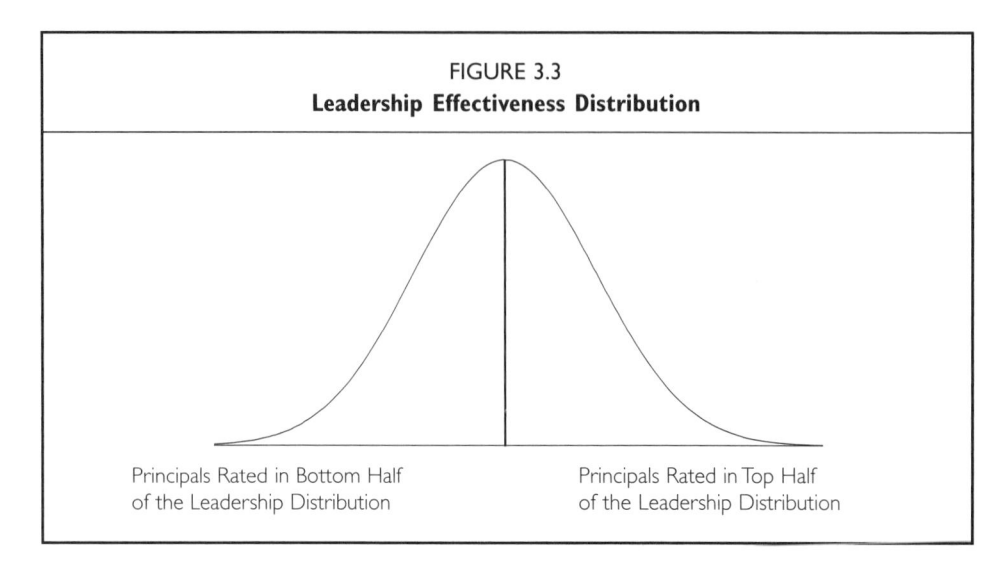

> **FIGURE 3.3**
> **Leadership Effectiveness Distribution**
>
> Principals Rated in Bottom Half of the Leadership Distribution | Principals Rated in Top Half of the Leadership Distribution

profound effect on student achievement. We believe that our general finding of a .25 average correlation is compelling and should stir school leaders to seek ways to improve their leadership skills. However, at least one other study with the same stated purpose as ours reported a much weaker relationship between principal leadership and student achievement. Before we can legitimately make recommendations based on our findings, we must address this discrepancy.

Our Findings in Light of Other Studies

It is important to address the fact that our finding of an average correlation of .25 between principals' leadership behavior and student achievement is much higher than that reported in a meta-analysis conducted by Witziers, Bosker, and Kruger (2003). They reported an average correlation between leadership and student academic achievement of .02, indicating almost no relationship between leadership and achievement. To dramatize the point, their article is entitled "Educational Leadership and Student Achievement: The Elusive Search for an Association." Obviously our findings and conclusions differ substantially from theirs. Technical Note 6 (see p. 147) provides a detailed analysis of the reasons for these disparate findings. Briefly, though, three basic reasons explain the differences.

First, the study by Witziers and his colleagues was focused on schools in various countries, as opposed to our study of schools in the United States. To illustrate, of the 37 studies included in the Witziers meta-analysis, 25 were taken from the study of the International Association for the Evaluation of Educational

Achievement (IEA) on reading literacy in 25 countries (see Postlethwaite & Ross, 1993). These studies of literacy in countries other than the United States reported very low correlations between leadership and literacy achievement. When the IEA studies were excluded from their analysis, Witziers and his colleagues found that the correlation between leadership and achievement doubled. Additionally, studies from the Netherlands that were included in their meta-analysis characteristically reported no relationship (a correlation of .00) between leadership and student achievement. As stated by Witziers and his coauthors, "The results, both for the total sample and the sample without IEA data, show that in the Netherlands the effect size [correlation] is about zero" (p. 409). In short, studies outside of the United States characteristically reported very low correlations, bringing the overall average down considerably. When Witziers and his colleagues computed the average correlation for specific types of studies in the United States, they found it to be .11.

Another factor that explains the difference between the two studies in estimates of the overall effect of leadership on student achievement deals with the way that average correlations were computed. Our procedures for computing average correlations are reported in Technical Note 7 (see p. 149). Briefly, though, in our meta-analysis we computed average correlations within and between studies using a process that excluded conceptual and statistical outliers—those correlations that are very different from the others in a set based on conceptual or statistical criteria. A researcher typically excludes such outliers because they very likely involve factors that are extraneous to the construct that is the focus of a meta-analysis. In this case, that construct was school leadership (for a discussion see Lipsey & Wilson, 2001). In a number of situations, this resulted in the exclusion of extremely low correlations. Had we left these outliers in the analysis, the average correlation would have been lower than the .25 reported.

The third factor accounting for the disparity in findings is that our study corrected for *attenuation* in both the measures of student achievement and the measures of principal leadership. (See Technical Note 8 on p. 152 for a discussion.) Attenuation refers to the shrinkage in a correlation coefficient due to the lack of precision in the measurement instruments used in a study. In the case of our meta-analysis, some studies used questionnaires of leadership ability that had extremely low reliabilities. By definition, a measurement instrument that has low reliability will underestimate the correlation between leadership and student achievement. To illustrate, assume that in a given study the true correlation between leadership and student achievement is .30. However, the study measures principal leadership using a questionnaire that has a reliability of .64. Attenuation theory tells us that the true correlation will be reduced by a factor equal to the square root of the reliability (for a discussion, see Hunter & Schmidt, 1990a, 1990b, 1994). The square root of .64 is .80. Therefore, the correlation that will be computed in our example study will be .24 (.80 × .30) as opposed to .30—the true correlation. In other words, the correlation computed in the study underestimates the true correlation by .06.

In summary, our computed average correlation of .25 represents an estimate of the relationship between the leadership behavior of principals and the overall achievement of students in a school under the following conditions: schools are all from the United States or cultures similar to that in the United States; scores on leadership behavior are computed using sets of correlations that appear to be measuring the same constructs; and scores on leadership behavior and student achievement have been corrected for their lack of reliability.

We believe that an average correlation computed under these conditions is a more reasonable estimate of the relationship between principal leadership and student achievement—if not for the statistical reasons cited above, then for the lack of face validity of the alternative. To illustrate, consider the correlation of .02 found in the study by Witziers and his colleagues. If this represents the true relationship between principal leadership and student achievement, then educators must accept the conclusion that the leadership behavior of the principal in a given school has almost no effect on the achievement of the students in a school. If the principal provides strong guidance and support, the achievement of the students in the school will be about the same as would be expected if the principal provides no guidance and support. This conclusion flies in the face of common sense and the experience of literally tens of thousands of principals in the United States who have effected dramatic improvements in the achievement of students in their schools.

A Deeper Look

In Chapter 1 we cautioned against overemphasizing the average correlation computed within a meta-analysis. Specifically, the recognized founder of modern meta-analysis, Gene Glass (in Robinson, 2004) cautions: "The result of a meta-analysis should never be an average; it should be a graph" (p. 29). In keeping with Glass's recommendation, consider Figure 3.4, which is a bar graph of the correlations from our meta-analysis.

The figure depicts a wide of range of correlations from the studies in our meta-analysis. From one perspective, each of the correlations represents a separate

FIGURE 3.4
Distribution of Correlations

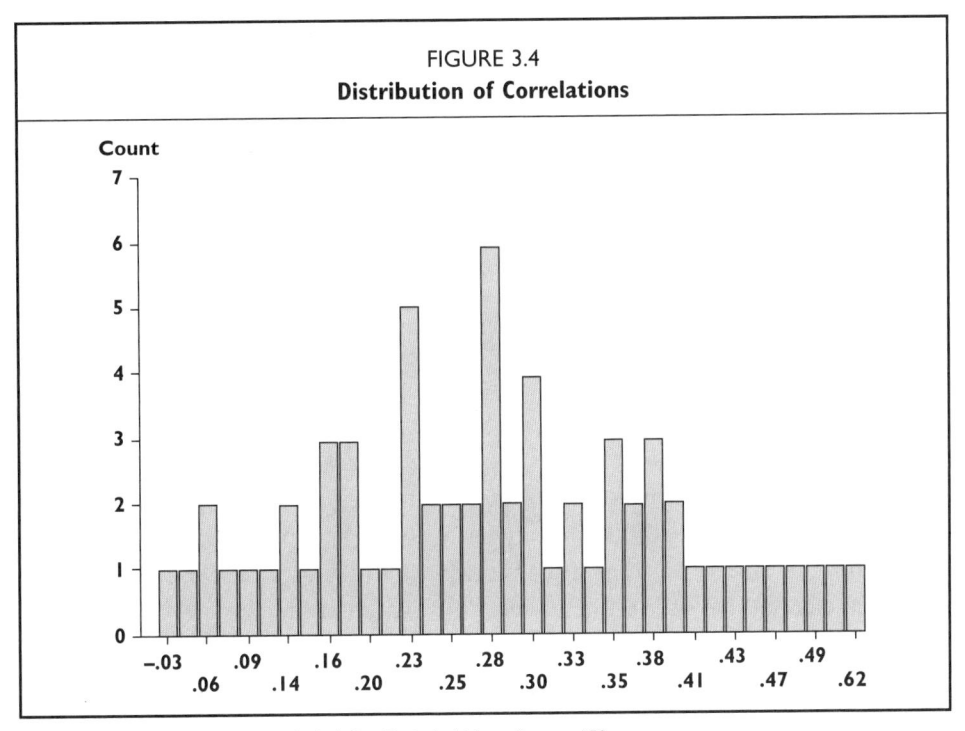

Note: Outliers have been excluded. See Technical Note 8 on p. 152.

estimate of the "true relationship" between overall leadership behavior by the principal and student achievement. That is, each study assumed or hoped that the principals and schools being examined represented the principals and schools all across the country. (See Technical Note 9 on p. 153 for a discussion of this concept.) If we consider the extreme estimates in Figure 3.4, we obtain very different perspectives on the effect of school leadership. To illustrate, consider .62, the largest positive correlation in the figure. If this represents the true relationship between school leadership and student achievement, it means that an *increase* in leadership behavior from the 50th percentile to the 84th is associated with an *increase* in student achievement from the 50th to the 73rd percentile. But now let's consider the extreme negative correlation of −.03. If this represents the true relationship between school leadership and student achievement, it means that an *increase* in leadership behavior from the 50th percentile to the 84th is associated with a *decrease* in student achievement from the 50th percentile to the 49th.

A logical question would ask how studies on the same topic can produce such discrepant results. Again, Glass provides guidance. He recommends that answering this question should be the primary purpose of meta-analysis. Specifically, in his book on meta-analysis entitled *How Science Takes Stock* (1997), Hunt quotes Glass as commenting:

> What I've come to think meta-analysis really is—or rather, what it ought to be—is not a single-number summary such as "This is what psychotherapy's effect is" but a whole array of study results that show how relationships between treatment and outcome change as a function of all sorts of other conditions—the age of the people in treatment, what kinds of problems they had, the training of the therapist, how long after therapy you're measuring change, and so on. That's what we really want to get—a total portrait of all those changes and shifts, a complicated landscape rather than a single central point. That would be the best contribution we could make. (p. 163)

Technically, attempts to answer the question regarding the different effects of leadership behavior on student achievement found in different studies are referred to as a search for moderator variables—variables that can affect the relationship between school leadership and student achievement. What, then, are the potential variables that could explain the differences in findings depicted in Figure 3.4? We considered the effect of a number of moderator variables. These are discussed in Technical Note 10 (see p. 153). Here we discuss two of them.

One moderator variable we considered was the quality of the studies involved in our meta-analysis. We rated each study high, medium, or low in its quality. This allowed us to determine whether the quality of a study's methodology accounted for some of the differences in the reported correlations. Our complete findings for this moderator variable are reported in Technical Note 10. Figure 3.5 summarizes the highlights of those findings.

As depicted in Figure 3.5, studies that were rated highest in quality of methodology produced the largest average correlation between principal leadership and student achievement. The studies that were rated lowest produced the lowest

FIGURE 3.5
Quality of Studies

Quality	Average r	Number of Studies	Number of Schools
High	.31	22	820
Medium	.23	28	1,212
Low	.17	14	567

Note: Because we excluded outliers in our analysis, the total number of studies reported in this figure is 64 as opposed to 69, and the total number of schools is 2,599 as opposed to 2,802. See Technical Note 7 for an explanation of how we identified outliers.

FIGURE 3.6
Levels of Schools

Level of School on Which Studies Focused	Average r	Number of Studies	Number of Schools
Elementary	.29	36	1,175
Middle School/Junior High	.24	6	323
High School	.26	9	325
K–8	.15	7	277
K–12	.16	6	499

Note: Because we excluded outliers in our analysis, the total number of studies reported in this figure is 64 as opposed to 69, and the total number of schools is 2,599 as opposed to 2,802. See Technical Note 7 on p. 149 for an explanation of how we identified outliers.

average correlation. Although it would be inappropriate to draw hard and fast conclusions from the findings, Figure 3.5 does provide some evidence that the relatively strong average correlation we found between principal leadership and student achievement was probably not an artifact of poor research design. Indeed, taken at face value, Figure 3.5 implies that the stronger the research design the higher the correlation—those studies that were more precise in the way they measured leadership, the way they defined leadership, and so on, found stronger relationships between leadership and student achievement.

Another moderator variable we considered was the level of the school included in studies. It might be the case that the relationship between leadership and student achievement is substantially different at one set of grade levels than it is at another. The findings regarding this variable are reported in Figure 3.6.

Again, no hard and fast conclusions should be drawn from Figure 3.6. Taken at face value, however, the figure indicates little difference in the effect of principal leadership from elementary school to middle school/junior high to high school. Although the correlations are not identical for these three levels of schooling, they are probably too close to be considered "different" from a statistical perspective. With this qualification noted, it is interesting that the average correlations for studies that encompassed K–8 and K–12 are quite a bit lower than those focusing on more specific grade levels. We could find no obvious reason why these studies produced lower correlations. Perhaps the breadth of these studies weakened their ability to accurately measure principal leadership, student academic achievement, or both. However, this is speculation only.

In all, we examined the impact of eight moderator variables on the size of the correlation between principal leadership and student academic achievement. Technical Note 10 reports our findings for all eight and discusses what can and cannot be concluded from our analysis. In general, though, our analysis of moderator variables didn't offer any obvious explanations for the differences in correlations between principal leadership and student achievement. Another area of investigation, however, did. That area of investigation involved specific types of leadership behavior. We consider those specific types of leadership behaviors in Chapter 4.

Summary and Conclusions

In broad terms, our meta-analysis indicates that principals can have a profound effect on the achievement of students in their schools. We also found that the studies we included in our meta-analysis reported different size correlations between principal leadership and student achievement—some very large and positive, some low and negative. Our attempts to explain these differences using moderator variables such as study quality and level of schooling did not produce any straightforward explanations.

Part 2

Practical Applications

4

The 21 Responsibilities of the School Leader

The average correlation of .25 produced in our meta-analysis was based on principal leadership defined in very general terms. However, researchers and theorists in school leadership have cautioned that such generality doesn't tell us much in a practical sense. For example, Wimpleberg, Teddlie, and Stringfield (1989) have exhorted that research on principal leadership not only must attend to general characteristics of behavior such as "has a vision," but also must identify specific actions that affect student achievement. Consequently, we examined the 69 studies in our meta-analysis looking for specific behaviors related to principal leadership. We identified 21 categories of behaviors that we refer to as "responsibilities." They are listed in Figure 4.1 on p. 42 along with their correlations with student achievement.

Our review in Chapter 2 of various theories and theorists should make clear that these 21 responsibilities are not new findings within the literature on leadership, though others may have given them different names. Indeed, as mentioned in Chapter 2, Cotton (2003) identified 25 responsibilities quite similar to ours. (See Appendix B for a comparison of our responsibilities and Cotton's.) To a great extent, our findings validate the opinions expressed by leadership theorists for decades. However, our 21 responsibilities provide some new insights into the nature of school leadership. Here we briefly consider each of the 21 responsibilities.

1. Affirmation

Affirmation is the extent to which the leader recognizes and celebrates school accomplishments—and acknowledges failures. It is related to some of the behaviors described in Chapter 2 in the discussion of transactional leadership and many

FIGURE 4.1
The 21 Responsibilities and Their Correlations (r) with Student Academic Achievement

Responsibility	The Extent to Which the Principal…	Average r	95% CI	No. of Studies	No. of Schools
1. Affirmation	Recognizes and celebrates accomplishments and acknowledges failures	.19	.08 to .29	6	332
2. Change Agent	Is willing to challenge and actively challenges the status quo	.25	.16 to .34	6	466
3. Contingent Rewards	Recognizes and rewards individual accomplishments	.24	.15 to .32	9	465
4. Communication	Establishes strong lines of communication with and among teachers and students	.23	.12 to .33	11	299
5. Culture	Fosters shared beliefs and a sense of community and cooperation	.25	.18 to .31	15	819
6. Discipline	Protects teachers from issues and influences that would detract from their teaching time or focus	.27	.18 to .35	12	437
7. Flexibility	Adapts his or her leadership behavior to the needs of the current situation and is comfortable with dissent	.28	.16 to .39	6	277
8. Focus	Establishes clear goals and keeps those goals in the forefront of the school's attention	.24	.19 to .29	44	1,619
9. Ideals/Beliefs	Communicates and operates from strong ideals and beliefs about schooling	.22	.14 to .30	7	513
10. Input	Involves teachers in the design and implementation of important decisions and policies	.25	.18 to .32	16	669
11. Intellectual Stimulation	Ensures faculty and staff are aware of the most current theories and practices and makes the discussion of these a regular aspect of the school's culture	.24	.13 to .34	4	302
12. Involvement in Curriculum, Instruction, and Assessment	Is directly involved in the design and implementation of curriculum, instruction, and assessment practices	.20	.14 to .27	23	826

FIGURE 4.1 *(continued)*
The 21 Responsibilities and Their Correlations (r) with Student Academic Achievement

Responsibility	The Extent to Which the Principal…	Average *r*	95% CI	No. of Studies	No. of Schools
13. Knowledge of Curriculum, Instruction, and Assessment	Is knowledgeable about current curriculum, instruction, and assessment practices	.25	.15 to .34	10	368
14. Monitoring/ Evaluating	Monitors the effectiveness of school practices and their impact on student learning	.27	.22 to .32	31	1,129
15. Optimizer	Inspires and leads new and challenging innovations	.20	.13 to .27	17	724
16. Order	Establishes a set of standard operating procedures and routines	.25	.16 to .33	17	456
17. Outreach	Is an advocate and spokesperson for the school to all stakeholders	.27	.18 to .35	14	478
18. Relationships	Demonstrates an awareness of the personal aspects of teachers and staff	.18	.09 to .26	11	505
19. Resources	Provides teachers with materials and professional development necessary for the successful execution of their jobs	.25	.17 to .32	17	571
20. Situational Awareness	Is aware of the details and undercurrents in the running of the school and uses this information to address current and potential problems	.33	.11 to .51	5	91
21. Visibility	Has quality contact and interactions with teachers and students	.20	.11 to .28	13	477

Note: *95% CI* stands for the interval of correlations within which one can be 95% sure the true correlation falls (see Technical Note 9, p. 153). *No. of Studies* stands for the number of studies that addressed a responsibility. *No. of schools* stands for the number of schools involved in computing the average correlation.

of the leadership behaviors identified by Collins (2001) in his research on businesses that have gone from "good to great."

At its core this responsibility involves a balanced and honest accounting of a school's successes and failures. Cottrell (2002) explains that one of the biggest challenges facing school-level administrators is directly addressing performance issues—both positive and negative. Although it is somewhat easy to recognize and acknowledge the positive, it is rather difficult to recognize the negative. He notes that a typical school includes staff members who might be classified as 30 percent superstars, 50 percent middle stars, and 20 percent falling stars. He further explains that it is natural to recognize exceptional performance from the superstars as well as to ignore inferior performance from the falling stars. Yet both must be addressed explicitly. He states, "You simply cannot ignore performance issues and expect your superstars to stick around very long" (p. 40). In a summary of research on leadership accountability, Lashway (2001) frames the issue in terms of accountability: "For many, 'accountability' just means delivering results" (p. 2). He adds that in this era of standards, accountability should encompass consequences, both positive and negative, that are based on results.

The specific behaviors and characteristics associated with this responsibility as found in our meta-analysis are the following:

- Systematically and fairly recognizing and celebrating the accomplishments of students
- Systematically and fairly recognizing and celebrating the accomplishments of teachers
- Systematically and fairly recognizing the failures of the school as a whole

To illustrate, the principal executes the responsibility of Affirmation when she acknowledges that a certain group of students or the school as a whole has raised scores on the state test by 5 percentile points. Affirmation is exhibited when the principal announces at a faculty meeting that members of the social studies faculty have just had an article accepted for publication in a professional journal. The principal demonstrates the responsibility of Affirmation when he announces to the faculty that they have not met the goal they set of decreasing student referrals during the third quarter.

2. Change Agent

It is not uncommon for a school (or any other complex organization) to keep certain practices in place and unchallenged for years and even decades simply because of their historical status. In contrast, the responsibility of *Change Agent* refers to the leader's disposition to challenge the status quo. Many of the characteristics of this responsibility fit well within the discussion in Chapter 2 on transformational leadership. It is one of the defining features of total quality management (TQM). Underpinning the responsibility of acting as a Change Agent is the leader's willingness to temporarily upset a school's equilibrium. Fullan (2001) explains that an effective leader has the ability "to disturb them [staff] in a manner that approximates the desired outcome" (pp. 45–46). He further comments that change agents don't "live more peacefully, but . . . they can handle more uncertainty—and conflict—and are better at working through complex issues in ways that energize rather than deplete the commitment of the organizational members" (p. 15).

Silins, Mulford, and Zarins (2002) provide a different perspective on the responsibility of Change Agent. They note that effective change agents are leaders who "protect those who take risks" (p. 618). They further explain that effective leadership involves "the extent to which staff feel empowered to make decisions and feel free to experiment and take risks" (p. 619). Finally, Clarke (2000) notes:

> Seeing successful school improvement as the ability to live with contested and problematic issues is a more realistic and developmentally helpful way of preparing for sustained reform. This way of operating implies an acceptance that conflict is a necessary dynamic of good reform and healthy learning environment. (p. 350)

Specific behaviors and characteristics associated with this responsibility and identified in our meta-analysis are the following:

- Consciously challenging the status quo
- Being willing to lead change initiatives with uncertain outcomes
- Systematically considering new and better ways of doing things
- Consistently attempting to operate at the edge versus the center of the school's competence

To illustrate, the responsibility of Change Agent is practiced when the school leader poses a question such as this: Is our homework policy really helping students learn, or is it indirectly punishing those students who don't have much help at home? The school leader demonstrates the responsibility of Change Agent when he makes a commitment to implement a new reading program for at least two years to give it adequate time to work. The school leader exhibits the responsibility of Change Agent when he says to the faculty, "Perhaps we are becoming too comfortable with ourselves. What could we be doing that we are not?"

3. Contingent Rewards

Contingent Rewards refers to the extent to which the school leader recognizes and rewards individual accomplishments. In Chapter 2 we identified this behavior as one of the defining features of transactional leadership. One might expect that recognizing individual accomplishments is standard operating procedure in schools. However, singling out individual teachers for recognition and reward appears to be rare in K–12 education. Specifically, some believe that the "egalitarian" culture of

K–12 education, in which everyone must be considered equal regardless of competence, works against the implementation of this responsibility (see Friedkin & Slater, 1994).

This tendency notwithstanding, a great deal of discussion has addressed the importance of contingent rewards in schools. Nunnelley, Whaley, Mull, and Hott (2003) explain that "the administrative leader must be proactive in recognizing the varying abilities of staff members" (p. 56). Buckingham and Clifton (2001) note that "many different kinds of prestige should be made available to reflect the many different perfect performances the organization wants to encourage" (p. 241). Kouzes and Posner (1999) emphasize the fact that contingent rewards send messages to teachers and administrators alike:

> In recognizing individuals, we sometimes get lost in the ceremonial aspects. We think about form, but we forget substance. Recognitions are reminders; quite literally, the word *recognize* comes from the Latin to "know again." Recognitions are opportunities to say to everyone, "I'd like to remind you one more time what's important around here. Here's what we value." (p. 19)

Specific behaviors and characteristics associated with this responsibility and identified in our meta-analysis are the following:

- Using hard work and results as the basis for rewards and recognition
- Using performance versus seniority as a primary criterion for rewards and recognition

To illustrate, the principal demonstrates the responsibility of Contingent Rewards when he singles out and praises a teacher who has put in extra time for the last month working with students whose reading comprehension scores are below grade level. The principal executes the responsibility of Contingent Rewards when she rewards teachers whose students have made exceptional progress with a trip to a local conference on best practices.

4. Communication

Communication refers to the extent to which the school leader establishes strong lines of communication with and between teachers and students. This responsibility seems self-evident—good communication is a critical feature of any endeavor in which people work in close proximity for a common purpose. In Chapter 2, we mentioned it in conjunction with instructional leadership, total quality management (TQM), and theories of leadership promoted by virtually every theorist reviewed in that chapter. Scribner, Cockrell, Cockrell, and Valentine (1999) explain that effective communication might be considered the glue that holds together all the other responsibilities of leadership. One might say that effective communication is an implicit or explicit feature of most aspects of leadership. Similar sentiments have been expressed by Elmore (2000), Fullan (2001), and Leithwood and Riehl (2003).

The specific behaviors and characteristics associated with this responsibility as defined in our meta-analysis are the following:

- Developing effective means for teachers to communicate with one another
- Being easily accessible to teachers
- Maintaining open and effective lines of communication with staff

To illustrate, the school leader displays the responsibility of Communication when he sets up and presides over informal, biweekly, after-school discussion sessions at which teachers can discuss their concerns. The school leader demonstrates the responsibility of Communication when she initiates a monthly newsletter distributed to all faculty members describing significant decisions she has made or is considering.

5. Culture

By definition, every school has a culture. As Hanson (2001) explains:

> Schools also have their own unique cultures that are shaped around a particular combination of values, beliefs, and feelings. These school cultures emphasize what is of paramount importance to them as they strive to develop their knowledge base in a particular direction, such as producing outstanding football teams, high SAT scores, disciplined classrooms and skilled auto mechanics, or sending kids to college who come from inner-city urban schools. Although the culture of a school is not visible to the human eye, its artifacts and symbols reflect specific cultural priorities. (p. 641)

Like the responsibility of Communication, *Culture* is implicit or explicit in virtually every theory and in the principles espoused by every theorist discussed in Chapter 2. Although a culture is a natural by-product of people working in close proximity, it can be a positive or negative influence on a school's effectiveness. An effective leader builds a culture that positively influences teachers, who, in turn, positively influence students. As Leithwood and Riehl (2003) explain:

> Leaders act through and with other people. Leaders sometimes do things, through words or actions, that have a direct effect on the primary goals of the collective, but more often their agency consists of influencing the thoughts and actions of other persons and establishing policies that enable others to be effective. (p. 8)

Fostering a school culture that indirectly affects student achievement is a strong theme within the literature on principal leadership. For example, Scribner,

Cockrell, Cockrell, and Valentine (1999) assert that building principals can do little to directly affect student achievement. Consequently, an effective culture is the primary tool with which a leader fosters change.

In keeping with these various sentiments, our study defined the responsibility of Culture as the extent to which the leader fosters shared beliefs and a sense of community and cooperation among staff. We found the following behaviors associated with this responsibility as a result of our meta-analysis:

- Promoting cohesion among staff
- Promoting a sense of well-being among staff
- Developing an understanding of purpose among staff
- Developing a shared vision of what the school could be like

To illustrate, a principal deploys the responsibility of Culture when she takes time at faculty meetings to point out and praise examples of teachers working together. The principal practices the responsibility of Culture when he has an extended discussion with faculty regarding the underlying purpose and mission of the school.

6. Discipline

One important task of the school principal is to protect teachers from undue distractions. It is an acknowledged aspect of instructional leadership, and many theorists address it directly or indirectly. Elmore (2000) explains that "school leaders are hired and retained based largely on their capacity to buffer teachers from outside interference." (p. 7). He goes on to say, "Buffering consists of creating structures and procedures around the technical core of teaching." (p. 6). The structures and procedures Elmore speaks of are those that protect instructional time. Specifically, he notes that "there is a role for leaders in moving non-instructional issues out of the way to prevent them from creating confusion and distraction in school systems, schools, and classrooms" (p. 24). Youngs and King (2002) have also highlighted the importance of protecting or shielding teachers. In describing the behaviors of one highly successful principal, they explain that "she buffered the school from the potentially negative effects of the new district initiatives." (p. 662).

The acts of "buffering" and "protection" converge to form our responsibility of *Discipline*. Specifically, Discipline refers to protecting teachers from issues and influences that would detract from their instructional time or focus. We prefer the term *discipline* to *buffering* or *protection* because it conveys the message that this responsibility is perhaps a natural consequence of attending to the primary work of schools—teaching.

Specific behaviors and characteristics associated with this responsibility as identified in our meta-analysis are the following:

- Protecting instructional time from interruptions
- Protecting teachers from internal and external distractions

To illustrate, the school leader uses the responsibility of Discipline when she establishes and enforces a policy that no announcements are to be made during instructional time. The school leader executes the responsibility of Discipline when he handles an issue with the local media in a way that does not involve individual teachers.

7. Flexibility

Flexibility refers to the extent to which leaders adapt their leadership behavior to the needs of the current situation and are comfortable with dissent. It is associated with transformational leadership as well as the theories of Bennis (2003), Collins (2001), and Spillane (Spillane & Sherer, 2004). Fullan (2001) explains flexibility in the following way:

> To recommend employing different leadership strategies that simultaneously and sequentially combine different elements seems like complicated advice, but developing this deeper feel for the change process by accumulating insights and wisdom across situations and time may turn out to be the most practical thing we can do. . . . (p. 48)

Deering, Dilts, and Russell (2003) describe this responsibility in terms of "mental agility." Lashway (2001) emphasizes the acceptance of diverse opinions. He notes that effective leaders "encourage and nurture individual initiative . . . leaders must protect and encourage the voices of participants who offer differing points of view" (p. 8).

Specific behaviors associated with this responsibility and identified in our meta-analysis are the following:

- Adapting leadership style to the needs of specific situations
- Being directive or nondirective as the situation warrants
- Encouraging people to express diverse and contrary opinions
- Being comfortable with making major changes in how things are done

To illustrate, the responsibility of Flexibility is demonstrated when the principal determines that he must directly intervene in a decision being made by members of the mathematics department because it will have negative consequences for other faculty members. The principal executes the responsibility of Flexibility when she decides to refrain from giving her opinion regarding the adoption of a new textbook to ensure that teachers feel ownership over the decision.

8. Focus

One common opinion expressed by researchers and theorists alike is that schools are quite willing to try new things—perhaps too much so. As Elmore (2002) explains, "The pathology of American schools is that they know how to change. They know how to change promiscuously and at the drop of a hat. What schools do not know how to do is to improve, to engage in sustained and continuous progress toward a performance goal" (p. 1). Fullan (1993) echoes these comments, noting, "It is probably closer to the truth to say that the main problem in public education is not resistance to change but the presence of too many innovations mandated or adopted uncritically and superficially on an ad hoc fragmented basis" (p. 23). An effective school leader ensures that change efforts are aimed at clear, concrete goals.

In keeping with comments like these, the responsibility of *Focus* refers to the extent to which the leader establishes clear goals and keeps those goals in the forefront of the school's attention. Effective execution of this responsibility provides a safeguard against expending vast amounts of energy and resources on school improvement initiatives that go nowhere. As described by Leithwood and Riehl (2003), "Leadership involves purposes and direction. Leaders know the ends toward which they are striving. They pursue goals with clarity and tenacity, and are accountable for their accomplishments" (p. 7).

Specific behaviors and characteristics associated with this responsibility and identified in our meta-analysis are the following:

• Establishing concrete goals for curriculum, instruction, and assessment practices within the school
• Establishing concrete goals for the general functioning of the school
• Establishing high, concrete goals, and expectations that all students will meet them
• Continually keeping attention on established goals

To illustrate, the school leader executes the responsibility of Focus when she and the staff set a goal that by the end of the year the curriculum will be aligned with the state standards and the state test in all subject areas. The responsibility of Focus is demonstrated when the school leader and the faculty set a goal that by the end of the year 65 percent of the students will be at standard or above in mathematics.

The school leader displays the responsibility of Focus when she reminds faculty members of the school goals at faculty meetings.

9. Ideals/Beliefs

It might be said that human beings are at their best when they operate from a set of strong ideals and beliefs. De Pree (1989) explains:

> Beliefs are connected to intimacy. Beliefs come from policies or standards or practices. Practice without belief is a forlorn existence. Managers who have no beliefs but only understand methodology and quantification are modern-day eunuchs. They can never engender competence or confidence. (p. 55)

Bennis (2003) places well-articulated ideals and beliefs at the core of effective leadership. Youngs and King (2002) view beliefs as a subtle but powerful force used by a principal to effect change. They explain that "one prominent way in which principals shape school conditions and teaching practices is through their beliefs." (pp. 643–644). Cottrell (2002) echoes Bennis's (2003) position by offering the following advice to leaders: "Guard your integrity like it's your most precious management possession" (p. 52).

Specific behaviors and characteristics associated with this responsibility and identified in our meta-analysis are the following:

- Possessing well-defined beliefs about schools, teaching, and learning
- Sharing beliefs about school, teaching, and learning with the staff
- Demonstrating behaviors that are consistent with beliefs

To illustrate, the principal exhibits the responsibility of Ideals/Beliefs when she begins the school year by writing and distributing to faculty members a description of her belief that a school must pay particular attention to students who come from educationally disadvantaged backgrounds. The responsibility of Ideals/Beliefs is demonstrated when the principal explains a decision he has made in terms of his belief that academic achievement is not the only measure of success in a school.

10. Input

Input refers to the extent to which the school leader involves teachers in the design and implementation of important decisions and policies. It is associated with transformational leadership, TQM, and instructional leadership. Silins, Mulford, and Zarins (2002) attest to the importance of this responsibility by noting that a school's effectiveness is proportional to "the extent to which teachers participate in all aspects of the school's functioning—including school policy decisions and review—share a coherent sense of direction, and acknowledge the wider school community" (p. 618). They further explain that effective leadership is a function of "the extent to which the principal works toward whole-staff consensus in establishing school priorities and communicates these priorities and goals to students and staff, giving a sense of overall purpose" (p. 620). De Pree (1989) refers to this responsibility as "participative management":

> Everyone has the right and the duty to influence decision making and to understand the results. Participative management guarantees that decisions will not be arbitrary, secret, or closed to questioning. Participative management is not democratic. Having a say differs from having a vote. (pp. 24–25)

Finally, Cottrell (2002) warns of the consequences of not attending to this responsibility:

> They [principals] forget to take the time to listen to their people. Soon they become insensitive to the needs and desires of the individuals on the team. Arrogance, out-of-control egos, and insensitivity are part of the management land trap. Don't allow yourself to fall into that trap—listen to your people! (p. 87)

Specific behaviors and characteristics associated with this responsibility and identified in our meta-analysis are the following:

- Providing opportunities for staff to be involved in developing school policies
- Providing opportunities for staff input on all important decisions
- Using leadership teams in decision making

To illustrate, the school leader demonstrates the responsibility of Input when he institutes the use of an "honest reaction box" outside his office. Faculty members may place signed or unsigned comments in the box. The principal reads all comments and offers the topics for discussion at faculty meetings. The school leader employs the responsibility of Input when she shares information about an important topic with the faculty and asks for their guidance on the decision.

11. Intellectual Stimulation

Intellectual Stimulation refers to the extent to which the school leader ensures that faculty and staff are aware of the most current theories and practices regarding effective schooling and makes discussions of those theories and practices a regular aspect of the school's culture. Supovitz (2002) refers to this characteristic as the extent to which the leader engages staff in meaningful dialogue regarding research and theory. As a result of his review of the research on leadership accountability,

Lashway (2001) links this responsibility to the change process. He explains that "deep changes require deep learning, and leaders must build teacher learning into the everyday fabric of school life" (p. 7). Fullan (2001) describes this responsibility in terms of the need for "knowledge building, knowledge sharing, knowledge creation, knowledge management" (p. 77). Finally, Kaagan and Markle (1993) explain:

> Discussing educational issues is something that the diverse actors in the education drama rarely get to do. Merely providing the time and resources to support team development around these issues seems to have a marked pay-off. By making overtly collective and open reflections that up to now have remained singular and closed, there emerges a strong will and capacity to innovate. (p. 11)

Specific behaviors and characteristics associated with this responsibility and identified in our meta-analysis are the following:

- Continually exposing staff to cutting-edge research and theory on effective schooling
- Keeping informed about current research and theory on effective schooling
- Fostering systematic discussion regarding current research and theory on effective schooling

To illustrate, the principal executes the responsibility of Intellectual Stimulation when he institutes a book group to study the differing philosophies underlying the whole-language and phonics-based approaches to reading because the school is considering the adoption of a new reading program that combines the two. The responsibility of Intellectual Stimulation is demonstrated when the principal hires a speaker to talk about economic trends and how they are affecting the job market, and then uses the presentation as a springboard for a discussion of how well the school is preparing students for the future.

12. Involvement in Curriculum, Instruction, and Assessment

This responsibility addresses the extent to which the principal is directly involved in the design and implementation of curriculum, instruction, and assessment activities at the classroom level. This type of hands-on support has been a staple of discussions regarding school leadership for decades. Like the responsibility of Visibility (discussed later), *Involvement in Curriculum, Instruction, and Assessment* is considered critical to the concept of instructional leadership.

Stein and D'Amico (2000) attest to the importance of this responsibility by noting that knowledge of subject matter and pedagogy should be as important to administrators as it is to teachers. As a result of their synthesis of the research on leadership, researchers at the National Institute on Educational Governance,

Finance, Policymaking, and Management (1999) noted that an administrator's ability and willingness to provide input regarding classroom practices was one of the most highly valued characteristics reported by teachers. In that same brief, the authors reported that in one large school district in the Northwest, both the superintendent and the principals regularly visited classrooms with the goal of learning to recognize and describe good teaching and to provide better instructional feedback to teachers. Relative to this responsibility, Reeves (2004) emphasizes the principal's involvement in assessment practices. He explains that in an effective school

> the principal personally evaluates student work and participates in collaborative scoring sessions in which the percentage agreement by the faculty is measured and posted. The principal personally reviews faculty-created assessments as part of each teacher evaluation and coaching meeting. (p. 50)

Specific behaviors and characteristics associated with this responsibility as defined by our meta-analysis are the following:

- Being directly involved in helping teachers design curricular activities
- Being directly involved in helping teachers address assessment issues
- Being directly involved in helping teachers address instructional issues

To illustrate, the school leader demonstrates the responsibility of Involvement in Curriculum, Instruction, and Assessment when she regularly meets with teachers to review the use of end-of-quarter tests that have been developed to determine if they can be improved. The school leader also executes this responsibility when she meets with members of the science department to discuss how they will ensure that the required science courses address the content of the science section on the state test.

13. Knowledge of Curriculum, Instruction, and Assessment

Whereas Involvement in Curriculum, Instruction, and Assessment deals with a hands-on approach to classroom practices, *Knowledge of Curriculum, Instruction, and Assessment* addresses the extent to which the leader is aware of best practices in these domains. The focus here is on the acquisition and cultivation of knowledge, whereas the responsibility of Involvement in Curriculum, Instruction, and Assessment is action oriented. Fullan (2001) attests to the importance of this responsibility by explaining that a principal's knowledge of effective practices in curriculum, instruction, and assessment is necessary to provide guidance for teachers on the day-to-day tasks of teaching and learning. Elmore (2000) adds that "leadership is the guidance and direction of instructional improvement" (p. 13). To accomplish this, principals must be students of best practices. Reeves (2004) echoes that an extensive knowledge base regarding best practices is necessary to mentor teachers. To develop an extensive knowledge base, Fullan (2001) recommends that principals meet monthly with other administrators to stay abreast of current advances in curriculum, instruction, and assessment.

As straightforward and obvious as this responsibility might appear, some believe that it receives little attention in practice. To illustrate, in a 1999 policy brief, researchers at the National Institute of Educational Governance, Finance, Policymaking, and Management noted that "instructional knowledge has traditionally received little emphasis in the hiring process for principals' jobs" (paragraph 4). When describing the results of a study of interview protocols used with principals, the researchers noted that "people who did well in other stages of interviewing could not accurately describe the lessons they had seen" (paragraph 4).

Specific behaviors and characteristics identified in our meta-analysis and associated with this responsibility are the following:

- Possessing extensive knowledge about effective instructional practices
- Possessing extensive knowledge about effective curricular practices
- Possessing extensive knowledge about effective assessment practices
- Providing conceptual guidance regarding effective classroom practices

To illustrate, the principal demonstrates the responsibility of Knowledge of Curriculum, Instruction, and Assessment when she attends a conference featuring new research on instructional practices. This responsibility is also evident when the principal reads a book on the research supporting a comprehensive school reform program the school is considering adopting.

14. Monitoring/Evaluating

As a result of a review of almost 8,000 studies, Hattie (1992) concluded that "the most powerful single modification that enhances achievement is feedback." According to Hattie, "the simplest prescription for improving education must be 'dollops of feedback' " (p. 9). However, feedback does not occur automatically. It is a function of design. Creating a system that provides feedback is at the core of the responsibility of *Monitoring/Evaluating*. More specifically, within our meta-analysis this responsibility refers to the extent to which the leader monitors the effectiveness of school practices in terms of their impact on student achievement.

As a result of his study of successful schools, Elmore (2000) concluded that "superintendents and system-level staff were active in monitoring curriculum and instruction in classrooms and schools." (p. 26). Others have related this responsibility to the act of evaluation. For example, De Pree (1989) explains that performance reviews, when done well, represent a strong leverage point in the management of a school. Kaagan and Markle (1993) note that in the most effective schools "constant evaluation" is a norm.

Specific behaviors and characteristics associated with this responsibility and identified in our meta-analysis are the following:

- Continually monitoring the effectiveness of the school's curricular, instructional, and assessment practices
- Being continually aware of the impact of the school's practices on student achievement

To illustrate, the responsibility of Monitoring/Evaluating is enacted when the school leader implements standards-based report cards and uses the information from those report cards to determine the extent to which the school is meeting its goal to increase the number of students who are at or above standard in writing. The school leader also exhibits this responsibility by systematically observing the implementation of the new science program.

15. Optimizer

As a result of their study involving more than 1,200 K–12 teachers, Blase and Kirby (2000) identified optimism as a critical characteristic of an effective school leader. They note that the principal commonly sets the emotional tone in a school for better or for worse. Kelehear (2003) explains that at appropriate times an effective leader is willing to bolster a change initiative with his optimism and energy. For Kelehear, the creation of an optimistic emotional tone is a strategy that the principal should execute at appropriate times. Kaagan and Markle (1993) describe the benefit of a positive emotional tone as an environment where "new ideas and innovation abound" (p. 5).

Aligned with these sentiments, the responsibility of *Optimizer* refers to the extent to which the leader inspires others and is the driving force when implementing a challenging innovation. Specific behaviors and characteristics associated with this responsibility and identified in our meta-analysis are the following:

- Inspiring teachers to accomplish things that might be beyond their grasp
- Being the driving force behind major initiatives
- Portraying a positive attitude about the ability of staff to accomplish substantial things

To illustrate, the principal displays the responsibility of Optimizer when she distributes a summary of the research supporting the new standards-based report card the staff is considering implementing. The responsibility of Optimizer is evident when the principal announces to the faculty that she understands that implementing standards-based report cards will have difficult moments and will take time, but that she will provide support and the necessary resources until implementation is effectively completed.

16. Order

The fact that order, as opposed to chaos, is good for a school is self-evident. In terms of leadership behavior of principals, the relevant questions are, What are the defining characteristics of an orderly school and how is order established?

Order in any dynamic environment is created by structure. The explicit structures in an environment inhibit certain events and facilitate others. Fritz (1984) explains this dynamic in the following way: "Once a structure exists, energy moves through that structure by the path of least resistance. In other words, energy moves where it is easiest for it to go" (p. 4). Following this theme, we defined *Order* in our meta-analysis as the extent to which the leader establishes a set of standard operating principles and routines.

In the context of schools, Nunnelley, Whaley, Mull, and Hott (2003) define order as clear boundaries and rules for both students and faculty. In an analysis of successful schools in a large metropolitan area, Supovitz (2002) identified order as a necessary condition: "groups need structures that provide them with the leadership, time, resources, and incentives to engage in instructional work" (p. 1618). In the context of standards-based education, Lashway (2001) explains: "This means not only finding the time and money but reshaping routine policies and practices. Staffing, scheduling, and other seemingly mundane issues can have a major impact on the school's capacity to meet new standards" (p. 1). He goes on to say: "Daily routines can hinder or help teacher learning, and they also send important signals about the organization's priorities" (p. 4).

In our meta-analysis, the responsibility of *Order* involved the following specific behaviors:

• Establishing routines for the smooth running of the school that staff understand and follow
  • Providing and reinforcing clear structures, rules, and procedures for staff
  • Providing and reinforcing clear structures, rules, and procedures for students

To illustrate, the responsibility of Order is executed when the school leader establishes and implements a procedure for equitable access to the copy machine. He also demonstrates this responsibility when he establishes and implements an equitable system for monitoring the lunchroom.

17. Outreach

A school is not an island. Rather, it functions in a complex context that must be addressed if the school is to be highly effective. The responsibility of *Outreach* refers to the extent to which the leader is an advocate and a spokesperson for the school to all stakeholders. Cotton (2003) affirms the importance of this factor, explaining that the principal must have a willingness and an ability to communicate to individuals both inside and outside the school. Benecivenga and Elias (2003) add that partnerships are required to effectively run a school, and these partnerships necessarily extend beyond the boundaries of the school to the community at large. They note that Comer (2003) echoes this same sentiment when he says, "It takes a village to raise a child." They further explain that "educational leaders must ensure that local police and fire departments, community newspapers, local private and public agencies and civic groups, and local government officials participate in the culture of the school community" (p. 70).

Specific behaviors and characteristics associated with this responsibility are the following:

- Ensuring that the school complies with all district and state mandates
- Being an advocate of the school with parents
- Being an advocate of the school with the central office
- Being an advocate of the school with the community at large

To illustrate, the principal demonstrates the responsibility of Outreach when she systematically reviews all district regulations to ensure that her school is in compliance. The responsibility of Outreach also is employed when she regularly sends a memo to the superintendent detailing the latest accomplishments of the school.

18. Relationships

A case can be made that effective professional relationships are central to the effective execution of many of the other responsibilities. In the context of our meta-analysis, the responsibility of *Relationships* refers to the extent to which the school leader demonstrates an awareness of the personal lives of teachers and staff. To foster this responsibility, Elmore (2000) recommends that principals should "rely more heavily on face-to-face relationships than on bureaucratic routines" (p. 32). He further notes, "In the panoply of rewards and sanctions that attach to accountability systems, the most powerful incentives reside in the face-to-face relationships among people in the organization, not in external systems" (p. 31). Citing research and theory on emotional intelligence, Fullan (2001) describes the importance of the school leader's forming emotional bonds with and among teachers that help staff and administrators stay aligned and focused during times of uncertainty.

Specific behaviors and characteristics associated with this responsibility as identified in our meta-analysis are the following:

- Being informed about significant personal issues within the lives of staff members
- Being aware of personal needs of teachers
- Acknowledging significant events in the lives of staff members
- Maintaining personal relationships with teachers

To illustrate, the school leader executes the responsibility of Relationships when sending flowers in the name of the school to the family of a teacher who has lost a loved one. The school leader also exhibits this responsibility when he makes an effort to say hello to every teacher in the school at least once a day and to ask teachers how they are doing.

19. Resources

Resources are to a complex organization what food is to the body. In the context of school leadership, Deering, Dilts, and Russell (2003) explain that resources important to a school extend well beyond books and materials. They state:

> To be successful, leaders need to create organizations fluid enough to respond quickly to new circumstances. This involves the alignment of several levels of resources necessary to analyze, plan, and take action in response to opportunities and threats that the future brings. (p. 34)

Fullan (2001) expands the concept even further:

> Another component of school capacity concerns the extent to which schools garner technical resources. Instructional improvement requires additional resources in the form of materials, equipment, space, time, and access to new ideas and to expertise. (pp. 64–65)

One of the most frequently mentioned resources important to the effective functioning of a school is the professional development opportunities for teachers.

Elmore (2000) explains that "heavy investments in highly targeted professional development for teachers and principals in the fundamentals of strong classroom instruction" (p. 28) are critical to the success of a school. In their discussion of professional development, Nunnelley, Whaley, Mull, and Hott (2003) include professional growth plans. They explain that ". . . the principal is obligated to making sure strong professional growth plans are enacted" (p. 56).

In keeping with comments such as these, within our meta-analysis the responsibility of *Resources* refers to the extent to which the leader provides teachers with materials and professional development necessary for the successful execution of their duties. Specific behaviors associated with this responsibility found within our meta-analysis are the following:

- Ensuring that teachers have the necessary materials and equipment
- Ensuring that teachers have the necessary staff development opportunities to directly enhance their teaching

To illustrate, the principal demonstrates the responsibility of Resources when she meets with every teacher once a month to ask what materials they need. This responsibility is also deployed when the principal schedules a staff development session on a topic that teachers have explicitly requested.

20. Situational Awareness

Situational Awareness addresses leaders' awareness of the details and the undercurrents regarding the functioning of the school and their use of this information to address current and potential problems. In a summary of the research on leadership accountability, Lashway (2001) describes this responsibility in the following way: "Deep change requires knowing what is happening, distancing the ego from daily events, and honestly appraising the state of the organization" (p. 8). Deering, Dilts, and Russell (2003) describe this responsibility as anticipatory leadership. They exhort principals to identify "clues of coming opportunities and hints about emerging threats. With the openness and mental agility of truly anticipatory leadership throughout the organization, the organization is well positioned to survive and prosper" (p. 33).

Specific behaviors and characteristics associated with this responsibility and identified in our meta-analysis are the following:

- Accurately predicting what could go wrong from day to day
- Being aware of informal groups and relationships among the staff
- Being aware of issues in the school that have not surfaced but could create discord

To illustrate, the school leader demonstrates the responsibility of Situational Awareness when he studies the schedule in an attempt to identify hidden problems that it creates for teachers or students. He also executes this responsibility when he meets with a group of teachers who he has heard are disappointed in a decision he has recently made.

21. Visibility

The responsibility of *Visibility* addresses the extent to which the school leader has contact and interacts with teachers, students, and parents. As explained in Chapter 2, this responsibility is commonly associated with instructional leadership. Whitaker (1997) describes the importance of visibility in the following way:

> The research has demonstrated the great need for strong instructional leadership in schools and has identified several common characteristics of effective leaders. One of those characteristics, extremely important in the life of a school and often neglected, is that of being a visible principal. (p. 155)

Fink and Resnick (2001) add that effective principals "are in teachers' classrooms every day, and it is difficult to draw the line between observations that have an evaluative intent and those that are part of the professional support system" (p. 606). Blase and Blase (1999) echo these comments, explaining that highly effective principals are in classrooms on a routine basis. The proposed effect of Visibility is twofold: first, it communicates the message that the principal is interested and engaged in the daily operations of the school; second, it provides opportunities for the principal to interact with teachers and students regarding substantive issues.

Specific behaviors and characteristics associated with this responsibility as found in our meta-analysis are the following:

- Making systematic and frequent visits to classrooms
- Having frequent contact with students
- Being highly visible to students, teachers, and parents

To illustrate, the principal exemplifies the responsibility of Visibility when she attends school football, basketball, and baseball games as frequently as possible. This responsibility is also demonstrated when the principal makes daily visits to classrooms simply to ask teachers and students how things are going.

Examining the Relative Effect of the Responsibilities

Again, we must point out that the 21 responsibilities identified in our meta-analysis are not new to the literature on leadership. Each one has been mentioned explicitly or implicitly by a host of researchers and theorists. Indeed, we refer to these behaviors as responsibilities because they are, or at least should be, standard operating procedures for effective principals. Perhaps this wide array of behaviors explains why it is so difficult to be an effective school leader. The variety of skills a leader must master is daunting indeed.

What is new to the leadership literature is the quantification of the relationship each responsibility has with student academic achievement. The quantified relationship for each responsibility is reported as the correlation in the third column of Figure 4.1, pp. 42–43. These correlations are interesting. However, probably the most important information depicted in Figure 4.1 is the 95 percent confidence interval reported in the fourth column. Technical Note 9 (p. 153) discusses confidence intervals in some detail. Here we should simply note that a confidence interval that does not include the value .00 indicates that a correlation is significant at the .05 level. Recall from the discussion in Chapter 1 that when a researcher says her findings are significant at the .05 level, she is stating that the reported results could happen by chance 5 times in 100 or less if there is no real relationship between the variables under investigation (in this case the variables under investigation are student academic achievement and the 21 leadership responsibilities). Figure 4.1 illustrates that all 21 of the responsibilities we identified have a statistically significant relationship with student achievement.

This is perhaps the first time in the history of leadership research in the United States that we can point to a set of competencies (responsibilities) that are research based. We believe this to be a significant addition to the knowledge base regarding school leadership.

We would like to emphasize that in the preceding discussion, we listed the 21 responsibilities in alphabetic order. We did so to communicate the message that they are all important. Indeed, as demonstrated in the next chapter, their rank order changes when they are viewed from a different perspective. When we list the 21 responsibilities in order of their strength of relationship with student achievement, some interesting patterns emerge. To illustrate, consider Figure 4.2. Again, we caution that interpreting the rank order depicted in Figure 4.2 in a rigid fashion would be a mistake. For example, it would be ill-advised to conclude that Situational Awareness is the most important responsibility and Relationships is the least important based on their relative positions in Figure 4.2.

Probably what is most striking about Figure 4.2 is how close the correlations are in size. Twenty of 21 correlations, or 95 percent, are between the values of .18 and .28. Specifically, the responsibility of Relationships has a correlation of .18 and the

FIGURE 4.2
21 Responsibilities Listed in Order of Correlation with Student Academic Achievement

Correlation with Achievement	Responsibility
.33	Situational Awareness
.32	
.31	
.30	
.29	
.28	Flexibility
.27	Discipline Outreach Monitoring/Evaluating
.26	
.25	Culture Order Resources Knowledge of Curriculum, Instruction, and Assessment Input Change Agent
.24	Focus Contingent Rewards Intellectual Stimulation
.23	Communication
.22	Ideals/Beliefs
.21	
.20	Involvement in Curriculum, Instruction, and Assessment Visibility Optimizer
.19	Affirmation
.18	Relationships

responsibility of Flexibility has a correlation of .28. Contrasting these extremes using the interpretation of correlations introduced in Chapter 1 provides a useful perspective. A correlation of .18 implies that an increase in a principal's effectiveness in Relationships from the 50th percentile to the 84th percentile is associated with an increase in a school's achievement from the 50th percentile to the 57th percentile. An increase in a principal's effectiveness in terms of Flexibility from the 50th percentile to the 84th percentile is associated with an increase in a school's achievement from the 50th percentile to the 61st percentile. Although their relative effects differ somewhat, clearly the responsibilities of Relationships and Flexibility can have a substantial influence on student achievement.

Because the responsibility of Situational Awareness has the largest correlation, .33, we should at least comment on it. Recall that this responsibility addresses the extent to which the principal is aware of the details and undercurrents in the running of the school and uses this information to address current and future problems. According to Figure 4.1, the correlation for this responsibility involves the fewest number of schools (91) and the second-fewest number of studies (5). Had a few more studies involving a few more schools been found, the correlation of .33 might have shrunk considerably. However, it makes intuitive sense that a school leader must understand the innermost workings of the school at the nuts-and-bolts level to be effective. The more one knows about the inner workings of an organization, the more one is able to lead and manage that organization.

Summary and Conclusions

Our meta-analysis defined 21 leadership responsibilities. Although each has been addressed in the theoretical literature for decades, the fact that they have a statistically significant relationship with student achievement, as indicated by our meta-analysis, is an important new addition to the research and theoretical literature. Our findings indicate that all are important to the effective execution of leadership in schools.

5

Two Types of Change

Although the 21 responsibilities described in Chapter 4 are useful in their own right, they tell us little about how the responsibilities relate to one another. It seems logical that the responsibility of Relationships, let's say, might be related to Communication, which might be related to Culture, and so on. To address this issue of relatedness, we conducted a factor analysis using the responses to a questionnaire designed to measure principals' behavior in terms of the 21 responsibilities. The specifics of that factor analysis and the questionnaire we used are described in Technical Note 11 (p. 161). In brief, though, a factor analysis helps identify the underlying traits (factors) that are common to a number of observable characteristics. In this case, the observable characteristics are the 21 leadership responsibilities.

The primary finding from our factor analysis was that two traits or factors seem to underlie the 21 responsibilities. These two factors are first-order change and second-order change.

First- and Second-Order Change

One of the constants within K–12 education is that someone is always trying to change it—someone is always proposing a new program or a new practice. Many of these programs and practices are well thought-out, well articulated, and even well researched. Yet many, maybe even most, educational innovations are short-lived. Cuban (1987) has chronicled the fate of a number of innovations, all of which were basically sound. Some of the more visible ones that have not endured are programmed instruction, open education, the Platoon System, and flexible scheduling.

A question posed by Cuban and many others is, Why did these innovations fail? Our factor analysis provides a possible and plausible explanation. Specifically, our factor analysis (as well as our collective experience) indicates that the leadership supporting an innovation must be consistent with the order of magnitude of the change represented by that innovation. If leadership techniques do not match the order of change required by an innovation, the innovation will probably fail regardless of its merits. Some innovations require changes that are gradual and subtle; others require changes that are drastic and dramatic. For the purposes of this discussion, we refer to these categories of change as first-order change and second-order change, respectively.

First-order change is incremental. It can be thought of as the next most obvious step to take in a school or a district. Second-order change is anything but incremental. It involves dramatic departures from the expected, both in defining a given problem and in finding a solution. In other publications we have described the difference between first- and second-order change as that between "incremental change" and "deep change" (see Waters, Marzano, & McNulty, 2004a, 2004b). Incremental change fine-tunes the system through a series of small steps that do not depart radically from the past. Deep change alters the system in fundamental ways, offering a dramatic shift in direction and requiring new ways of thinking and acting.

Using other names and terminology, a great many theorists have discussed this basic dichotomy. For example, Heifetz (1994) discusses the distinction between first- and second-order change by describing Type I, Type II, and Type III problems. He notes that Type I problems are those for which there is a reasonable expectation that traditional solutions will suffice. Type II problems are those that might be fairly well defined, but for which no clear-cut solution is available. Type III problems are those for which current ways of thinking do not provide a solution. Whereas Type I and Type II problems typically require first-order change, Type III problems require second-order change.

Argyris and Schön (1974, 1978) address the distinction between first- and second-order change in their discussion of single-loop learning and double-loop learning. Single-loop learning occurs when an organization approaches a problem from the perspective of strategies that have succeeded in the past. When a particular strategy is successful, it reinforces its utility. If a strategy is not successful, another is tried until success is achieved. In a sense, then, single-loop learning teaches us which of our current set of strategies works best in different situations. Double-loop learning occurs when no existing strategy suffices to solve a given problem. In these situations, the problem must be conceptualized differently or new strategies must be conceived. Double-loop learning, then, expands an organization's view of the world while adding new strategies to an organization's repertoire.

The Difficulty of Second-Order Change

The common human response is to address virtually all problems as though they were first-order change issues. It makes sense that we would tend to approach new problems from the perspective of our experiences—as issues that can be solved using our previous repertoire of solutions. Argyris and Schön (1974) explain this tendency in terms of "mental maps." They argue that individuals and organizations have mental maps regarding how to act in situations. When faced with a new situation, we consult one or more of our mental maps. Unfortunately, solutions to most recurring modern-day problems require a second-order perspective. Heifetz (1994) notes:

> For many problems, however, no adequate response has yet been developed. Examples abound: poverty at home and abroad, industrial competitiveness, failing schools, drug abuse, the national debt, racial prejudice, ethnic strife, AIDS, environmental pollution. No organizational response can be called into play that will clearly resolve these kinds of problems. (p. 72)

Fritz (1984) explains the tendency to approach all situations as first-order change issues in the following way:

> A common rule of thumb in life is to have a formula about how things should work, so that if you learn the formula, you will always know what to do. From a reactive-responsive orientation, this notion is very appealing, because with such a formula you would hypothetically be prepared to respond appropriately to any situation. Unfortunately, at best this would prepare you for situations that are predictable and familiar. Your mastery of those situations would be similar to that of a well-trained mouse in a maze. From the orientation of the creative, on the other hand, the only rule of thumb about process is not to have a rule of thumb. (p. 73)

Finally, Fullan (2001) explains: "The big problems of the day are complex, rife with paradoxes and dilemmas. For these problems, there are no once-and-for-all answers" (p. 73).

The comments of Heifetz, Fritz, and Fullan are apropos to schools that approach persistent problems in the same manner year after year. Witness the decades-old problem of the achievement gap between children from poverty versus children not from poverty. This issue has been a focus of educational reform for decades. Indeed, it was part of President Lyndon Johnson's War on Poverty in the mid-1960s. In spite of decades of attention, the problem persists. Clarke

(2000) explains that to change schools in response to issues like this one, we need to develop new ways of thinking about them:

> We need to develop a new language of improvement that is better designed to respond to the problems of the present and lead into the future, rather than one that is designed around the solution of problems belonging to an age gone by. (p. 48)

With all due respect to Clarke's advice, words like these are perhaps too easily spoken, for undertaking second-order change is never a small task. In fact, second-order change is so complex that it is best not entered into lightly. Indeed, Prestine (1992) cautions that second-order change cannot be approached hesitantly. Sizer asserts that second-order change calls for decisive, swift action: "I'm increasingly persuaded that schools that go slow and a little at a time end up doing so little that they succeed in only upsetting everything without accruing the benefits of change" (in Fullan, 1993, p. 8).

The differences in first- and second-order change, combined with the natural inclination to approach all changes as first order in nature, provide a plausible explanation for the failed innovations chronicled by Cuban (1987). Perhaps these innovations represented second-order changes in education but were managed and led in a manner more appropriate to first-order change. Consider, for example, open education, identified by Cuban as a failed innovation with research supporting it. Indeed, Hedges and Olkin's (1985) review of the research on open education indicates that it had a positive effect on students' attitudes and achievement. Yet it was short-lived. On the surface, it might appear that open education represented a simple alteration in the physical structure of schools—it used large open spaces where different groups of students might be simultaneously involved in different activities. However, this simple physical change required alterations in scheduling protocols, in how teachers prepare for instruction and interact with one another, in how content is presented, and more. In short, open education required second-order change regarding the running of a school. A failure to recognize this fact coupled with the natural inclination to approach all innovations as first-order change might have caused those leading the innovation to employ inappropriate leadership behaviors. Ultimately, this led to the downfall of the innovation.

Leadership for First- Versus Second-Order Change

Clearly the distinction between first-order change and second-order change is an important one, particularly for schools. From the perspective of the findings from our meta-analysis, it raises the basic question, Which of the 21 responsibilities are appropriate to first-order change and which are appropriate to second-order change?

Leadership for First-Order Change: Managing the Daily Life of a School

The results of our factor analysis indicated that all 21 responsibilities are important to first-order change at least to some degree. This makes intuitive sense. Within our meta-analysis, the 21 responsibilities were exhibited in a wide variety of schools in a wide variety of situations. However, our factor analysis indicated not all 21 responsibilities are equally important to first-order change. Here is how the responsibilities ranked in relationship to first-order change as found in our factor analysis (see Technical Note 12 on p. 168 for a discussion of how this rank order was computed):

1. Monitoring/Evaluating
2. Culture
3. Ideals/Beliefs
4. Knowledge of Curriculum, Assessment, and Instruction
5. Involvement in Curriculum, Assessment, and Instruction
6. Focus
7. Order
8. & 9. Affirmation; Intellectual Stimulation (a tie in rank order)
10. Communication
11. Input
12. Relationships
13. Optimizer
14. Flexibility
15. Resources
16. Contingent Rewards
17. Situational Awareness
18. Outreach
19. Visibility
20. Discipline
21. Change Agent

This listing provides an interesting perspective on leadership for first-order change. It provides a different perspective on the relative importance of the 21 responsibilities from that implied in Figure 4.2 (p. 63). There we cautioned that it would be a mistake to overinterpret the ranking in Figure 4.2. Likewise, here we caution that the ranking in the list above should not be considered a negative mandate on the lower-ranked responsibilities. Change Agency, Discipline, Visibility, and other lower-ranked responsibilities must receive as much attention in the day-to-day operations as Monitoring/Evaluating, Culture, Ideals/Beliefs, and other highly ranked responsibilities.

Saying that all 21 responsibilities are related to first-order change is another way of saying that all 21 should define the standard operating procedures in a school. This notion is reflected in our subtitle for this section, "Managing the Daily Life of a School." First-order change is a by-product of the day-to-day operations of the school. The routine business of schooling demands corrections and alterations that, by definition, are first order in nature. The responsibilities, then, can be considered the management tools of effective school leaders. Figure 5.1 restates the 21 responsibilities in terms of specific management behaviors.

The list in Figure 5.1 is daunting. If all of these responsibilities are necessary to effectively manage the day-to-day operations of a school, how can a school leader possibly accomplish the task? We offer a solution to this problem in Chapter 7. Here we simply note that our factor analysis provided evidence of the complexity and breadth of the task of leading and managing a school through the routine changes and adjustments encountered throughout a school year.

Leadership for Second-Order Change

Unlike first-order change, we found that second-order change is related to seven of the 21 responsibilities in our factor analysis. They are the following:

1. Knowledge of Curriculum, Instruction, and Assessment
2. Optimizer
3. Intellectual Stimulation
4. Change Agent
5. Monitoring/Evaluating
6. Flexibility
7. Ideals/Beliefs

Again, these responsibilities are listed in rank order according to their relationship with second-order change. Considered at face value, this listing indicates that a principal seeking to provide leadership for a second-order change initiative should have the following priorities:

1. Being knowledgeable about how the *innovation* will affect curricular, instructional, and assessment practices and providing conceptual guidance in these areas (Knowledge of Curriculum, Instruction, and Assessment).

FIGURE 5.1
The 21 Responsibilities and Day-to-Day Management of a School

Managing a school involves . . .

1. Establishing an effective monitoring system to provide feedback on the effectiveness of the school's curriculum, instruction, and assessment practices and their effect on student achievement (Monitoring/Evaluating).
2. Building and maintaining a culture in which a common language is employed, ideas are shared, and staff members operate within the norms of cooperation (Culture).
3. Operating from a well-articulated and visible set of ideals and beliefs regarding schooling, teaching, and learning (Ideals/Beliefs).
4. Seeking out and keeping abreast of research and theory on effective practices in curriculum, instruction, and assessment (Knowledge of Curriculum, Instruction, and Assessment).
5. Actively helping teachers with issues regarding curriculum, instruction, and assessment in their classrooms (Involvement in Curriculum, Instruction, and Assessment).
6. Establishing concrete goals relative to student achievement as well as curriculum, instruction, and assessment practices in the school, and keeping these prominent in the day-to-day life of the school (Focus).
7. Establishing procedures and routines that give staff and students a sense of order and predictability (Order).
8. Recognizing and celebrating the legitimate successes of individuals within the school as well as the school as a whole; also recognizing and acknowledging failures when appropriate (Affirmation).
9. Fostering knowledge of research and theory on best practices among the staff through reading and discussion (Intellectual Stimulation).
10. Establishing and fostering clear lines of communication to and from the staff as well as within the staff (Communication).
11. Establishing and fostering procedures that ensure that staff members have input into key decisions and policies (Input).
12. Attending to and fostering personal relationships with the staff (Relationships).
13. Providing an optimistic view of what the school is doing and what the school can accomplish in the future (Optimizer).
14. Inviting and honoring the expression of a variety of opinions regarding the running of the school and adapting one's leadership style to the demands of the current situation (Flexibility).
15. Ensuring that the staff members have the necessary resources, support, and professional development to effectively execute the teaching and learning process (Resources).
16. Expecting and recognizing superior performance from the staff (Contingent Rewards).
17. Being keenly aware of the mechanisms and dynamics that define the day-to-day functioning of the school and using that awareness to forecast potential problems (Situational Awareness).
18. Being an advocate of the school to all relevant constituents and ensuring that the school complies with all important regulations and requirements (Outreach).
19. Being highly visible to teachers, students, and parents through frequent visits to classrooms (Visibility).
20. Protecting staff members from undue interruptions and controversies that might distract them from the teaching and learning process (Discipline).
21. Being willing to challenge school practices that have been in place for a long time and promoting the value of working at the edge of one's competence (Change Agent).

2. Being the driving force behind the new *innovation* and fostering the belief that it can produce exceptional results if members of the staff are willing to apply themselves (Optimizer).
3. Being knowledgeable about the research and theory regarding the *innovation* and fostering such knowledge among staff through reading and discussion (Intellectual Stimulation).
4. Challenging the status quo and being willing to move forward on the *innovation* without a guarantee of success (Change Agent).
5. Continually monitoring the impact of the *innovation* (Monitoring/Evaluating).
6. Being both directive and nondirective relative to the *innovation* as the situation warrants (Flexibility).
7. Operating in a manner consistent with his or her ideals and beliefs relative to the *innovation* (Ideals/Beliefs).

A number of aspects of this listing provide insight into leadership for second-order change. First, notice that the generalizations are couched in terms of an *innovation*. This is because second-order change manifests itself only in the context of a specific issue that is being addressed or a problem that is being solved. It is not something abstract or subtle. One does not engage in second-order change by simply talking about it. Fritz (1984) warns of the dangers of grandiose talk that is not followed by concrete action:

> This strategy is often employed by people who "hold the vision" while ignoring what is going on around them. These are the idle dreamers who give real visionaries a bad name. Not to confuse a creator with a dreamer. Dreamers only dream, but creators bring their dreams into reality. Only an accurate awareness of reality and an accurate awareness of your vision will enable you to form structural tension as an important part of the creative process. (p. 118)

Second, three of the seven responsibilities that are important aspects of second-order change are also listed as top priorities in the context of first-order change: Monitoring/Evaluating, Ideals/Beliefs, and Knowledge of Curriculum, Instruction, and Assessment. We might infer that behaviors within these responsibilities are vital to *any* type of change. Whether an innovation represents a small change (first-order) or a large change (second-order), a principal must establish a monitoring system that allows her to identify effective versus ineffective practices in curriculum, instruction, and assessment and evaluate the impact on student achievement. To do so, the principal must have and seek out knowledge of best practices in curriculum, instruction, and assessment. As a foundation for actions, the principal must communicate a strong set of ideals and beliefs. However, the principal's behavior must be consistent with the ideals and beliefs espoused. Behavior that is inconsistent with announced ideals and beliefs undermines any change initiative, large or small. Argyris and Schön (1974) discuss this dynamic by referring to "espoused theories" as opposed to "theories-in-use":

> When someone is asked how he would behave under certain circumstances, the answer he usually gives is his espoused theory of action for that situation. This is the theory of action to which he gives allegiance, and which, upon request, he communicates to others. However, the theory that actually governs his actions is this theory-in-use. (pp. 6–7)

Argyris and Schön further explain that leaders all too often espouse one set of ideals and beliefs yet operate from another—theories-in-use contradict their espoused theories. Apparently such a discrepancy rapidly erodes trust in the leader's fitness to manage.

Third, three of the seven responsibilities important to second-order change are ranked low in terms of their relative importance to first-order change. Specifically, the responsibility of Change Agent is important to second-order change but is rated last in relative importance to first-order change. This makes intuitive sense. Behaviors such as challenging the status quo seem far more appropriate to second-order change than to first-order change. Similarly, the responsibilities of Optimizer and Flexibility, although critical to second-order change, are ranked 13th and 14th, respectively, in importance to first-order change. Again this makes sense. Leadership behaviors that focus on the long-term potential of an innovation (Optimizer) and adapting to a changing landscape (Flexibility) are probably not vital to the incremental, predictable alterations that characterize first-order change but might be critical to large leaps that are not logical extensions of the past.

Perhaps the most revealing aspect of our factor analysis is that some responsibilities are negatively affected by second-order change. These responsibilities are the following:

1. Culture
2. Communication
3. Order
4. Input

As before, these responsibilities are listed in terms of the strength of relationship with second-order change. However, in this case that relationship is negative. That is, Culture has the strongest negative relationship with second-order change, and so on. It is important to understand that although the specific behaviors within these responsibilities have a negative relationship with second-order change, this does not mean that the school leader actively tries to subvert these responsibilities. It does mean that the school leader might pay a certain price for the implementation of a second-order change innovation. Specifically, a principal seeking to provide leadership for second-order change might have to endure the following perceptions:

- Team spirit, cooperation, and common language have deteriorated as a result of the innovation (Culture).
- Communication has deteriorated as a result of the innovation (Communication).
- Order and routine have deteriorated as a result of the innovation (Order).
- The level of input from all members of the staff has deteriorated as a result of the innovation (Input).

Note that the statements are all couched in terms of staff perceptions of the second-order change innovation being implemented. Again, within second-order change, a leader does not try to subvert any of the 21 responsibilities. However, the leader realizes that some staff members might perceive things deteriorating as a result of the innovation. Researchers have alluded to this phenomenon. For example, Fullan (2001) notes that "the more accustomed one becomes to dealing with the unknown, the more one understands that creative breakthroughs are always preceded by periods of cloudy thinking, confusion, exploration, trial and stress; followed by periods of excitement, and growing confidence as one pursues purposeful change, or copes with unwanted change" (p. 17). Heifetz (1994) explains the phenomenon in terms of the expression of competing values: "The inclusion of competing value perspectives may be essential to adaptive success" (p. 23). Fullan (1993) further explains that the process of second-order change is sometimes quite messy:

> "Ready, fire, aim" is the more fruitful sequence if we want to take a linear snapshot of an organization undergoing major reform. Ready is important; there has to be some notion of direction, but it is killing to bog down the process with vision, mission, and strategic planning before you know enough about dynamic reality. Fire is action and inquiry where skills, clarity, and learning are fostered. Aim is crystallizing new beliefs, formulating mission and vision statements, and focusing strategic planning. Vision and strategic planning come later. (pp. 31–32)

Finally, Fullan (1993) adds that "those individuals and organizations that are most effective do not experience fewer problems, less stressful situations, and greater fortune, they just deal with them differently" (p. 91).

The implications of the findings on second-order change from our factor analysis are far-reaching. At the most elementary level the message is that second-order change is a horse of a different color from a leadership perspective. To successfully implement a second-order change initiative, a school leader must ratchet up his idealism, energy, and enthusiasm. Additionally, the school leader must be willing to live through a period of frustration and even anger from some staff members. No doubt this takes a great personal toll on a school leader and might explain why many promising practices in education have not led to improved student achievement and ultimately have been abandoned. In Chapter 7 we address some specific ways that a school leader can manage second-order change.

Summary and Conclusions

Our factor analysis provided insight into how the 21 responsibilities interact and are applied. When involved in the day-to-day first-order changes and corrections that a school faces, the school leader must attend to all 21 responsibilities as a regular aspect of managing the school. When involved in second-order change initiatives that are dramatic departures from the past, the leader must emphasize 7 responsibilities. Additionally, the leader might have to endure the perception among some staff members that behavior relative to 4 of the 21 responsibilities has eroded.

6

Doing the Right Work

One critical aspect of leadership that was not evident from our meta-analysis or factor analysis was the type of work a school selects as its focus. Each year, every school in the United States formally or informally identifies something it will work on to maintain or (ideally) to improve student achievement. Many of these decisions become evident as school improvement plans. Harvard scholar Richard Elmore contends that the selection a school makes within these improvement plans is a critical factor in the school's ability to improve student achievement. Specifically, in a study commissioned by the National Governors Association, Elmore (2003) concluded that

> knowing the right thing to do is the central problem of school improvement. Holding schools accountable for their performance depends on having people in schools with the knowledge, skill, and judgment to make the improvements that will increase student performance. (p. 9)

Elmore points out that the school reform effort in the United States is plagued by falsehoods, one of which is that schools fail because teachers and administrators don't work hard enough: "These falsehoods include believing that schools fail because the people in them—administrators, teachers, and students—don't work hard enough and that they are lazy, unmotivated, and self-serving" (p. 9). For Elmore, the downfall of low-performing schools is not their lack of effort and motivation; rather, it is poor decisions regarding what to work on. So the problem in low-performing schools is not getting people to work, it is getting people to do the "right work."

What, then, are the various types of work a school might engage in, and which work is the right work? In this chapter, we consider two general approaches to this issue: (1) using a Comprehensive School Reform (CSR) model and (2) designing a site-specific approach.

Using a CSR Model

One approach to selecting the right work is to adopt a Comprehensive School Reform model. Specifically, the Comprehensive School Reform Program is a federally funded initiative that provides grants to schools that adopt proven comprehensive reform models (see Borman, Hewes, Overman, & Brown, 2003). The purpose of this effort is to provide research-based approaches to enhancing student achievement, particularly in low-performing schools. The U.S. Department of Education (2002) defines a Comprehensive School Reform model in terms of a wide array of features. For example, such a model is one that

- Has been found through scientifically based research to significantly improve the academic achievement of students.
- Provides high-quality professional development.
- Provides for meaningful involvement of parents and community.
- Employs proven methods for student learning, teaching, and school management.

A number of CSR models have been reviewed (see Herman et al., 1999; Northwest Regional Educational Laboratory, 2000). Among the more popular and well-researched ones are Direct Instruction, the School Development Program, and Success for All.

Direct Instruction was developed by Siegfried Engelmann and is available through the National Institute of Direct Instruction in Eugene, Oregon. Designed to be used in grades K through 6, its primary goal is to improve students' academic achievement in reading, language arts, and mathematics to such an extent that students are functioning above grade level by the end of 5th grade. It involves highly interactive lessons, use of small groups organized by performance levels, and frequent monitoring of student progress. Direct Instruction is meant to be used in the regular classroom as opposed to a pull-out program.

The School Development Program was designed by James Comer and is available from the School Development Program in New Haven, Connecticut. Its goal is to mobilize the community of adults to support student success. Designed to be used in grades K through 12, the School Development Program employs three teams: a school planning team, a student and staff support team, and a parent team. The teams have a common focus around three operations: design of a comprehensive school plan, effective staff development, and monitoring and assessing student progress. Finally, all three teams adhere to three principles: no-fault discussions, consensus decisions, and collaboration.

Success for All was developed by Robert Slavin and Nancy Madden and is available through the Success for All Foundation in Baltimore, Maryland. Developed for grades K through 8, the primary goal of Success for All is to ensure that every student learns to read effectively. It involves the use of cooperative learning and one-to-one tutoring, which are bolstered by a family support team and an on-site facilitator and building advisor.

The comprehensive meta-analysis by Borman, Hewes, Overman, and Brown (2003) reviews 29 CSR models including Direct Instruction, the School Development Program, and Success for All. It is probably accurate to say that the conventional wisdom regarding these programs is that they all have proven track records in their ability to enhance student achievement. Indeed, the first criterion in the list from the Department of Education is that the program has been found to improve student achievement through scientifically based research. However, the comprehensive meta-analysis by Borman and his colleagues provides an interesting perspective on the research supporting these CSR models.

Their meta-analysis suggests at least three generalizations about the CSR models that are relevant to the discussion in this book. First, among the 29 CSR models reviewed by Borman and his colleagues, costs to a school vary greatly. First-year (start-up) personnel costs range from a low of $0 to a high of $208,361. Median first-year personnel costs are $13,023. First-year nonpersonnel costs range from $14,585 to $780,000, with a median cost of $72,926. In short, adopting a CSR model can be a fairly expensive proposition. If a school selects one of the more expensive models, it would be well advised to carefully examine the model's chances of enhancing student achievement in that particular school.

Second, the extent to which the 29 CSR models have research supporting their effectiveness varies considerably. For example, one CSR model had studies involving 182 schools, whereas another model had a study involving 1 school. Additionally, the effect of the CSR models on student achievement varies considerably. To illustrate, consider Figure 6.1.

The percentages reported in Figure 6.1 are based on 1,111 standardized mean difference effect sizes reported in the meta-analysis by Borman and his colleagues. Standardized mean difference effect sizes (henceforth referred to as standardized mean differences) are explained in Technical Note 13 (p. 168). Briefly, a standardized mean difference tells you how many standard deviations the average score in the group of students who used the CSR model is above or below the average score

FIGURE 6.1
Distribution of Effect Sizes for Comprehensive School Reform Models

Effect Size Interval	Percent	Cumulative Percent
−2.00 to **−2.13**	.27	.27
−1.00 to −1.99	1.50	1.77
−.01 to −.99	33.12	34.89
.00 to .99	54.91	89.80
1.00 to 1.99	4.23	94.03
2.00 to 2.99	1.10	95.13
3.00 to 3.99	1.00	96.13
4.00 to 4.99	1.10	97.23
5.00 to 5.99	1.10	98.33
6.00 to 6.99	1.00	99.33
7.00 to **7.83**	1.00	100.33

of the group of students who did not use the CSR model. The standardized mean differences reported in Figure 6.1 range from −2.13 to +7.83. This indicates a rather large discrepancy in the findings from the studies on the 29 CSR models. The low standardized mean difference of −2.13 indicates a large *negative* effect for the CSR model involved. Specifically, it indicates that the average achievement for students in the experimental group—the school employing the CSR model—was 2.13 standard deviations less than the average achievement of the school not using the CSR approach. In other words, the average achievement score for the CSR school in this study was at the 2nd percentile of the non-CSR school. Taking this large negative effect size at face value, one might conclude that a typical student in the CSR school would lose a great deal of ground to the typical student in the non-CSR school.

The high standardized mean difference of 7.83 reported in Figure 6.1 indicates a large *positive* effect for the CSR model involved. Specifically, it indicates that the average achievement score of the school employing the CSR model was 7.83 standard deviations higher than the average score of students in the control group—that is, the average student in the CSR group was above the 99.9999999th percentile of the control group.

CSR models, then, appear to have a highly uneven effect on student achievement. Some studies indicate that a given CSR model produces extremely large positive effects on student achievement; others indicate that a given CSR model produces negative effects. In fact, 34.89 percent of the 1,111 effect sizes in the meta-analysis by Borman and his colleagues were below zero, indicating that in about 35 percent of the studies reviewed in that meta-analysis, the group that did not use a given CSR model outperformed the group that did.

Third, CSR models have a perplexing pattern of effects over time. Borman and his colleagues explain the long-term effects of CSR models in the following way:

> After the 5th year of implementation, CSR effects begin to increase substantially. Schools that had implemented CSR models for 5 years showed achievements that were nearly twice those found for CSR schools in general, and after 7 years of implementation, the effects were more than two and [one] half times the magnitude of overall CSR impact of d = .15 [i.e., the standardized mean difference is .15]. The small number of schools that had outcome data after 8 to 14 years of CSR model implementation achieved effects that were three and a third times larger than the overall CSR effect. (p. 153)

From these comments, we might conclude that if a school can simply stick with a CSR model for five years, then it can expect dramatic achievement gains. However, a careful analysis of the findings provides another interpretation. The average effect size for first-year implementation of CSR models is .17. Standardized mean differences for years two, three, and four are .14, .15, and .13, respectively. This indicates that the effects of CSR models stay basically the same or decrease slightly over the first four years. In the fifth year, the standardized mean difference increases rather dramatically to .25. Finally, the effect size increases to an impressive high of .50 after the 8th to 14th year.

One obvious interpretation of this pattern of effect sizes is that schools must persist in their efforts with any given CSR model, expecting moderate gains for the first four years, followed by rather dramatic gains. However, one finding from the meta-analysis by Borman and his colleagues implies a different interpretation. Specifically, they analyzed a number of factors that had a relationship with the magnitude of the effect size—whether the standardized mean difference for a given study was large or small. One characteristic they identified was the extent to which the CSR model provided ongoing staff development to facilitate implementation. They found that the more staff development support for a given CSR model, the *lower* the effect size associated with the model. (See Technical Note 14 on p. 169 for a more detailed discussion of this finding.) This appears to directly contradict the interpretation that long-term adherence to a CSR model will pay off if a school simply perseveres long enough. If this were the case, one would expect that staff development would enhance the effect of a CSR model. Borman and his coauthors do not discuss this anomaly. However, one interpretation is that CSR models are most effective when they are adapted. That is, only when schools adapt a CSR model to their specific situation does it positively affect student achievement. This interpretation is supported by a separate study of the impact of CSR programs on schools with diverse populations.

Datnow, Borman, Stringfield, Overman, and Costellano (2003) conducted a four-year study of CSR implementation in 13 culturally and linguistically diverse elementary schools. One of the more interesting findings is that a majority of the schools in the study abandoned the CSR model they were attempting to implement:

> In summary, at the end of our four-year study, five of the thirteen schools were still continuing to implement their reform designs with moderate to high levels of intensity. Reforms expired in six of thirteen schools we studied; two other schools were still formally associated with their reform but at very low levels. (p. 153)

This does not bode well for school leaders who might rigidly employ a CSR model as the "right work" in their school. The implication is that CSR models must be adapted if they are to be sustained. Of the five schools in the Datnow study that persisted with CSR implementations, all relied heavily on site-specific adaptations.

Although the Datnow study dealt exclusively with schools that had culturally and linguistically diverse populations, the research and theory on school change strongly support the importance of adaptations. Specifically, the work of Hall, Hord, and Loucks (Hall & Hord, 1987; Hall & Loucks, 1978; Hall, Loucks, Rutherford, & Newlove, 1975; Hord, Rutherford, Huling-Austin, & Hall, 1987) demonstrates that schools must alter the specifics of an innovation to meet the unique needs of their students and community. Indeed, for Hall, Hord, and Loucks, the highest level of implementation of an innovation is defined by adaptation.

In summary, many fine CSR models have been developed. Certainly a school looking for the right work should consider these models. However, rigid adoption of a CSR model does not appear to be a fail-safe method of improving student achievement.

Designing a Site-Specific Approach

The second approach to identifying the right work to undertake in a school is to design a site-specific intervention—to create or identify an intervention that addresses the specific needs of the school. The logic behind this option is that every school is different in some way. Consequently, no predesigned comprehensive school reform program will address the unique characteristics of a given school.

To design a site-specific intervention, a school must begin with a model or framework of those factors that can be altered in a school to enhance student achievement. A number of such models have been developed for this purpose, including those by Levine and Lezotte (1990), and Sammons (1999). The model that we use in this chapter was developed by Marzano (2003) and is described in *What Works in Schools: Translating Research into Action*. That model postulates 11 factors that might be the focus of school reform. These factors are listed in Figure 6.2.

Note that these factors are organized into three broad categories—school-level factors, teacher-level factors, and student-level factors. The school-level factors are those that are typically a function of school policy, such as safety and order. In other words, they represent issues that individual teachers cannot address comprehensively. Rather, these issues typically involve schoolwide initiatives or operating procedures.

The teacher-level factors involve issues that individual teachers can address effectively, such as instructional strategies and classroom management. Finally, the student-level factors involve issues such as home atmosphere that are typically not addressed by schools but can be if a school is willing to implement specific types of schoolwide programs.

Before we consider each of these factors in depth, it is important to explain that the factors are limited to those that can be substantively changed without access to extraordinary financial resources. That is, each of the 11 factors represents an area of change that is actually doable. We should also note that by definition some powerful interventions have been excluded from the list, such as increasing the number of days in the school year and providing a tutor for every student who is experiencing difficulty in school. These interventions would surely have powerful effects on student achievement, but they are probably beyond the resources currently available to most schools. The factors in Figure 6.2 might be considered a pragmatic set because they can be addressed immediately, without access to extraordinary resources. Each of these factors has specific, defining features and action steps that might be identified as the right work in a given school.

FIGURE 6.2
Factors in the "What Works in Schools" Model

School-Level Factors
- Guaranteed and viable curriculum
- Challenging goals and effective feedback
- Parent and community involvement
- Safe and orderly environment
- Collegiality and professionalism

Teacher-Level Factors
- Instructional strategies
- Classroom management
- Classroom curriculum design

Student-Level Factors
- Home environment
- Learned intelligence and background knowledge
- Motivation

Source: *What Works in Schools: Translating Research into Action* by Robert J. Marzano, 2003, p. 10. Copyright © 2003 ASCD.

Factor 1: Guaranteed and Viable Curriculum

As the title indicates, this factor addresses two interrelated aspects of the curriculum in a school—the extent to which the curriculum is *guaranteed* and the extent to which it is *viable*. Although viability is mentioned second in this factor, we consider this aspect of the curriculum first, because it is a necessary condition for a curriculum to be guaranteed.

Viability refers to whether the stated curriculum can be adequately taught in the instructional time available to teachers. Although this issue might sound like a nonsequitur, it is one of the most troublesome currently facing K–12 schools. Specifically, 49 of 50 states (with Iowa being the lone exception) have standards documents representing what students should know and be able to do in selected subject areas. Typically these subject areas are mathematics, language arts, science, social studies (which include history, civics, and geography), health and physical education, and the arts. Although the standards movement is well intended and many state standards documents are well written, the standards movement has created what some call a crisis of coverage. Simply stated, state standards documents usually identify far more content than teachers can adequately teach in the instructional time available.

To illustrate, in a study of the amount of time it would take to teach the content currently found in national and state-level standards documents, Marzano, Kendall, and Gaddy (1999) concluded that teaching the content in those documents would require 71 percent more instructional time than is now available. More pointedly, if schools were to teach all of the content as stated in those documents without adding days to the school year, they would have to extend schooling by about 10 years. To be viable, then, a curriculum must fit within the parameters of available instructional time, and this obviously requires substantial trimming of the content.

Once a curriculum is trimmed to the point where it is viable, it can be *guaranteed*. This means that a school imposes the constraint that classroom teachers must address specific content in specific courses at specific grade levels. The casual observer of K–12 education might assume that schools and districts already impose such constraints, but this is not the case. To illustrate, in discussing how teachers approach textbooks, Stevenson and Stigler (1992) note that even when all teachers in a school or a district use the same textbook series, different teachers omit different topics. Consequently, a school or district has no way of knowing what students have been taught. Hirsch (1996) addresses the same phenomenon, noting that "the idea that there exists a coherent plan for teaching content within the local district, or even within the individual school, is a gravely misleading myth" (p. 26).

Given the lack of a guaranteed and viable curriculum in many schools and districts, a school might identify one or more of the following action steps as the right work:

- Identify and communicate the content considered essential for all students versus that considered supplemental.
- Ensure that the essential content can be addressed in the amount of time available for instruction.
- Ensure that teachers address the essential content.
- Protect the instructional time available to teachers.

Factor 2: Challenging Goals and Effective Feedback

One of the strongest generalizations from the research literature is that feedback is a robust instructional activity that can be used in a variety of situations. In fact, in a review of almost 8,000 studies, Hattie (1992) concluded that feedback is the single most powerful educational tool available to educators. Marzano (2000b, 2003) has noted that the best way to provide the type of feedback suggested by the research is to use report cards like the one shown in Figure 6.3.

Note that the top section of the report card in Figure 6.3 looks quite traditional in its presentation of overall grades. Obviously, overall grades do not provide the level of feedback that Hattie alludes to. However, the bottom section of the report card does provide that level of feedback because it reports scores for specific topics in each subject area. The example in Figure 6.3 uses a 100-point scale. Marzano (2000b) illustrates how a report card based on a 4-point scale might be used. Whether a 100-point scale, a 4-point scale, or some other scale is used, the central feature of a report card like that shown in Figure 6.3 is that each student receives feedback on specific aspects of knowledge and skill every grading period (for example, every nine weeks). Scores for these grading periods can be reported in a transcript that also keeps track of student achievement at the topic level. (For a complete discussion, see Marzano 2000b, 2003.)

It is important to note that a report card like that depicted in Figure 6.3 is possible only if teachers are asked to keep track of relatively few topics per grading period and they are provided with computer software that performs the routine but laborious tasks of archiving data, computing averages, combining scores across topics, and the like. Currently, computer software is available that allows teachers to keep track of assessment data on specific areas of knowledge and skill on a day-to-day basis; allows for the aggregation of information gathered by teachers into report cards like that in Figure 6.3; and allows for the aggregation of information from report cards into transcripts.

FIGURE 6.3
Sample Standards-Based Report Card

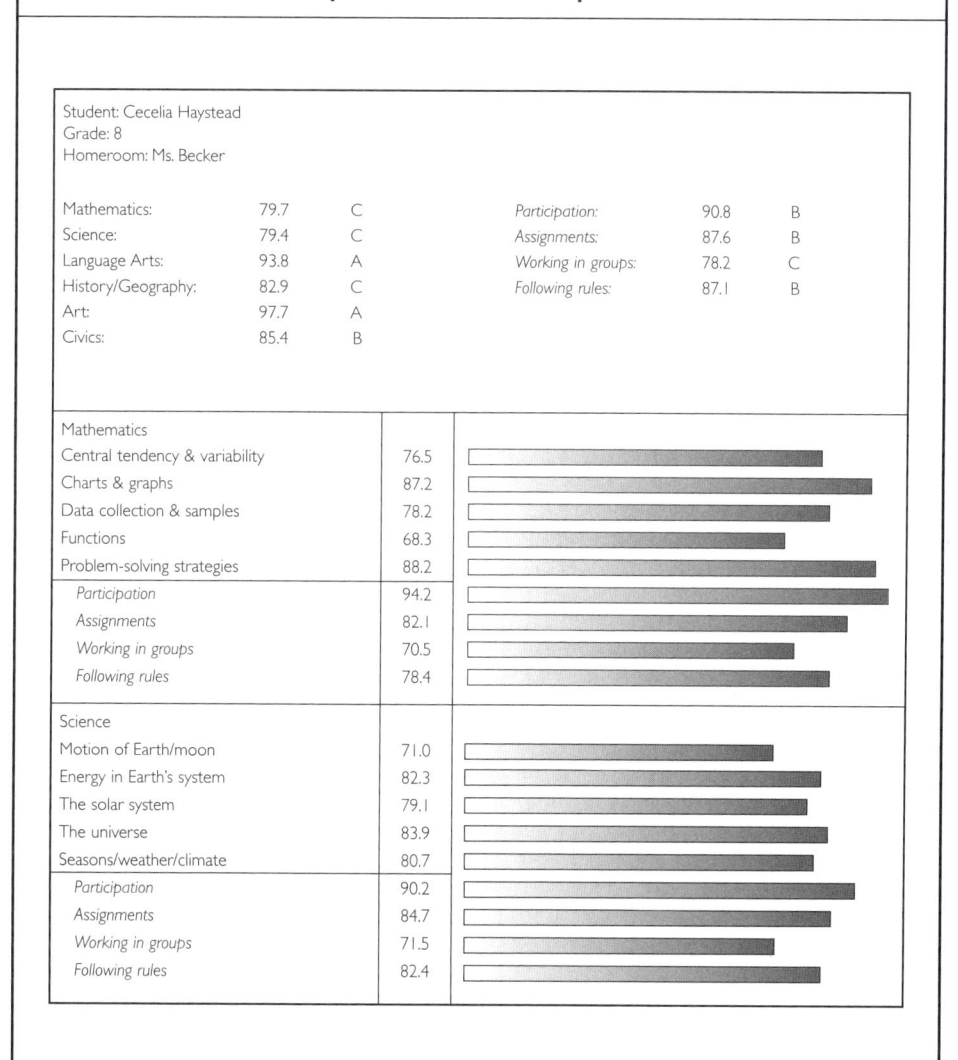

Student: Cecelia Haystead
Grade: 8
Homeroom: Ms. Becker

Mathematics:	79.7	C		Participation:	90.8	B
Science:	79.4	C		Assignments:	87.6	B
Language Arts:	93.8	A		Working in groups:	78.2	C
History/Geography:	82.9	C		Following rules:	87.1	B
Art:	97.7	A				
Civics:	85.4	B				

Mathematics	
Central tendency & variability	76.5
Charts & graphs	87.2
Data collection & samples	78.2
Functions	68.3
Problem-solving strategies	88.2
Participation	94.2
Assignments	82.1
Working in groups	70.5
Following rules	78.4
Science	
Motion of Earth/moon	71.0
Energy in Earth's system	82.3
The solar system	79.1
The universe	83.9
Seasons/weather/climate	80.7
Participation	90.2
Assignments	84.7
Working in groups	71.5
Following rules	82.4

(continued)

FIGURE 6.3 (continued)
Sample Standards-Based Report Card

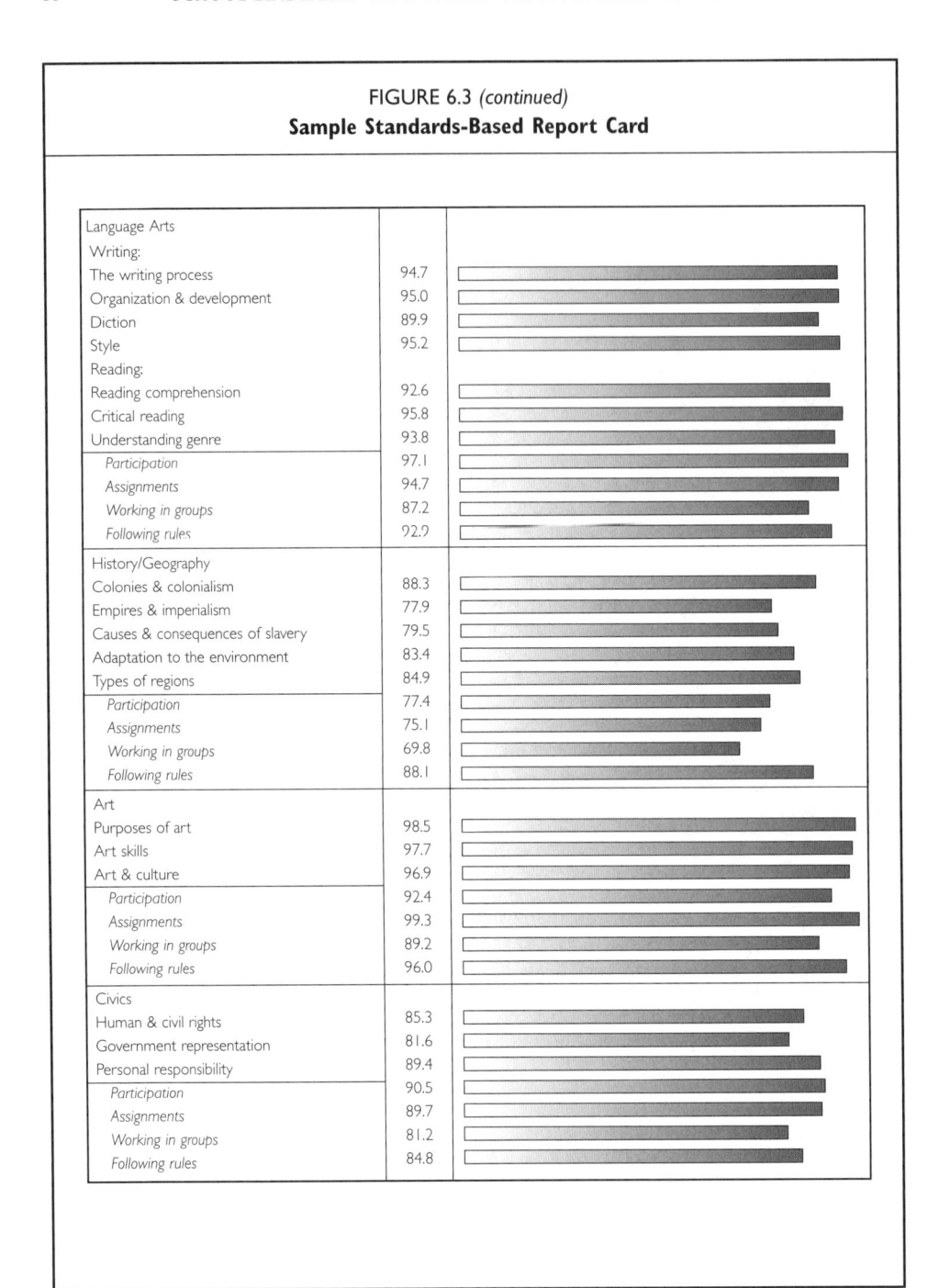

Language Arts		
Writing:		
The writing process	94.7	
Organization & development	95.0	
Diction	89.9	
Style	95.2	
Reading:		
Reading comprehension	92.6	
Critical reading	95.8	
Understanding genre	93.8	
Participation	97.1	
Assignments	94.7	
Working in groups	87.2	
Following rules	92.9	
History/Geography		
Colonies & colonialism	88.3	
Empires & imperialism	77.9	
Causes & consequences of slavery	79.5	
Adaptation to the environment	83.4	
Types of regions	84.9	
Participation	77.4	
Assignments	75.1	
Working in groups	69.8	
Following rules	88.1	
Art		
Purposes of art	98.5	
Art skills	97.7	
Art & culture	96.9	
Participation	92.4	
Assignments	99.3	
Working in groups	89.2	
Following rules	96.0	
Civics		
Human & civil rights	85.3	
Government representation	81.6	
Personal responsibility	89.4	
Participation	90.5	
Assignments	89.7	
Working in groups	81.2	
Following rules	84.8	

Source: *What Works in Schools: Translating Research into Action* by Robert J. Marzano, 2003, pp. 41–42. Copyright © 2003 ASCD.

With the implementation of a guaranteed and viable curriculum (Factor 1) and the support of technology for the record-keeping conventions important to this second factor, a school can identify challenging goals for the school as a whole as well as for individual students, and then provide the systematic, specific feedback that will generate the learning alluded to by Hattie (1992). Consequently, a school might select one or more of the following action steps as the right work:

• Implement an assessment and record-keeping system that provides timely feedback on specific areas of knowledge and skills for specific students.
• Establish and monitor specific, challenging achievement goals for the school as a whole.
• Establish and monitor specific, challenging achievement goals for each student.

Factor 3: Parent and Community Involvement

This factor deals with the support of and involvement in the school by parents and community. It involves at least three related elements: communication, participation, and governance.

Communication refers to the extent to which a school has developed good lines of communication both *to* and *from* parents and community. Vehicles for such communication typically include newsletters, phone calls, home visits, and parent-teacher conferences. Additionally, the use of e-mail and chat rooms via the Internet has greatly expanded capabilities for effective two-way communication.

Participation refers to the extent to which parents and community are involved in the day-to-day running of the school. Involvement in the school might be evident as parent and community volunteers perform functions such as classroom aides; hallway, lunchroom, and playground monitors; office clerical assistants; and guest lecturers and presenters.

Governance refers to the extent to which the school has established structures that allow for parents and community to be involved in decision making relative to school policy. Tangri and Moles (1987) explain the rationale for parent and community involvement in school governance in the following way: "The concept of parent [and community] participation in educational decision making is closely linked to democratic ideals of citizen participation in the affairs of government" (p. 520). Typically, vehicles for involvement by parents and community in school governance involve the creation of formal teams like the parent team within Comer's School Development Program (Comer, 1984, 1988) and site-based management teams.

Relative to this factor, a school might select one or more of the following action steps as the right work:

• Establish vehicles for communication between schools and parents and the community.

• Establish multiple ways for parents and community to be involved in the day-to-day running of the school.

• Establish governance vehicles that allow for the involvement of parents and community members.

Factor 4: Safe and Orderly Environment

A school that has a safe and orderly environment is one in which students and teachers alike *are* safe and *perceive* that they are safe from both physical and psychological harm. Safety and order as described here has been recognized by many as a necessary condition for effective schooling (Chubb & Moe, 1990; Mayer, Mullens, Moore, & Ralph, 2000). Indeed, national goals have even been established regarding this factor. For example, in 1994 the Goals 2000: Educate America Act (National Education Goals Panel, 1994) stated that by the year 2000, every school "will offer a disciplined environment conducive to learning" (p. 13). To address this factor, a school must implement rules and procedures at the school level and involve students in their design and implementation.

To address this factor, a school might select one or more of the following action steps as the right work:

• Establish rules and procedures for behavioral problems that might be caused by the school's physical characteristics or the school's routines.

• Establish schoolwide rules and procedures for general behavior.

• Establish and enforce appropriate consequences for violations of rules and procedures.

• Establish a program that teaches self-discipline and responsibility to students.

• Establish a system that allows for the early detection of students who have high potential for violence and extreme behaviors.

Factor 5: Collegiality and Professionalism

Collegiality and professionalism refer to the manner in which the staff members in a school interact and the extent to which they approach their duties as professionals. This factor is related to what researchers in the 1970s referred to as "school climate" (Brookover & Lezotte, 1979; Brookover et al., 1978). Brookover and colleagues (1978) attested to the importance of this factor, noting, "We believe that the differences in school climate explain much of the difference in academic achievement between schools that is normally attributed to composition" (p. 303). It should be noted that Brookover's concept of climate was quite broad in scope. What is referred to here as collegiality and professionalism is closer to what Deal and Kennedy (1983) refer to as "organizational climate":

> The organizational climate in a school has been defined as the collective personality of a school based upon an atmosphere distinguished by the social and professional interactions of the individuals in the school. (p. 14)

In operation, collegiality and professionalism are a function of implicit or explicit norms of behavior among staff members. These norms serve to create relationships that are professional in nature while also being cordial and friendly. This factor also includes structures that allow teachers to be an integral aspect of the important decisions in a school. Finally, this factor involves professional development that is focused, skill-oriented, and cohesive from session to session and year to year.

Three action steps are associated with this factor:

• Establish norms of conduct and behavior that engender collegiality and cooperation.

• Establish governance structures that allow for teacher involvement in decisions and policies for the school.

• Provide teachers with meaningful staff development activities.

Factor 6: Instructional Strategies

Figure 6.2, p. 82, identifies the first five factors as school-level factors. As indicated by their associated action steps, they involve schoolwide interventions. This sixth factor—instructional strategies—and the next two (classroom management and classroom curriculum design) address aspects of day-to-day classroom life.

One of the more obvious characteristics of effective teachers is that they have at their disposal a wide array of instructional strategies. Various researchers have promoted lists of allegedly effective instructional strategies. For example, eight categories of general instructional strategies have been identified based on the review of research jointly reported by Fraser, Walberg, Welch, and Hattie (1987) and Hattie (1992). Based on the research by Marzano (Marzano, 1998; Marzano, Gaddy, & Dean, 2000; Marzano, Pickering, & Pollock, 2001), the following nine categories of instructional strategies have been promoted:

• Identifying similarities and differences
• Summarizing and note taking
• Reinforcing effort and providing recognition

- Homework and practice
- Nonlinguistic representations
- Cooperative learning
- Setting objectives and providing feedback
- Generating and testing hypotheses
- Cues, questions, and advance organizers

Regardless of the specific list that is used, strategies should be organized into some type of framework for instructional design. Hunter (1984) proposed a design for individual lessons. More recently, Marzano (2003) has proposed a design for planning units. It involves the four categories depicted in Figure 6.4.

The first category includes those instructional strategies that deal with monitoring progress, balancing individual work with group work, reinforcing effort, and celebrating success. These activities are typically employed regularly and systematically throughout a unit. The second category includes those strategies that deal with assessing final goal attainment and celebrating success at the end of the unit. They provide a strong finish for a unit. The third category involves strategies that help students understand and assimilate new information that is presented to them. The final category includes instructional strategies that help students review, practice, and apply content.

One action step is associated with this factor, although as the framework in Figure 6.4 illustrates, it is multidimensional, involving a wide array of instructional strategies:

- Provide teachers with an instructional framework for planning units that employs research-based strategies.

Factor 7: Classroom Management

One can argue that classroom management is the foundation of effective teaching. In fact, in a major review of the research literature, Wang, Haertel, and Walberg (1993) identified classroom management as the factor that has the greatest impact on student achievement out of a list of 228 variables. This makes intuitive sense—a classroom that is chaotic as a result of poor management not only doesn't enhance achievement, it might even inhibit it.

Marzano, Marzano, and Pickering (2003) identify five aspects of effective classroom management. The first is the design and implementation of classroom rules and procedures. The second is the design and implementation of appropriate consequences for violations of rules and procedures. The third element addresses the relationship between teacher and students. More specifically, to

FIGURE 6.4
Categories for Instructional Strategies

Category I—Monitoring progress, balancing individual work with group work, reinforcing effort, and celebrating success:

- Having students work individually
- Having students work in cooperative groups
- Having students work in groups based on their knowledge and skill in specific topics
- Giving students periodic feedback on learning goals
- Asking students to keep track of their progress on the learning goals
- Periodically celebrating legitimate progress toward learning goals
- Pointing out and reinforcing examples of effort

Category II—Assessing final goal attainment and celebrating success at the end:

- Providing students with clear evaluations of their progress on each learning goal
- Having students evaluate themselves on learning goals and compare their evaluations with the teacher's
- Recognizing and celebrating the accomplishment of specific goals for specific students

Category III—Helping students understand and assimilate new information that is presented to them:

- Asking questions that help students identify what they already know about the content
- Providing students with direct links between new content and old content
- Providing students with ways of organizing the new content or thinking about the new content
- Asking students to take notes on the content
- Asking students to construct verbal and written summaries of the content
- Asking students to represent new content as pictures, pictographs, symbols, graphic representations, physical models, or dramatic enactments
- Asking students to create mental images for new content

Category IV—Helping students review, practice, and apply content:

- Asking students to revise their notes, correcting errors and adding detail
- Asking students to revise their pictures, pictographs, symbols, graphic representations, and physical models, correcting errors and adding detail
- Asking students to revise their mental images, correcting errors and adding detail
- Assigning homework and in-class activities that require students to practice skills and processes
- Assigning homework and in-class activities that require students to compare content, classify content, create metaphors with content, and create analogies with content
- Engaging students in projects that require them to generate and test hypotheses through problem-solving tasks, decision-making tasks, investigation tasks, inquiry tasks, systems analysis tasks, and invention tasks

Adapted by permission from *What Works in Schools* by Robert J. Marzano. Copyright © 2003 ASCD.

establish an optimal relationship with students, a teacher must exhibit two types of behaviors: (1) those that communicate appropriate levels of dominance (that is, those that signal that the teacher is in charge and can be trusted to provide behavioral and academic guidance) and (2) those that communicate appropriate levels of cooperation (that is, those that signal to students that the teacher is concerned about the individual needs of students and is willing to have the class function as a team). The fourth aspect of effective classroom management involves the teacher's use of strategies that heighten his awareness of all activities in the classroom, with particular emphasis on identifying and thwarting any potential problems. The final aspect of effective classroom management addresses the extent to which the teacher maintains a healthy emotional objectivity regarding management issues.

Consequently, if classroom management is its focus, a school might identify one or more of the following action steps as the right work:

- Have teachers articulate and enforce a comprehensive set of classroom rules and procedures.
- Have teachers use specific strategies that reinforce appropriate behavior and recognize and provide consequences for inappropriate behavior.
- Institute a schoolwide approach to discipline.
- Help teachers develop a balance of moderate dominance and moderate cooperation in their dealings with students.
- Provide teachers with an awareness of the needs of different types of students and ways of alleviating those needs.
- Have teachers employ specific strategies to maintain or heighten their awareness regarding the actions of students in their classes.
- Have teachers employ specific strategies that help them maintain a healthy emotional objectivity with their students.

Factor 8: Classroom Curriculum Design

Classroom curriculum design refers to those decisions teachers make to adapt the content found in textbooks, state standards documents, and district curriculum guides to the needs of their particular students. Such decisions are needed because students from school to school and even from classroom to classroom within a single school might vary greatly in their background knowledge and readiness for the topics being taught. Consequently, classroom teachers must adapt the activities and content in the textbooks, standards documents, and curriculum guides assigned to them.

When executing their adaptations, one of the first things teachers must do is to decide which information and skills are to be the focus of a given topic specified in their textbook, standards document, or curriculum guide. To illustrate, based on one or more of these documents, a 4th grade teacher might have to address the topic of fractions. However, many aspects of this topic could provide the focus of instruction, such as the relationship between fractions and decimals or the nature and comparative characteristics of common fractions such as one-half, one-fourth, and one-fifth. Additionally, important skills within the general topic of fractions include converting fractions to decimals and adding fractions with different denominators. To determine which information and skills should be the focus of instruction for specific students, a teacher must consider what those students already know about the topic. Obviously, these decisions cannot be made by textbooks or by those who design standards or curriculums. Such decisions must be made on a class-by-class, even student-by-student, basis.

Another classroom curricular decision a teacher must make is to identify activities to use to ensure that students are exposed to new content multiple times in a variety of ways. This is necessary because to fully understand and integrate new knowledge, students must have opportunities to process information in a variety of ways from a variety of perspectives. Additionally, these opportunities must be presented multiple times with a well-thought-out progression of difficulty.

A third curricular decision a teacher must make is to identify which skills are to be mastered by students and which skills are to be only introduced. Skills are types of procedural knowledge. To be useful, procedural knowledge must be learned until it becomes automatic—that is, an individual can execute the skill or process fluently with little or no conscious thought. Unfortunately, this level of learning requires a great deal of extended practice, so much so that it would be impossible for a teacher to adequately address all procedures found in textbooks, standards documents, or curriculum guides. Consequently, a teacher may introduce many skills within a given semester but teach only a few to the requisite level of automaticity. (For a discussion, see Marzano, Kendall, & Gaddy, 1999.) Again, teachers must use their knowledge of the background and readiness of the students in their class to make such determinations.

A fourth curricular decision a teacher must make is how to present the information within a topic or how to present a set of topics in a way that highlights their similarities. Highlighting similarities between topics is at the heart of knowledge transfer. Again, such links cannot be forged without knowing the background of individual students. An organizational scheme that would provide obvious connections between topics for one group of students might not provide such links for another group of students.

The final curricular decision a teacher must make is how to provide students with complex tasks that require them to apply their new knowledge in ways that expand their original understanding of the knowledge. Such tasks include making decisions based on new knowledge, solving problems based on new knowledge, and testing hypotheses based on new knowledge.

With this factor in mind, a school might select one or more of the following action steps as the right work:

- Have teachers identify the important information and skills in the topics they are required to address.
- Have teachers present new content multiple times using a variety of activities.
- Have teachers distinguish between those skills and processes that they will teach to a level of mastery and those that they will only introduce.
- Have teachers present content in groups or categories that demonstrate the critical features of the content.
- Have teachers engage students in complex tasks that require addressing content in multiple ways.

Factor 9: Home Environment

The last three factors in Figure 6.2 (p. 82) are labeled "student-level factors." They represent characteristics that are part of the general background students bring with them to school each day. In past decades, many people assumed that these student background factors were beyond the reach of schools. The three listed in Figure 6.2 are anything but that. Although they are the products of environmental influences outside the school, each can be significantly affected by focused schoolwide efforts.

The first of these three student-level factors is home environment. As the name indicates, this deals with the extent to which the environment in the home supports academic success. One of the more compelling research findings relative to this factor is that home environment can be orchestrated to positively affect student academic achievement regardless of the income, occupation, or education level of the parents or guardians in the home (White, 1982).

At least three aspects of home environment determine whether it supports academic achievement. The first is the extent to which parents and guardians communicate to their children about school and how they do so. Parents and guardians who communicate effectively have frequent and systematic discussions with children regarding school, encourage their children regarding school, and provide resources to help them with their schoolwork.

The second element characteristic of a supportive home environment is supervision. This involves the extent to which parents and guardians monitor their children's activities, such as time spent doing homework, when their children return home from school, what they do after school, how much they watch television, and what type of programs they watch.

The third characteristic of this factor is parenting style. Of the three general parenting styles—authoritative, authoritarian, and permissive—the authoritative style has the strongest positive relationship with student academic achievement, followed by the authoritarian style. The permissive style does little to support academic achievement.

One action step is associated with this factor:

• Provide training and support to parents to enhance their communication with their children about school, their supervision of their children, and their ability to communicate expectations to their children within the context of an effective parenting style.

Factor 10: Learned Intelligence and Background Knowledge

This factor, learned intelligence and background knowledge, gets its name from the fact that one of the strongest predictors (if not the strongest predictor) of academic achievement is the background knowledge students have regarding the content being taught (Bloom, 1976; Dochy, Segers, & Buehl, 1999). Interestingly, background knowledge—particularly academic background knowledge—is akin to what psychologists refer to as crystallized intelligence, or the type of intelligence that is learned as opposed to innate.

Techniques for enhancing academic background knowledge can be organized into two basic categories: direct approaches and indirect approaches. Direct approaches are those that involve students in out-of-school activities that are academically oriented. These experiences include field trips to historical sites, cultural events, plays, museums, and so on. Direct experiences also include involving students in mentoring relationships that pair an adult with the means to provide students with a wide variety of out-of-school academic experiences and a student who wishes to be involved in such a relationship. Ideally, the adult in the pair possesses the same background as the student and is of the same ethnicity.

Indirect experiences are those that generate "virtual" experiences that enhance students' academic background knowledge. Two types of indirect experiences that fit well into the current culture of K–12 education are wide reading and direct vocabulary instruction in terms that are important to the academic subjects students encounter in school.

The following action steps associated with this factor might be selected by a school as the right work:

• Involve students in programs that directly increase the number and quality of life experiences they have.

• Involve students in a program of wide reading that emphasizes vocabulary development.

• Provide direct instruction in vocabulary terms and phrases that are important to specific subject matter content.

Factor 11: Motivation

The final student-level factor is motivation. It refers to the extent to which students are motivated to be engaged in academic tasks from both external and internal sources. Drive theory, attribute theory, and self-worth theory provide some guidance regarding ways to motivate students via external sources (see Covington, 1992). One technique is to provide students with feedback regarding their knowledge gain. When students perceive that they have progressed in the acquisition of knowledge or skill, they tend to increase their level of effort and engagement regardless of their relative standing compared with other students. Another external approach to motivation is to involve students in gamelike tasks that focus on academic content, because games and gamelike activities are inherently interesting. If academic content is embedded in a game or gamelike activity, students tend to be engaged in the task and consequently learn the embedded content even if they are not interested in the content per se.

Self-system theory (see Csikszentmihalyi, 1990; Harter, 1999; Markus & Ruvolo, 1990) provides guidance as to techniques for enhancing or capitalizing on students' internal motivation. One approach is to involve students in long-term projects of their own design (see Marzano, Paynter, & Doty, 2004). However, to truly tap into sources of internal motivation, students must have the freedom to select the topics and specific goals of their projects, and have the necessary time and resources to complete them. This implies setting aside some specific time during the school week for students to work on such open-ended tasks. The time lost to traditional academic subjects due to these student-directed projects might be made up by the halo effect such projects generate. That is, the energy and engagement created by these tasks might spill over into traditional academic subject areas. A second approach to internal motivation is to provide students with an understanding of the dynamics of human motivation and consequently their own behavior in and out of school. Such an understanding allows students some measure of control over their own levels of motivation in various situations.

If student motivation is its focus, a school might select one or more of the following action steps as the right work:

- Provide students with feedback on their knowledge gain.
- Provide students with tasks and activities that are inherently engaging.
- Provide opportunities for students to construct and work on long-term projects of their own design.
- Teach students about the dynamics of motivation and how those dynamics affect them.

Summary and Conclusions

The school leader's ability to select the right work is a critical aspect of effective leadership. It might be the case that teachers and administrators in a low-performing school are working "hard" but not working "smart" in that they select interventions that have little chance of enhancing student academic achievement. Two categories of possible interventions are comprehensive school reform (CSR) models and site-specific approaches. Whereas CSR models are generally thought to have proven track records in their effect on student achievement, the research indicates that the effect of any given CSR model can vary greatly from site to site. A good rule of thumb is that CSR models should be adapted over time to meet the specific needs of a school. When a site-specific approach is used, a school designs its own intervention based on some theory or model of effective schooling. An 11-factor model, encompassing 39 possible action steps, can help a school identify the focus of its work. Whether a school uses this model or some other model, employing a site-specific approach involves designing an intervention that is specific to the needs and context of a given school.

7

A Plan for Effective School Leadership

According to an old proverb, "A vision without a plan is just a dream. A plan without a vision is just drudgery. But a vision with a plan can change the world." In the first six chapters of this book, we presented the rationale for and the results of our meta-analysis and our factor analysis. Our meta-analysis resulted in the identification of 21 responsibilities that define the role of a school leader. Our factor analysis resulted in the realization that leadership is different depending on whether a school is engaged in first-order change or second-order change. Finally, we found that the work of Richard Elmore added an important explanatory dimension to our findings. His conclusion that identifying the right work is critical to the success of a school helps us understand the conditions that mediate the impact of school leadership.

All these findings help us better understand school leadership. However, in isolation they do not constitute a plan—a set of coordinated actions that a school leader can take to enhance the achievement of students in schools. In this chapter, we attempt to do just that—organize our findings and conclusions into a plan of action that will help any school leader articulate and realize a powerful vision for enhanced achievement of students.

Our proposed plan involves five steps:

1. Develop a strong school leadership team.
2. Distribute some responsibilities throughout the leadership team.
3. Select the right work.
4. Identify the order of magnitude implied by the selected work.
5. Match the management style to the order of magnitude of the change initiative.

Step 1: Develop a Strong School Leadership Team

One of the findings from our meta-analysis is that 21 responsibilities characterize the job of an effective school leader. Although this list appears inordinately long, it is not; other researchers who have synthesized the research on leadership have identified equally long lists. Recall from the discussion in Chapter 2 that Cotton (2003) identified 25 responsibilities much like ours. We believe that anyone who attempts to synthesize the research on school leadership will have similar results. In short, our research and that of others validates the conclusion that leading a school requires a complex array of skills. However, the validity of this conclusion creates a logical problem because it would be rare, indeed, to find a single individual who has the capacity or will to master such a complex array of skills. How does one reconcile the fact that effective school leadership requires 21 responsibilities but that the mastery of all 21 is beyond the capacity of most people? Taken at face value, this situation would imply that only those with superhuman abilities or the willingness to expend superhuman effort could qualify as effective school leaders.

Fortunately, a solution exists if the focus of school leadership shifts from a single individual to a team of individuals. If school leadership is the responsibility of a leadership team within a school as opposed to the principal acting as lone leader, all 21 responsibilities can be adequately addressed. As we saw in Chapter 2, a variety of theorists (such as Elmore, Fullan, and Spillane) have addressed this concept of shared leadership directly and indirectly in a variety of theories. For us, it is the concept of a *purposeful community* that provides guidance as to how a leadership team might best be developed and maintained. Specifically, we believe that a strong leadership team is the natural outgrowth of a purposeful community. In other words, crafting the school into a purposeful community is a necessary condition for the design of an effective leadership team.

Crafting a Purposeful Community

We define a purposeful community as *one with the collective efficacy and capability to develop and use assets to accomplish goals that matter to all community members through agreed-upon processes.* Four important concepts are embedded in this definition. First is the concept of *collective efficacy,* which is group members' shared perception or belief that they can dramatically enhance the effectiveness of an organization. According to Goddard, Hoy, and Hoy (2004), the collective efficacy of the teachers in a school is a better predictor of student success in schools than is the socioeconomic status of the students. In simple terms, collective efficacy is the shared belief that "we can make a difference."

The second concept important to our definition of a purposeful community is *the development and use of all available assets*. Assets can be tangible or intangible (Kaplan & Norton, 2004). Tangible assets include financial and physical resources, the number of personnel in a school and the talents they bring, technology, and access to information. Intangible assets involve a shared vision, shared assumptions about what is important within the school, and shared ideals and beliefs about the core mission of the school.

The third concept important to the definition of a purposeful community is that it *accomplishes goals that matter to all community members*. Communities come in many types and forms. Purposeful communities are distinguished from "accidental communities" by their strong, well-articulated reasons for existing. They are not a product of serendipity; rather, members decide whether they wish to be part of the community. This is not a new idea; it has been well defined within discussions of "intentional communities." For example, in *Making the Grade*, Wagner (2002) writes:

> Historically, most communities were created by accident. They were usually the result of some physical proximity or immediate shared need. Sometimes they furthered the goals and growth and development of their members, sometimes they didn't—as any long-time resident of a small town will tell you. By contrast, an "intentional community" is created for a purpose. In fact, the term "intentional community" was first widely used to describe efforts of the nineteenth-century utopians to create communities whose goal was the intellectual and spiritual growth of its members. (pp. 148–149)

The fourth concept important to our definition of a purposeful community is *agreed-upon processes*. These are processes that enhance communication among community members, provide for efficient reconciliation of disagreements, and keep the members attuned to the current status of the community.

These four elements provide a template for the actions that the school leader must take. More pointedly, of the 21 responsibilities, the school leader must execute certain ones to develop a purposeful community from which a strong leadership team can be constructed. We believe that at least 9 of the 21 responsibilities are necessarily the purview of the principal and are the foundations for establishing a purposeful community. The 9 responsibilities are the following:

- Optimizer
- Affirmation
- Ideals/Beliefs
- Visibility
- Situational Awareness

- Relationships
- Communication
- Culture
- Input

Each of the four critical aspects of a purposeful community is dependent on the school leader's effective execution of one or more of these 9 responsibilities.

To create the *collective efficacy* that typifies a purposeful community, the school leader must effectively execute the responsibilities of Optimizer and Affirmation. The principal must be the champion (Optimizer) for the belief that the staff operating as a cohesive group can effect substantive change. Unfortunately, a number of researchers and theorists believe that school faculties do not typically operate from the shared belief that as a group they can make a difference (DuFour, 1998, 2004; Sergiovanni, 2004). Rather, teachers tend to operate from the perspective that their contribution to student learning is more a function of their individual efforts than the collective efforts of the staff. Given these isolationist tendencies, it is the job of the school leader to foster a belief in the power of collective efficacy. Sergiovanni (2004) refers to this shift in perspective as developing a "community of hope."

In specific terms, the principal might begin the school year with a thoughtful dialogue regarding the importance of a team approach to schooling, providing examples that illustrate the power of operating as a team. In recent years, Collins's (2001) book *Good to Great,* about companies that have not only endured economic hard times but prospered, has captured the attention of educators throughout the country. His concept of "getting the right people on the bus" fits nicely into a discussion of the power of collective efficacy. For Collins, the bus is a metaphor for the organization—in this case, the school. The "right people" is a metaphor for a group of like-minded individuals who are willing to subsume their personal ambitions under the common good of the institution.

Sergiovanni (2004) reminds us that the belief in collective efficacy must be backed up by fact—evidence that it works. The school leader accomplishes this by executing the responsibility of Affirmation—recognizing and celebrating the legitimate successes of individuals within the school and the school as a whole. Such acknowledgment provides evidence to the faculty that their efforts are producing tangible results. To do this, the principal might devote a portion of each faculty meeting to acknowledging accomplishments of the school as a whole and individuals working toward the common good of enhanced student achievement.

The second concept critical to a purposeful community is the *development and use of available assets*. As mentioned, assets can be tangible or intangible. The tangible assets such as books and equipment can be addressed effectively by the leadership team in the execution of the responsibility of Resources. (We suggest how the leadership team might do this in Step 2; see Figure 7.1, pp. 108–109.) However, the development of intangible assets such as shared visions, shared assumptions, and shared ideals is a by-product of actions by the principal. Such actions are exhibited when the principal executes the responsibility of Ideals/Beliefs. Ideals/Beliefs might be one of the more difficult responsibilities for the school leader to execute. Recall from the discussion in Chapter 4 that disclosing one's ideals and beliefs is a very intimate act (De Pree, 1989). Goleman, Boyatzis, and McKee (2002) contend that such willingness to self-disclose is a critical component of emotional intelligence.

Carrying out the responsibility of Ideals/Beliefs, the school leader might articulate his ideals and beliefs about the nature and purpose of schooling and invite teachers to share theirs, in an attempt to identify commonalities. In K–12 schools, such commonalities should be easy to come by because teachers and administrators probably share common reasons for entering the teaching profession, many of which deal with making a positive difference in the lives of others. When consciously operating from these "higher" principles, human beings are willing to expend vast amounts of energy and experience a heightened sense of satisfaction when doing so (Bandura, 1997; Csikszentmihalyi, 1990; Harter, 1999).

The third defining characteristic of a purposeful community is that it *accomplishes goals that matter to all community members*. The critical phrase here is "all community members." The driving force behind this concept is that all the members of the school staff believe that their day-to-day efforts serve common goals. Certainly the discussions regarding shared ideals and beliefs will go a long way to this end. However, in the complex swirl of activity that characterizes the day-to-day life of most schools, even the most meaningful discussions are easily forgotten. It is up to the building principal to keep the common goals articulated in those discussions alive for all staff members. The principal does so through actions, not words. Specifically, five responsibilities are involved in this aspect of a purposeful community: Visibility, Situational Awareness, Relationships, Communication, and Culture.

Visibility requires the principal to have frequent contact with teachers and students. These contacts would typically be evident as informal and unscheduled encounters as the principal walks through the building observing classes in progress, chatting with teachers and students, and observing sports events and other extracurricular activities. The principal's strong presence communicates that administration and staff are a team working together in all aspects of the school.

Situational Awareness refers to the principal's awareness of the details and undercurrents of running the school. Obviously, effective execution of the responsibility of Visibility will make it easier to execute Situational Awareness. As part of creating a purposeful community, Situational Awareness involves knowing the positive and negative dynamics that occur between individuals in the school, and using this information to forecast and head off potential problems. For example, the principal might become aware that a certain teacher or a certain group of teachers feels disenfranchised. Rather than wait for these feelings to show themselves in a negative manner, the principal would meet with the teacher or teachers, inviting them to discuss their issues openly.

The responsibility of Relationships might be considered to be the bedrock of the principal's efforts to establish a purposeful community. Along with an awareness of specifics of the professional lives of faculty and staff in a building, the principal should be aware of their personal lives, appropriately commenting on and reacting to critical events.

The responsibility of Culture involves the creation of a cooperative environment among staff within the context of a shared sense of purpose. Certainly the execution of the other responsibilities will contribute to establishing an appropriate culture. However, the principal should take overt action to this end. Schmoker (2001) proposes the simple device of bimonthly or monthly meetings at which teachers who are responsible for common subject areas, grade levels, or both meet to discuss instructional issues. One standing issue at all these meetings would be the level of consistency between the school's actual operations and its espoused ideals and beliefs.

The fourth defining feature of a purposeful community is *agreed-upon processes*. As stated earlier, these processes enhance communication among members of the community, provide for efficient reconciliation of disagreements, and make apparent the health (or lack thereof) of the community. The effective execution of the responsibility of Input addresses these issues. Recall from Chapter 4 that Input involves ensuring that all staff members in the school have a voice in the running of the school. At one level, input can be directly to the principal. A vehicle for this might be a standing open-door policy that gives every faculty member ready access to the principal. At a more formal level, the principal might schedule systematic meetings with every faculty member to seek out suggestions on how the school might be run more effectively. Additionally, each faculty meeting might include time for staff members to identify areas of concern regarding the running of the school.

Although these various actions are labor intensive, they are probably preconditions for a purposeful community, which itself is a precondition for a strong leadership team.

Setting Up and Maintaining a Leadership Team

A school will probably never reach a point at which people can stop working toward a purposeful community. To use a well-worn phrase, a purposeful community is more of a journey than it is a destination. Consequently, the school leader can begin setting up a leadership team in concert with the crafting of a purposeful community. There are no hard-and-fast rules for designing a leadership team. However, experience has shown us that at least two generalizations seem to apply to a well-functioning leadership team.

The first is that the members of the leadership team should be volunteers. This means that membership should not be based on some form of rotation wherein each staff member must serve a certain period of time. No doubt, membership on the team will require extra work and extra energy. The only way that this effort can be expected of leadership team members is if they volunteer their services because of their extraordinary commitment to the effective functioning of the school. One way of thinking of the leadership team, then, is that it is a group of individuals highly committed to the general well-being of the school. Members share a "culture of commitment" regarding the school. This is not to say that individuals who fail to volunteer for service on the team are uncommitted. Rather, individuals might not volunteer simply because they have issues outside school that are priorities at a given point in time. Every educator experiences times when professional life must take a backseat to personal life. Most likely the leadership team will be populated by individuals whose professional life is one of their highest priorities—at least for the time being.

The second generalization regarding the leadership team is that it is important to establish strong operating principles and agreements. A leadership team will have a "way of working together" that will develop as a function of serendipity or design. Strong operating principles help ensure that the way the team works together is productive, not destructive. A team's operating principles should be what the team turns to when the predictable conflict associated with change (particularly second-order change) occurs. Accordingly, operating principles should be broad and powerful statements that reflect values, or "truths," that transcend the differences that can divide groups in times of stress or conflict. The following are some operating principles we have found to be particularly powerful.

- **Significance.** We address "questions that matter," leading to a deep and broad positive impact on learning and practice. We continually review new and existing work against our goals and emerging issues so that we focus our resources appropriately.
- **Quality.** Our work and our approach exemplify the highest professional standards, withstanding critical scrutiny and exhibiting state-of-the-art practice. We review our work and hold ourselves accountable for our processes and results, striving for continuous improvement.
- **Responsibility.** We operate for the public good and are accountable for our work, the way in which we conduct it, and our interactions with each other. Our ultimate goal is to identify, develop, and share information and techniques that improve student learning. We assess our work and welcome direct and honest feedback so we can learn, grow, and remain relevant to those we serve.
- **Integrity.** We strive to create and maintain an environment of trust, respect, and common values. We treat each other and those we serve with fairness and respect. What we say and do supports who we aspire to be and what we have set out to accomplish.
- **Ethics.** Our work and our approach reflect fair, just, and compassionate understanding and insight. This results in opportunities for success for all children and those who serve them, regardless of race, culture, location, socioeconomic status, or discipline.
- **Openness.** Our decision-making process is transparent to both internal and external audiences. This means that faculty, staff, and the community we serve have an opportunity to understand how we make decisions and learn what decisions were made. To expand the base of knowledge in education, we regularly communicate key knowledge and learning to internal and external audiences.

Along with identifying operating principles, the leadership team must formalize agreements among team members to make the principles operational. These agreements should be commitments that team members make to one another describing the behaviors that staff members who are not on the team will be able to observe in day-to-day interactions. One of the agreements should address the importance of team members holding each other accountable for honoring their agreements.

Step 2: Distribute Some Responsibilities Throughout the Leadership Team

With a leadership team established, the next step is to distribute the 12 responsibilities throughout the leadership team. This is not to say that the principal should exclude himself from the execution of these responsibilities. Rather, these remaining 12 can be considered the joint work of the leadership team, with the principal functioning as a key member of that team. Here we describe how the leadership team might address a few of the 12 distributed responsibilities.

Knowledge of Curriculum, Instruction, and Assessment involves the acquisition and cultivation of knowledge regarding best practices in curriculum, instruction, and assessment. It seems reasonable that a team of committed people can address this responsibility more effectively than any one individual. For example, different members of the leadership team might be responsible for reading the current research and theory on different topics. Some team members might focus on curriculum, others on instruction, and others on assessment. The building principal operating as a member of the team would select one of these topics, but it would be the collective efforts of the team that would address this responsibility in a comprehensive manner.

As described in Chapter 4, whereas Knowledge of Curriculum, Instruction, and Assessment focuses on the acquisition of knowledge, Involvement in Curriculum, Instruction, and Assessment involves hands-on interactions with teachers. This responsibility manifests itself as direct involvement in day-to-day classroom practice. Again, the leadership team would distribute the work involved in executing this responsibility, with some members focusing on providing support and guidance for classroom teachers who want help with curricular issues, others focusing on instruction, and others focusing on assessment.

Flexibility refers to the ability and willingness to adapt leadership style to the needs of the current situation. One of the defining features of this responsibility is the ability to maintain what is referred to as the "balcony view" of an organization (Heifetz & Laurie, 2001; Heifetz & Linsky, 2002a). Heifetz and Linsky (2002b) explain the dynamics of the balcony view in the following way:

> *Get off the dance floor and onto the balcony.* Leadership is improvisational. It cannot be scripted. On one hand, to be effective a leader must respond in the moment to what is happening. On the other hand, the leader must be able to step back out of the moment and assess what is happening from a wider perspective. We call it getting off the dance floor and onto the balcony. It may be an original metaphor, but it's not an original idea. For centuries religious traditions have taught disciplines that enable a person to reflect in action. Jesuits call it *contemplation* in action. Hindus call it *Karma*

Yoga. We call it *getting onto the balcony* because that's a metaphor people can easily relate to. But it's critically important, and the reason why religious traditions have talked about it for so long is that it's hard to do . . . . It's hard, in the midst of action, to step back and ask yourself: What's really going on here? Who are the key parties to this problem? What are the stakes they bring to this issue? How will progress require us all to reevaluate our stakes and change some of our ways? (pp. 4–5)

Heifetz and Linsky further emphasize that the balcony view is difficult for individuals to achieve, as they imply by their many references to religious traditions. As a committed group, however, the leadership team is well equipped to achieve this perspective. Specifically, the leadership team might periodically ask questions such as these: What are the most critical issues currently facing us? What are our biggest weaknesses? What are our biggest strengths? What is the next best action to take as a leadership team? In some cases the leadership team might conclude that they must adopt a more open stance relative to the concerns of the staff and faculty. In other cases they might conclude that they must reaffirm the shared ideals and beliefs that underpin the school's efforts. In still other situations, the team might conclude that for the time being they should simply allow a certain amount of unrest to occur.

In short, 12 of the 21 responsibilities can be effectively distributed throughout the leadership team. Figure 7.1 on pp. 108–109 lists some actions the leadership team might take for each of the 12 distributed responsibilities.

Step 3: Select the Right Work

In Chapter 6 we considered the importance of a school's selecting the right work. The school leader might do a good job of crafting a purposeful community, out of which a strong leadership team arises; but if the school under the direction of the leadership team does not select work that has a high probability of enhancing student achievement, the hard work of the principal, the leadership team, and the school as a whole will be for naught—at least in terms of student academic achievement. A metaphor for the importance of this step might be a sailing vessel charged with the task of visiting ports of call that are interesting and instructive to the tourists on board. The captain of the ship might do well at assembling a fine crew and distributing the many chores aboard the ship. If the captain and crew select the wrong destinations given their charge, however, their work will not produce the desired result.

In schools, the "desired result" typically deals with student academic achievement. In Chapter 6 we identified 39 action steps that might be considered the right work in a given school. Figure 7.2, pp. 110–111, reviews these 39 action steps.

FIGURE 7.1
Distributed Responsibilities and Actions of the Leadership Team

Responsibility	Actions of the Leadership Team
Monitoring/Evaluating	• Provide feedback on classroom practices and student learning through multiple strategies (e.g., lesson study, student work, observations, and team planning). • Ensure that the aligned and intended curriculum is taught (e.g., through observations, team planning, and student work).
Knowledge of Curriculum, Instruction, and Assessment	• Ensure that professional development is focused on agreed-upon instructional and assessment practices within the intended curriculum. • Assess knowledge needed and acquired using informal methods (e.g., observation, surveys, student work, needs assessment).
Involvement in Curriculum, Instruction, and Assessment	• Develop and model techniques for effective lesson design that include (1) how to effectively communicate learning goals, (2) how to help students acquire and integrate their knowledge, (3) how to help students practice and review knowledge, and (4) how to determine if students have learned the knowledge.
Focus	• Adopt common agreements regarding student expectations and effort required to meet the established goals. • Communicate goals to staff and formally and informally keep them in the forefront of the conversations about student achievement.
Intellectual Stimulation	• Use study groups, demonstrated through a leadership team "fishbowl," to stimulate inquiry and reflection on the research around the focused goals. • Use language with peers that demonstrates knowledge of and respect for research on student learning.
Flexibility	• Respond to issues and concerns raised by staff in a direct, open, and transparent manner. • Develop mechanisms to support teachers through the change process. • Examine leadership team practices and make necessary changes. • Support the principal when situations require a more directive style of leadership.
Resources	• Allocate resources based on instructional priorities. Be transparent in this work. • Determine annual priorities for faculty learning. • Provide staff development opportunities that are coordinated with the school's focus and mission.
Contingent Rewards	• Support the implementation of policies and practices that are performance-based as opposed to seniority-based. • Recognize, both formally and informally, those whose work is congruent with the stated purpose and goals of the school.
Outreach	• Communicate positively with the community about the school. • Engage parents in activities that are meaningful and relevant to them.

FIGURE 7.1 (continued)
Distributed Responsibilities and Actions of the Leadership Team

Responsibility	Actions of the Leadership Team
Outreach (continued)	• Collect data regarding parent and community attitudes toward the school. Analyze results and design appropriate programs. • Promote the school's accomplishments through the media and central administration.
Discipline	• Establish agreed-upon policies and procedures for scheduling practices that do not interrupt instructional time. • Establish routines for communication that minimize or eliminate interruptions and distractions to classroom instruction.
Change Agent	• Model a "can do" attitude; formulate agreements about supporting initiatives, such as "no badmouthing the change." • Analyze change initiatives to determine implications for different stakeholders. • Lead structured dialogues to ascertain people's underlying assumptions, values, and beliefs. • Provide data that create sustained tension between what is and what could be. • Assess the magnitude of a change and identify levels of comfort and discomfort.
Order	• Help the principal execute routines and procedures. • Identify ways to improve the effectiveness and utility of established routines and procedures.

To identify the right work in a school, the 39 questions in Figure 7.2 might be posed to the entire faculty. To this end, the model from *What Works in Schools* (Marzano, 2003) involves an online survey that allows teachers within a building to respond to multiple items for each of the 39 action steps. Through 2004, more than 2,000 schools have administered the survey to staff members. For each item, teachers and administrators answer the following questions:

• To what extent do we engage in this behavior or address this issue?

• How much will a change in our practice on this item increase the academic achievement of our students?

• How much effort will it take to significantly change our practices regarding this issue?

The first question deals with how well the school is doing relative to the action steps. The second question deals with how much student achievement will be enhanced if the school improves on the issue addressed in the item. We consider

FIGURE 7.2
A Model for Identifying the "Right Work"

Factors		Action Steps
		Is the next best thing to do in our school to . . .
School-Level	Guaranteed and Viable Curriculum	1. Identify and communicate the content considered essential for all students versus that considered supplemental?
		2. Ensure that the essential content can be addressed in the amount of time available for instruction?
		3. Ensure that teachers address the essential content?
		4. Protect the instructional time available to teachers?
	Challenging Goals and Effective Feedback	5. Implement an assessment and record-keeping system that provides timely feedback on specific areas of knowledge and skill for specific students?
		6. Establish and monitor specific, challenging achievement goals for the school as a whole?
		7. Establish and monitor specific, challenging achievement goals for each student?
	Parent and Community Involvement	8. Establish vehicles for communication between schools and parents and the community?
		9. Establish multiple ways for parents and community to be involved in the day-to-day running of the school?
		10. Establish governance vehicles that allow for the involvement of parents and community members?
	Safe and Orderly Environment	11. Establish rules and procedures for behavioral problems that might be caused by the school's physical characteristics or the school's routines?
		12. Establish schoolwide rules and procedures for general behavior?
		13. Establish and enforce appropriate consequences for violations of rules and procedures?
		14. Establish a program that teaches self-discipline and responsibility to students?
		15. Establish a system that allows for the early detection of students who have high potential for violence and extreme behaviors?
	Collegiality and Professionalism	16. Establish norms of conduct and behavior that engender collegiality and cooperation?
		17. Establish governance structures that allow for teacher involvement in decisions and policies for the school?
		18. Provide teachers with meaningful staff development activities?
Teacher-Level	Instructional Strategies	19. Provide teachers with an instructional framework for planning units that employs research-based strategies?
	Classroom Management	20. Have teachers articulate and enforce a comprehensive set of classroom rules and procedures?

FIGURE 7.2 (continued)
A Model for Identifying the "Right Work"

Factors		Action Steps *Is the next best thing to do in our school to . . .*
Teacher-Level	Classroom Management	21. Have teachers use specific strategies that reinforce appropriate behavior and recognize and provide consequences for inappropriate behavior? 22. Institute a schoolwide approach to discipline? 23. Help teachers develop a balance of moderate dominance and moderate cooperation in their dealings with students? 24. Provide teachers with an awareness of the needs of different types of students and ways of alleviating those needs? 25. Have teachers employ specific strategies to maintain or heighten their awareness regarding the actions of students in their classes? 26. Have teachers employ specific strategies that help them maintain a healthy emotional objectivity with their students?
	Classroom Curriculum Design	27. Have teachers identify the important information and skills in the topics they are required to address? 28. Have teachers present new content multiple times using a variety of activities? 29. Have teachers make distinctions between those skills and processes that will be taught to a level of mastery and those that will only be introduced? 30. Have teachers present content in groups or categories that demonstrate the critical features of the content? 31. Have teachers engage students in complex tasks that require addressing content in multiple ways?
Student-Level	Home Environment	32. Provide training and support to parents to enhance their communication with their children about school, their supervision of their children, and their ability to communicate expectations to their children within the context of an effective parenting style?
	Learned Intelligence and Background Knowledge	33. Involve students in programs that directly increase the number and quality of life experiences students have? 34. Involve students in a program of wide reading that emphasizes vocabulary development? 35. Provide direct instruction in vocabulary terms and phrases that are important to specific subject matter content?
	Motivation	36. Provide students with feedback on their knowledge gain? 37. Provide students with tasks and activities that are inherently engaging? 38. Provide opportunities for students to construct and work on long-term projects of their own design? 39. Teach students about the dynamics of motivation and how those dynamics affect them?

Adapted by permission from *What Works in Schools* by Robert J. Marzano. Copyright © 2003 ASCD.

the third question in the next section. For now, let's illustrate how the first two questions might be used to identify the right work for a school.

Consider Action Step 2 in Figure 7.2. It deals with whether the content that teachers are expected to address can be adequately taught in the instructional time available to teachers. According to a recent analysis of the responses from the 2,000 schools that have taken the *What Works in Schools* survey (see Marzano, 2005), teachers commonly rate their school's performance on this item very low—they perceive that they do not have sufficient time to adequately address all the content they are expected to teach. Additionally, teachers commonly rate this item high in terms of the extent to which it will enhance student achievement in their schools. It is the confluence of these two response patterns that provides evidence for a school's next best work. Whether the action steps in Figure 7.2 are presented to the faculty as a formal survey or simply as discussion items at a faculty meeting, it should be possible to get a clear view regarding the right work for the school by identifying those items on which the school is not performing well *and* on which improved performance will enhance student academic achievement.

Step 4: Identify the Order of Magnitude Implied by the Selected Work

Step 3 should result in the identification of a specific area of work on which to focus. Ideally, the work identified is the most powerful next action the school can take to enhance the academic achievement of students. With its next work identified, the leadership team would consider the magnitude of change implied. One of the difficult aspects of identifying the magnitude of change for a given initiative is that one person's first-order change might be another's second-order change.

The phenomenon of first- versus second-order change is an internal event. It is defined by the way people react to a proposed innovation. Whether a change is perceived as first order or second order depends on the knowledge, experience, values, and flexibility of the individual or group perceiving the change. Figure 7.3 lists characteristics that typically determine whether an initiative is perceived as a first-order change or a second-order change.

To illustrate the characteristics depicted in Figure 7.3, consider the initiative of moving from a traditional report card to one that is standards-based. Specifically, Action Step 5 in Figure 7.2 addresses the implementation of an assessment and record-keeping system that provides timely feedback on specific types of knowledge and skills for specific students. One manifestation of this action step is a standards-based report card like that depicted in Figure 6.3 (see Chapter 6, p. 85). Depending on how they perceive this change initiative, some staff members will experience

FIGURE 7.3
Characteristics of First-Order Change and Second-Order Change

First-Order Change	Second-Order Change
• Is perceived as an extension of the past	• Is perceived as a break with the past
• Fits within existing paradigms	• Lies outside existing paradigms
• Is consistent with prevailing values and norms	• Conflicts with prevailing values and norms
• Can be implemented with existing knowledge and skills	• Requires the acquisition of new knowledge and skills
• Requires resources currently available to those responsible for implementing the innovations	• Requires resources currently not available to those responsible for implementing the innovations
• May be accepted because of common agreement that the innovation is necessary	• May be resisted because only those who have a broad perspective of the school see the innovation as necessary

the initiative as first-order change and others will experience it as second-order change.

The first characteristic listed in Figure 7.3 is the extent to which the proposed change is perceived as an extension of or a break from the past. Perhaps a specific teacher in the school has been experimenting with standards-based ways of reporting to her students for a few semesters or even a few years. Consequently, for her, changing the school report card to one like that depicted in Figure 6.3 is an extension of her experiences—the next logical step. However, for another teacher in the same school who has not been experimenting with new reporting systems, a new report card is not an extension of the past. That teacher would view the new report card as second-order change.

The second characteristic listed in Figure 7.3 is the extent to which the innovation is perceived as fitting within existing paradigms. To illustrate this characteristic, let's consider two other individuals in the school, both of whom are building vice principals. One of the two might perceive that the faculty in the school strongly favors using standards as the guiding force behind not only the school's reporting system but also the design of the curriculum and the type of tests that should be given. Indeed, that vice principal might regularly interact with teachers who hold this point of view. For this vice principal, the new report card fits well within the existing paradigm regarding schooling—it is a first-order change. However, the second vice principal systematically interacts with a group of teachers who perceive standards as a disruptive force in the functioning of the school and the intellectual freedom of teachers. That vice principal would perceive the new standards-based report card as a dramatic departure from the existing paradigm—a second-order change.

The remaining characteristics listed in Figure 7.3 follow suit. Depending on the characteristics an individual ascribes to an innovation, the individual will perceive the innovation as first or second order in nature. Within one school, different individuals or groups will ascribe different characteristics to an innovation, so that the magnitude of change associated with the innovation is different for various constituent groups in the school. How, then, does the school leader and leadership team ascertain the order of magnitude of the changes being proposed? We suggest two ways.

The first technique is to determine people's perceptions of how difficult it would be to implement the innovation. It makes intuitive sense that change initiatives that are perceived as second order will be thought of as more difficult than change initiatives that are first order in nature. This is where the third question in the *What Works in Schools* survey is of use. It asks: How much effort will it take to significantly change our practices regarding this issue? For faculty members who indicate that a great deal of effort will be required to significantly change the schools' practices, the innovation is most likely second order in nature. For those who indicate that little effort will be required, the innovation is most likely first order in nature.

The second technique is more direct; it is a simple extension of the characteristics listed in Figure 7.3. Specifically, the principal and the leadership team can address the following questions regarding the work that has been selected:

- Is the new work a logical and incremental extension of what we have done in the past?
- Does the new work fit within the existing paradigms of teachers and administrators?
- Is the new work consistent with prevailing values and norms?
- Can the innovations be implemented with the knowledge and skills that exist among the faculty and administrators?
- Can the innovations be implemented with resources that are easily available?
- Is there common agreement that the innovation is necessary?

If the principal and leadership team conclude that most of the staff would answer no to most of these questions, they have good evidence that the new work that has been selected is second order in magnitude.

Step 5: Match the Management Style to the Order of Magnitude of the Change Initiative

As a result of Step 4, the leadership team and the principal should have a fairly good indication of whether their new work is first order or second order in magnitude. As we have seen, leadership looks quite different for first-order versus second-order initiatives.

Managing First-Order Change

First-order change requires attention to all 21 responsibilities. As described in Step 1, the school principal must address at least nine of these responsibilities simply to craft a purposeful community. Again, these responsibilities are the following:

- Optimizer
- Affirmation
- Ideals/Beliefs
- Situational Awareness
- Visibility
- Relationships
- Communication
- Culture
- Input

The school leader must persist in effectively executing these nine responsibilities not only to nurture a purposeful community but also to support first-order change initiatives. This does not mean that the leadership team cannot participate in the effective execution of these responsibilities as a way of supporting the principal.

To illustrate how the leadership team might provide such support, let's briefly consider a few of the responsibilities. Recall from the discussion of Step 1 that the building principal executes the responsibility of Optimizer by being a champion for the belief that the staff operating as a cohesive group can produce powerful results. The leadership team might support this responsibility by identifying tasks that capitalize on the strengths of faculty members. To carry out the responsibility of Affirmation, the building principal might devote a portion of each faculty meeting to acknowledging the accomplishments of the school as a whole as well as individuals within the school. In support of this, the leadership team might systematically gather examples of these collective and individual accomplishments so that the principal will have a readily available list of examples. In short, the leadership team can provide concrete support for each of the nine responsibilities that pertain specifically to the principal. Figure 7.4 lists some other ways the leadership team might help the principal execute these responsibilities.

In addition to supporting the principal's responsibilities, the leadership team should continually attend to the 12 distributed responsibilities (see Figure 7.1, p. 108). In short, first-order change initiatives require attention to all 21 responsibilities. As discussed in Chapter 5, they are necessary ingredients in the day-to-day operations of a school.

Managing Second-Order Change

Second-order change requires a different approach to leadership. Recall from the discussion in Chapter 5 that seven responsibilities seem to be critical to effective leadership for second-order change. They are the following:

- Knowledge of Curriculum, Instruction, and Assessment
- Optimizer
- Intellectual Stimulation
- Change Agent
- Monitoring/Evaluating
- Flexibility
- Ideals/Beliefs

These are defined somewhat differently in second-order change situations than they are in first-order situations.

Within first-order change situations, Knowledge of Curriculum, Instruction, and Assessment refers to an understanding of best practices regarding curriculum, instruction, and assessment. Within second-order change, this responsibility involves an understanding of how the selected change initiative will affect current practices in curriculum, instruction, and assessment. For example, assume that a school has decided to institute a standards-based report card. Additionally, the leadership team has determined that the staff perceives the initiative as second order in magnitude. To effectively execute this responsibility, the school leader would carefully study how the new report card would affect the current curriculum. One thing she might discover is that the current curriculum, which consists of course outlines, provides teachers with wide latitude in the course content they may include and exclude. Implementation of a standards-based report card will greatly diminish this latitude. Because teachers will have to report on students' progress in certain areas of knowledge and skill, they will certainly have to address those areas of knowledge and skill in their classes. In effect, the new report card will standardize the curriculum and influence how every classroom teacher executes instruction and

FIGURE 7.4
Leadership Team Actions Supporting the Nine Responsibilities of a Principal

Responsibility	Actions of the Leadership Team
Optimizer	• Focus on staff strengths and help arrange work so that strengths are matched with tasks. • Celebrate successes. • Use data to illustrate progress toward goals.
Affirmation	• Develop structures that regularly recognize and celebrate accomplishments. • Take time in staff meetings to share and celebrate individual and school-wide learning (successes and failures). • Communicate student successes to parents and the community.
Ideals/Beliefs	• Forge shared agreements around the mission, vision, and purpose of the school. Help turn the adopted beliefs into observable behaviors. • Lead in the writing of instructional philosophies by content area. • Ask strategic questions about times when actions do not reflect agreed-upon purposes, goals, and agreements.
Situational Awareness	• Keep the principal informed about perceptions from within the school and from the community the school serves.
Visibility	• Support the principal in efforts to be visible: invite the principal into the classroom; model the idea of being comfortable with the principal in the classroom; ask the principal to work with groups of students regularly. • Remain highly visible around the school and encourage frequent contact with students both in and outside of the classroom.
Relationships	• Work hand in hand with the principal in acknowledging professional accomplishments of staff; celebrate the awarding of advanced degrees, professional honors, and so on. • Recognize significant events in the lives of staff, such as birthdays, marriages, and births. • Promote a caring culture and procedures that support staff in facing personal challenges and meeting obligations outside of school, such as those related to families and children.
Communication	• Help develop structures that promote the free flow of information with the staff, such as daily bulletins, common Web pages, professional sharing during faculty meetings, and joint planning time. • Model constructive disagreement and problem-solving skills. • Model positive communication; center conversations on learning.
Culture	• Model cooperation and cohesion; be promoters of the desired culture of the building. • Monitor school climate. • Lead structured dialogues around the purpose and vision of the school.
Input	• Model giving input in a positive manner. • Ask strategic questions about whether decisions and actions are aligned with school goals. • Actively seek staff input. • Ensure that all perspectives are addressed.

assessment. Understanding the impact the new report card will likely have on curriculum, instruction, and assessment might be critical to developing strategies to ensure the success of this innovation.

Within first-order change situations, the responsibility of Optimizer involves being a generally positive influence in the school. Within a second-order change situation, the role of Optimizer becomes more focused and intense. The school leader must be willing to be the driving force behind the change initiative and take a stand for its success. For example, relative to a standards-based report card, the school leader would systematically highlight the potential benefits of the new report card. Additionally, she would make it clear that she will do everything in her power to ensure the successful implementation of the new report cards.

Intellectual Stimulation within the context of first-order change involves fostering a knowledge of research and theory on best practices among the staff through reading and discussion. Again, within first-order change the emphasis is broad. Within second-order change the focus is on the innovation being implemented. In this case, reading and discussion would focus on standards-based report cards. The general thrust of this responsibility within second-order change is to stimulate the intellectual curiosity of faculty regarding the innovation.

The importance of the responsibility of Change Agent to second-order change is almost self-evident. In first-order change situations, this responsibility is centered on challenging unexamined school practices that have been in place for a long time. The intent is to generate new ideas for future consideration. Within second-order change situations, the responsibility of Change Agent shifts its emphasis to inspiring faculty and staff to operate at the edge of their competence. This shift in focus is necessary because by definition the school has undertaken a change initiative that will require teachers and administrators to perform at their best.

The responsibility of Monitoring/Evaluating in first-order change situations involves keeping track of students at a general level. If achievement trends indicate that students are not learning, adjustments are made in curriculum, instruction, and assessment. In second-order change situations, this responsibility involves a careful monitoring of the effects of the innovation. In the case of the standards-based report card, this would include examining the effects of the new report card on student learning along with the effects on classroom practices.

Like the responsibility of Change Agent, the importance of the responsibility of Flexibility to second-order change is fairly obvious. Given the uncertainty associated with second-order change initiatives, it is vital that the school leader adapt her leadership style to the demands of the current situation. At times the appropriate leadership behavior might be to provide information. At other times it might be to provide inspiration. At still other times the appropriate leadership behavior might be to offer no input or guidance, allowing dynamics among the faculty to play out on their own.

The final responsibility important to second-order change is Ideals/Beliefs. As we saw in Step 1, identifying shared ideals and beliefs regarding the nature and purpose of schooling is critical to establishing a purposeful community. Within second-order change situations, the focus is narrowed in that the leader addresses the extent to which the identified innovation is consistent with shared ideals and beliefs. While in the throes of a second-order change initiative, it is probably easy for faculty and staff to forget that they selected a given initiative because it was in keeping with their ideals and beliefs. A standards-based report card might have been selected because it was a logical consequence of the shared belief that a school should be able to identify specific strengths and weaknesses of every student. While executing the responsibility of Ideals/Beliefs, the school leader would strive to keep this reasoning in the forefront of discussions regarding the initiative.

We have described these examples regarding the seven responsibilities critical to second-order change in terms of the school leader. However, the leadership team can share in the execution of these responsibilities. Figure 7.5 lists some specific steps the team can take relative to these second-order change responsibilities.

As described in Chapter 5, second-order change not only involves emphasizing the seven responsibilities; it also involves the possible perception that things have deteriorated relative to the four responsibilities of Culture, Communication, Order, and Input.

Within the context of first-order change, Culture refers to the creation of a sense of team spirit and a cooperative atmosphere in the running of the school. It is accompanied by the creation and use of a common language regarding teaching, learning, and schooling. In a second-order change environment, some or many staff members may perceive that these elements have deteriorated. For example, if a school is adopting a standards-based report card, some staff members might believe that the initiative has diminished team spirit. Additionally, they might believe that the common language that previously characterized the school has suffered since the introduction of the new terminology of the standards-based report card.

The responsibility of Communication involves developing clear lines of communication to and from faculty members as well as among faculty members. Even though these lines of communication might still be open, during second-order change some faculty members might believe that the innovation has interrupted the flow of information. Those faculty members for whom standards-based report cards are a great departure from their current practice might logically perceive that they have few or no venues for expressing their concerns.

FIGURE 7.5
Leadership Team Responsibilities and Actions Important to Second-Order Change

Responsibility	Actions of the Leadership Team
Knowledge of Curriculum, Instruction, and Assessment	• Work individually with staff members regarding implementation of the innovation. • Attend staff development opportunities regarding the innovation.
Optimizer	• Speak positively about the innovation. • Provide examples of other schools that have successfully implemented the innovation. • Express a continued belief that the innovation will enhance student achievement. • Identify roadblocks and challenges to the innovation.
Intellectual Stimulation	• Include research about the innovation in conversations. • Ask questions that cause teachers to be reflective in their practices related to the innovation. • Lead discussions around current practices related to the innovation.
Change Agent	• Raise issues around achievement related to the innovation. • Share data related to other schools that have implemented the innovation. • Compare where the school is and where it needs to be in terms of implementing the innovation. • Demonstrate "tolerance for ambiguity" regarding the innovation.
Monitoring/Evaluating	• Look at both formative and summative assessments in relation to the innovation. • Conduct classroom walk-throughs related to the innovation.
Flexibility	• Continually adjust plans in response to progress and tension. • Use situational leadership regarding the innovation. • Use protocols that allow for input regarding the innovation without bogging down into endless discussion.
Ideals/Beliefs	• Communicate ideals and beliefs related to the innovation in formal and informal conversations and model through behaviors. • Ensure that practices related to the innovation are aligned with shared ideals and beliefs. • Ask strategic questions regarding the innovation when actions don't reflect agreed-upon purposes, goals, and understandings.

Order involves establishing procedures and routines that provide faculty and students with a sense of predictability. It makes sense that the perception regarding this responsibility could erode in a second-order change situation. The old way of doing things has been disrupted. Even if the "old" report cards were not as useful as the "new" report cards, they were familiar. The unfamiliar typically brings with it a sense of uncertainty.

Finally, the responsibility of Input will most probably suffer as a result of a second-order change. Whereas faculty and staff once felt that their voices were being heard and heeded, the implementation of the innovation serves for some as evidence that this is no longer the case.

It is important to emphasize the fact that the perceptions regarding these four responsibilities are just that—perceptions. For those who hold these perceptions, however, they are reality.

One approach the school leader can take is to simply ride out the storm—endure the fact that some staff members have become disenfranchised. This suggestion is not without merit. The realization that some faculty members within the school will not be happy about a given second-order change can provide a sense of freedom for a school leader. Rather than try to ensure that all staff members feel comfortable, the school leader can focus on the business of increasing the probability that the change initiative will succeed, recognizing that some discord is inevitable.

A more proactive approach would be for the school leader to charge members of the leadership team with focusing on the responsibilities that are casualties of the second-order initiative. That is, in cases in which the school leader might not be the person best suited to seek out those staff members who perceive that the culture of the school has deteriorated, members of the leadership team can serve as strong proxies. They might meet individually with disenfranchised members of the staff. During these meetings, members of the leadership team might simply listen to the concerns of the staff members with the intent of fully understanding and honoring their concerns. Team members would also ensure that the concerns expressed in these meetings would be communicated in full to the principal. In short, the leadership team can act as goodwill ambassadors for the second-order change initiative and liaisons between the faculty and administration.

Figure 7.6 lists some other actions the leadership team might take regarding these four responsibilities that are frequently the casualties of second-order change.

Summary and Conclusions

This chapter presented a five-step plan for effective school leadership—a plan based on the research and theory discussed in the preceding chapters. The first step involves developing a school leadership team based on the foundation of a purposeful community. The second step distributes 12 of the 21 leadership responsibilities to the members of the leadership team, leaving 9 responsibilities to the school principal. The third step involves considering 39 action steps from the *What Works in Schools* (Marzano, 2003) framework to identify the "right work"

FIGURE 7.6
Second-Order Change: Responsibilities That Suffer and Actions That Help

Culture	• Continually remind colleagues of the vision for the initiative and why it is important. • Model a "we're all in this together" attitude. • Find points of agreement that can serve as common ground during the implementation of the innovation. • In staff meetings, work in small groups generating explicit ideas and connections on how the innovation can advance the shared vision of the school and how it fits the shared purpose. • Provide differentiated support for teachers based on their response to the initiative. • Create time for staff to discuss the change and its implications.
Communication	• Discuss disagreements and contentions in staff and team meetings. • Probe for questions and concerns from colleagues and bring them to the leadership team for resolution. • Develop a transition plan with the principal that anticipates various responses and attempts to be proactive. • Communicate the transition plan to all stakeholders. • Create a unified front: Agree upon a consistent and uniform message. • Emphasize the fact that things will stabilize as the innovation becomes better defined and institutionalized.
Order	• Design effective decision-making procedures, problem-solving tools, and conflict resolution tools. • Model effective mediation strategies. • Communicate the fact that the innovation will disrupt the established routine to some extent. • Be consistent in using procedures that foster a sense of stability. • Take an active role in creating and implementing operational procedures.
Input	• Meet frequently with small groups to hear concerns and respond. • Actively seek input from staff. • Work to develop "ownership" rather than "buy-in" for the initiative. • Work with the principal to offer multiple opportunities to discuss the innovation openly and honestly. • Help the staff understand the stages and the implications of changes. • Explicitly communicate the ways in which input informs decisions. • Be transparent about the difference between decisions and input.

for the school. The fourth step involves analyzing the related work to determine if it is a first- or second-order change initiative for the faculty and staff. The fifth step matches the appropriate leadership behaviors to the order of the change implied by the selected work.

Epilogue

In this book we have presented the results of our research and attempted to translate our findings into a concrete plan that experienced and novice school leaders can use to enhance the academic achievement of students in their schools. We hope this plan is seen as a useful tool that is grounded in 35 years of research.

Perhaps more important than the use of our proposed plan is whether educational leaders at the building level and district level will seize the opportunity to make a profound difference in the achievement of their students through strong and thoughtful leadership. At no time in recent memory has the need for effective and inspired leadership been more pressing than it is today. With increasing needs in our society and in the workplace for knowledgeable, skilled, responsible citizens, the pressure on schools intensifies. The expectation that no child be left behind in a world and in an economy that will require everyone's best is not likely to subside.

We are all familiar with exhortations like "If it is to be, it is up to me," and "I used to ask, 'Why doesn't somebody do something?' until I realized that I am somebody." Although clichés, these statements carry with them particular relevance in today's world. The need for truly effective educational leadership is great. The time for improving our schools is short. The opportunity to lead is ours. As evidenced by the discussion in this book, we believe that the knowledge needed to make substantial, positive changes in the effectiveness of schools is available. The only thing left is to act. It is our hope that the information presented in this book will help principals and others translate their vision and aspirations into plans and their plans into actions that will change not only our schools, but potentially, the world.

Technical Notes

The following notes explain some of the more technical aspects of the findings presented in this book. They are not designed to be read sequentially. Rather, they make sense in the context of the discussion in Chapters 1 through 7. The notes are brief treatments of the topics addressed. For more detailed analyses consult standard statistical and methodological texts such as Cohen (1988); Cohen and Cohen (1975); Glass, McGaw, and Smith (1981); Glass, Willson, and Gottman (1975); Hunter and Schmidt (1990a, 1990b); Lipsey and Wilson (2001); and Loehlin (1992).

Technical Note 1: Interpreting the Correlation Coefficient in Terms of the *BESD* and Predicted Z Scores

Throughout this book, we discuss a number of relationships. In Figure 1.1 (Chapter 1, p. 4), the focus is on the relationship between the effectiveness of a school and student achievement. Many times throughout the book we focus on the relationship between school leadership and student achievement. This technical note describes the ways relationships between variables are represented and interpreted in this book. A useful place to start is the notion of the percentage of variance (*PV*) explained by a predictor variable.

It is generally accepted that the percentage of variance explained by a predictor (or independent) variable (e.g., the effectiveness of a school) relative to a predicted (or dependent) variable (e.g., student achievement) represents the strength of the relation between the two. Commonly, a "set" of predictor variables is used. For example, a given study might attempt to predict student achievement using (A) per pupil expenditures, (B) quality of the teaching staff, and (C) quality of principal's leadership. The predictor variables (A, B, and C) considered as a set would account for a proportion of the total variance in the predicted variable (student achievement). The index (PV) used to judge the influence of predictor variables is the ratio of variance accounted for by the predictor variables over the total variance of the predicted variable multiplied by 100.

$$PV = \frac{\text{percent of variance explained by predictor, or independent, variables}}{\text{percent of total variance in the predicted, or dependent, variable}} \times 100$$

An index closely related to PV is the correlation coefficient. We discuss the correlation coefficient in some depth in Technical Note 4. Here we simply note that when a single predictor, or independent, variable (e.g., principal leadership) is used with a predicted, or dependent, variable (e.g., student achievement), the relationship between the two can be expressed as r—the Pearson product-moment correlation. When multiple predictors (e.g., per pupil expenditures, quality of the teaching staff, and quality of principal's leadership) are used with a predicted variable, the relationship between the predictor variables, considered as a set, and the predicted variable is expressed as R—the multiple correlation coefficient. In both cases, the percentage of variance accounted for (PV) in the predicted (dependent) variable by the predictor (independent) variables is computed by squaring the correlation coefficient (i.e., r^2 or R^2) and multiplying by 100. In short, there is a strong conceptual and mathematical relationship between PV and the univariate and multivariate correlation coefficients.

As common as is the use of r^2, or R^2, and PV, they have been criticized as indicators of the relationship between predictor (independent) variables and the predicted (dependent) variable. Hunter and Schmidt (1990b) explain:

> The percent of variance accounted for is statistically correct, but substantively erroneous. It leads to severe underestimates of the practical and theoretical significance of relationships between variables. . . . The problem with all percent variance accounted for indices of effect size is that variables that account for small percentages of the variance often have very important effects on the dependent variable. (pp. 199–200)

Hunter and Schmidt use the correlation between aptitude and heredity reported by Jensen (1980) to illustrate this circumstance. This correlation is about

0.895, which implies that about 80 percent (0.895^2) of the variance in aptitude is a function of heredity, leaving only 20 percent of the variance due to environment ($r = 0.447$). The relative influence of heredity on aptitude and environment on aptitude, then, is about 4 to 1 from the percentage-of-variance perspective. However, regression theory (Cohen & Cohen, 1975) tells us that the correlations between heredity and aptitude (H) and between environment and aptitude (E) (after the influence of heredity has been partialed out) are analogous to the regression weights in a linear equation predicting aptitude from heredity and environment when dependent and independent variables are expressed in standard score form. (For this illustration, we will assume that heredity and environment are independent.) Using the quantities above, this equation would be as follows:

$$\text{Predicted Aptitude} = 0.895(H) + 0.447(E)$$

This equation states that an increase of one standard deviation in heredity will be accompanied by an increase of 0.895 standard deviations in aptitude. Similarly, an increase of one standard deviation in environment will be accompanied by an increase of 0.447 standard deviations in aptitude. (We explain this concept in more depth subsequently.) This paints a very different picture of the relative influences of heredity and environment on aptitude. Here the ratio is 2 to 1 as opposed to the ratio of 4 to 1 that results from the percentage-of-variance perspective.

The potentially misleading impressions created by the percentage-of-variance perspective has stimulated the use of the binomial effect size display (*BESD*). The *BESD* is one of the two primary ways we interpret correlation coefficients in this book. As described by Rosenthal and Rubin (1982), to employ the *BESD*, the predictor variable is thought of as being dichotomized into two distinct groups. One group might be the experimental group; the other might be the control group. Similarly, one group might be high performers on some variable; the other might be low performers on the same variable. In the *BESD* illustration used in Figure 1.1 (p. 4), the dichotomized independent variable is school effectiveness. If schools were rank-ordered in terms of their effectiveness they would most likely fall into a normal distribution. The top half of that distribution would be thought of as effective schools and the bottom half as ineffective schools. Similarly, when employing the *BESD*, the predicted variable is dichotomized into success or failure on some criterion measure. In Figure 1.1, the predicted variable is conceptualized as success or failure on some form of achievement test.

A common convention employed with the *BESD* is to assume that the expectation for the predicted variable is a success rate of 0.50. To compute the *BESD*, the correlation coefficient is divided by 2 and then added to and subtracted from the

FIGURE TN1.1
Binomial Effect Size Display with 1% of Variance (r = 0.10) Accounted for by Hypothetical Medical Treatment

	Alive	Dead	Total
Treatment Group	55%	45%	100%
Control Group	45%	55%	100%

Note: Constructed from data in *Statistical Power for the Behavioral Sciences* by J. Cohen, 1988, Hillsdale, NJ: Erlbaum, p. 534. In the title, r stands for the Pearson product-moment correlation coefficient.

expected success rate or 0.50. For example, if the *r* between predictor and predicted is 0.20, then 0.20 ÷ 2 = 0.10. The percentage of subjects in the experimental group or the high-performing group that would be expected to "succeed" on the predicted variable is computed as 0.50 + 0.10 = 0.60. The percentage of subjects in the experimental group or the high-performing group that would be expected to "fail" on the criterion measure is 0.50 − 0.10 = 0.40. The converse of these computations is used for the control group or the low-performing group. Rosenthal and Rubin (1982) make the case for the use of *BESD* as a realistic and useful representation of the size of the treatment effect when the outcome variable is continuous, provided that the groups are of equal size and variance.

Cohen (1988) dramatically illustrates the use of the *BESD* with an example from medicine. This is depicted in Figure TN1.1. The figure exemplifies a situation in which the independent variable (i.e., membership in the experimental or control group) accounts for only 1 percent of the variance in the dependent variable (i.e., *r* = 0.10). The assumption here is that the independent variable is some sort of medical treatment that accounts for 1 percent of the variance in the outcome measure, which is being alive or dead. Yet this 1 percent of explained variance translates into a 10-percentage-point difference in terms of patients who are alive (or dead) based on group membership. As Cohen (1988) notes,

> This means, for example, that a difference in percent alive between .45 and .55, which most people would consider important (*alive*, mind you!) yields *r* = .10, and "only 1% of the variance accounted for," an amount that operationally defines a "small" effect in my scheme.... "Death" tends to concentrate the mind. But this in turn reinforces the principle that the size of an effect can only be appraised in the context of the substantive issues involved. An r^2 of .01 is indeed small in absolute terms, but when it represents a ten percentage point increase in survival, it may well be considered large. (p. 534)

Abelson (1985) further dramatizes this same point. After analyzing the effect of various physical skills on the batting averages of professional baseball players, he found that the percentage of variance accounted for by these skills was a minuscule 0.00317—not quite one-third of 1 percent ($r = 0.056$). Commenting on the implications for interpreting education research, Abelson notes,

> One should not necessarily be scornful of minuscule values for percentage of variance explained, provided there is statistical assurance that these values are significantly above zero, and that the degree of potential cumulation is substantial. (p. 133)

Finally, Cohen (1988) exhorts, "The next time you read 'only X% of the variance is accounted for,' remember Abelson's paradox" (p. 535).

The second interpretation of a correlation coefficient frequently employed in this book is in a predictive sense—the extent to which performance on one variable predicts performance on another variable. In the examples above more than one predictor variable was involved. When a single predictor is involved, the general form of the prediction equation might be stated as follows:

$$\text{(Predicted Z score)} = \text{(Predictor Z score)} \times \text{(correlation)}$$

To interpret this equation, it is necessary to understand the concept of a Z score. A Z score is a transformation of a raw score to standard deviation units. A Z score of 1.00 means that a given raw score is one standard deviation above the mean of the distribution; a Z score of 2.00 means that a given raw score is two standard deviations above the mean, and so on. A useful aspect of Z scores is that they can be easily translated into percentile points on the unit normal distribution. A Z score of .00 means that an individual is at the 50th percentile; a Z score of 1.00 means that a person is at the 84th percentile; a Z score of –1.00 means that a person is at the 16th percentile. These conversions are accomplished by consulting a table depicting the unit normal distribution.

From the equation above, we see that the Z score of the predicted variable can be computed by multiplying the Z score on the predictor variable by the correlation coefficient. For example, let's assume that the correlation between the leadership of the principal in a school and the average academic achievement of students in a school is .25. Using the equation above, we can predict the average achievement of a school in Z score form if we know the Z score for that school regarding the leadership behavior of the principal. For example, let's assume that a certain school has a Z score of 1.00 on the predictor variable, principal leadership behavior. Because the correlation between principal leadership behavior and student achievement has been computed to be .25, we multiply the Z score of 1.00 on principal leadership by .25. Thus the formula predicts that a school with a Z score of 1.00 on principal leadership behavior will have a Z score of .25 on the average academic achievement of students in the school.

The prediction equation also demonstrates that a Z score of .00 on the predictor variable translates into a Z score of .00 on the predicted variable. In other words, a school with the mean score on the predictor variable will be predicted to have the mean score on the predicted variable. This allows us to make inferences about changes in the predictor variable associated with changes in the predictor variable. It is easiest to do this if we begin with the assumption that a school starts at the 50th percentile (i.e., a Z score of .00) on both the predictor and predicted variables. Again, using the correlation between leadership and student achievement of .25, the prediction equation indicates that a Z score of 1.00 on the predictor variable translates into a Z score of .25 on the predicted variable. Consequently, we can infer the following: An increase in principal leadership behavior from a Z score of .00 to 1.00 is associated with an increase in the average academic achievement of students in a school from a Z score of .00 to .25. Translating this into percentile terms, we can say that an increase in the predictor variable of one standard deviation is associated with an increase in the predicted variable from the 50th percentile to the 60th percentile because a Z score of .25 represents the 60th percentile on the unit normal distribution. It is important to note that when describing the relationship between an increase in leadership behavior and an increase in student achievement throughout the book, we have consistently used the term "associated with." A correlation between two variables does not demonstrate a causal relationship between the two variables, although it does not exclude such a relationship.

Technical Note 2: Estimating the Performance of Schools at the 99th Percentile

An explanation for the estimated impact of schools at the 99th percentile is presented in Marzano (2003). Briefly, though, to determine the impact on students of schools at the 99th percentile of the distribution, we assumed that schools are distributed normally in terms of their effectiveness. We also assumed that, on the average, schools account for 20 percent of the variance on student achievement, which translates to $r = 0.447$. That is, the average correlation between the qualities of a school and student achievement is 0.447. Based on the research of Scheerens and Bosker (1997), we assumed that the standard deviation of this distribution of correlations is 0.1068 (see Marzano, 2000a, pp. 57–58, for a discussion). Schools at the 99th percentile would be 2.33 standard deviations above the mean. That is, the correlation between the qualities of schools at the 99th percentile and student achievement is 0.694 (.447 + 2.33 x 0.1068). Using the *BESD*, this implies that in these schools 84.7 percent of the students would pass a test on which half are expected to pass. Additionally, only 15.3 percent of the students would fail the test.

Technical Note 3: General Features of Meta-Analysis

In general terms, it can be said that much of the research in education is designed to answer the following question: Does the relationship observed in this situation represent a true relationship or one that has occurred by chance? Explicit in this question are two elements: observed relationships and chance occurrence. Educational researchers examine many types of relationships—the relationship between using a specific reading program and student achievement in reading, the relationship between different instructional styles and student achievement, and so on. In terms of school leadership, educational research has typically focused on the relationship between specific behaviors of school principals and the achievement of students. There are many mathematical ways to express a relationship. In our meta-analysis we used the correlation coefficient. (See Technical Note 4 for a discussion of correlation coefficients.) The typical study we examined computed a correlation between the leadership of the principal and the average achievement of students in a sample of schools.

For illustrative purposes, assume that a particular study involved 20 schools and computed the correlation to be .20 between the leadership in those schools and the average achievement of the students in those schools. The correlation of .20 is a quantitative index of the "observed relationship" mentioned above. The second important concept mentioned above deals with whether this observed relationship could have happened by chance alone. To address this second concept, a researcher will "test the significance" of the observed correlation. Note that the following discussion of significance testing is a rudimentary one. For a more detailed and advanced discussion, consult Harlow, Mulaik, and Steiger (1997).

To test the statistical significance of an observed correlation, the researcher first considers the possibility that there is no real relationship between the two variables being studied. This is called the "null hypothesis." In terms of correlations, this is tantamount to assuming that the true correlation is .00. The researcher then (metaphorically) asks the question, How likely would it be to observe a correlation of .20 if there is no real relationship between principal leadership and student achievement (i.e., the true correlation is .00)? This is an important question because an observed correlation of .20 can occur even when the true correlation is .00. Through statistical analysis, the researcher can determine the probability of obtaining an observed correlation of .20 between principal leadership and the student achievement by chance. If this correlation could happen by chance 5 times or less in 100, the researcher will reject the null hypothesis of no relationship and conclude that there is a real relationship between principal leadership and student academic achievement. Another way of saying this is that the observed correlation of .20 is "significant" at the .05 level. If the chances of computing a correlation of .20 are 1 time in 100 or less when the null hypothesis is true, then the researcher reports that the correlation is significant at the .01 level, and so on.

In isolation, a single study tells a researcher what the chances are that an observed relationship (indicated by a correlation of .20 in our example) occurred by chance as described above. However, when research is limited to a single study, it is easy to make errors regarding the significance of an observed correlation. More specifically, it is not uncommon for a researcher conducting a single study to conclude that his observed correlation is "not significant" when, in fact, it is. In other words, it is not uncommon for a researcher to inaccurately conclude that there is no real relationship between two variables when, in fact, there is. This is because the statistical significance of a correlation is determined by the size of the correlation (in this case .20) and the size of the sample used to compute the correlation (in this case 20 schools). The smaller the true correlation, the larger the sample size must be for a researcher to conclude that it is significant.

To illustrate, consider Figure TN3.1. The figure provides an interesting perspective on our correlation of .20 computed on a sample of 20 schools. From Figure TN3.1 we see that a correlation of .20 requires a sample size of 72 to be considered significant at the .05 level. In other words, our observed correlation of .20 will automatically be considered nonsignificant at the .05 level even if it, in fact, represents a true relationship between these two variables. The researcher will conclude that there is no relationship between principal leadership and student achievement (i.e., the researcher will conclude that the true correlation is .00). But this would be an error by the researcher, produced solely by the fact that the sample consisted of only 20 schools. Had 72 schools been used and the observed correlation was computed to be .20, it would have been considered statistically significant.

This type of false conclusion (referred to as a Type II error) is all too common in the research on school leadership, primarily because the correlations between principal leadership behavior and student achievement are relatively low and many studies examining the relationship between principal behavior and student achievement employ small samples.

FIGURE TN3.1
Sample Sizes Needed for Significance at the .05 Level (One-tailed)

Correlation	Necessary Sample Size
.16	102
.17	92
.18	82
.20	72
.21	62
.23	52
.24	47
.26	42
.27	37
.30	32
.32	27
.36	22
.37	21
.38	19
.40	18
.41	17
.43	16
.44	15
.46	14
.48	13
.50	12

Note: The figures reported here have been rounded. For more accurate figures, consult standard statistical tables such as those reported by Downie & Heath (1965), p. 306.

Meta-analysis by its very nature helps to alleviate this situation. In simple terms, meta-analysis allows the researcher to combine correlations from different studies and examine the significance of the combined correlation from the perspective of the combined sample sizes. To illustrate, assume that a researcher finds three studies that examine the relationship between principal leadership and student achievement. Also assume that those studies computed the observed correlations and used the sample sizes depicted in Figure TN3.2.

Consulting Figure TN3.1 we see that none of these observed correlations is significant at the .05 level because none has the requisite sample size, given their reported correlation. Specifically, a correlation of .24 requires a sample size of 47 to be considered significant, a correlation of .32 requires a sample size of 27 to be considered significant, and a correlation of .18 requires a sample size of 82 to be considered significant. However, if we combine these correlations and their sample sizes using meta-analytic techniques, we find that the weighted average is .23 and is significant at the .05 level.

FIGURE TN3.2
Correlations and Sample Sizes of Three Hypothetical Studies

Study	Observed Correlation	Sample Size
1	.24	23
2	.32	20
3	.18	36

Herein lies the power of meta-analysis. It allows researchers to draw statistical conclusions about relationships based on a sample of all the studies that have been done as opposed to one study at a time. In practical terms, it allows researchers to find meaningful relationships that would otherwise never be identified from the perspective of individual studies. The reader should note that the discussion of meta-analysis presented here is highly simplistic. For more detailed and accurate treatments see Lipsey and Wilson (2001), Hedges and Olkin (1985), and Glass, McGaw, and Smith (1981).

Technical Note 4: Methods Used to Compute Correlations in the Meta-Analysis

The basic purpose of our meta-analysis was to examine the relationship between leadership (at both general and specific levels) and student academic achievement. The correlation coefficient was used as the index of relationship. In more specific terms, the product-moment correlation was used to quantify the linear relationship between leadership and student academic achievement. The formula for the product-moment correlation is

$$r_{xy} = \frac{\text{Summation } Z_x Z_y}{(N-1)}$$

where

r_{xy} stands for the product-moment correlation between variable x and variable y,

Z_x = the Z score or standard score for a given raw score on variable x,

Z_y = the Z score or standard score for a given raw score on variable y, and

N = the number of pairs of scores in the set. (Note that the formula above estimates the population correlation. When a correlation is intended as a descriptive statistic for a set of data, N as opposed to N–1 is used as the denominator in the equation.)

Stated in words, the product-moment correlation might be described as the average product of the Z scores for pairs of raw scores (see Magnusson, 1966, for a detailed discussion).

As described in Technical Note 1, one of the uses of the product-moment correlation is to predict an individual's score on one variable based on knowledge of the individual's score on the other variable. The equation for such a prediction is

$$Z'_y = r_{xy} Z_x$$

Described in words, this equation states that the predicted Z score or standard score on variable y (indicated by the apostrophe) is equal to the correlation between x and y multiplied by the Z score or standard score on x. As Magnusson (1966) explains:

> When we know an individual's observed standard score on x (Z_x) and the correlation coefficient for the relation between scores on the x-distribution and scores on the y-distribution, we can obtain the best possible prediction of the individual's standard score on y by multiplying Z_x by the correlation coefficient. (p. 39)

In many of the reports analyzed for our meta-analysis, product-moment correlations were reported. In other cases, however, the product-moment correlation had to be computed or imputed from available data. Correlations were computed or imputed in four situations.

1. Path Analytic Studies

Path analytic studies attempt to quantify the pattern of relationships among a set of variables. Figure TN4.1 depicts a path diagram. In the diagram, the capital letters X, Y, Z, W, L, and A represent a set of interrelated variables. A might be student academic achievement, L might be the general leadership ability of the principal, Z might represent the principal's knowledge of instructional practices, Y might represent the principal's energy level, X might represent the principal's desire to create change, and W might represent the principal's past experience with the change process. The lowercase letters—a, b, c, d, e, f, g, h—represent path coefficients and have numeric values that range from −1.00 to +1.00 (when expressed in standardized form; see Loehlin, 1992, for a discussion). For example, assume that the path coefficients above have the following values:

a = .25
b = .31
c = .41
d = .21
e = .13
f = .41
g = .31
h = .12

These path coefficients are analogous to standardized partial regression coefficients (Loehlin, 1992, p. 13). They tell us the extent to which a change in the variable at the tail end of an arrow translates into a change in the variable at the head of the arrow. Because they are "standardized" regression coefficients, the changes in the variables are expressed in Z score form. To illustrate, the path coefficient *a* of .25 indicates that a one standard deviation change in L is accompanied by a .25 standard deviation change in A. Because they are "partial" regression coefficients, they express the impact of one variable on another with the rest of the variables in the set held constant.

Because path coefficients are derived from correlations, they can be used to reconstruct the correlations from which they were computed. In simple terms, the correlation between two variables is the sum of the direct and indirect paths between them. Direct paths involve a single arrow, and indirect paths involve multiple arrows. Three rules must be followed when reconstructing correlations (see Loehlin, 1992; Wright, 1960, for a discussion):

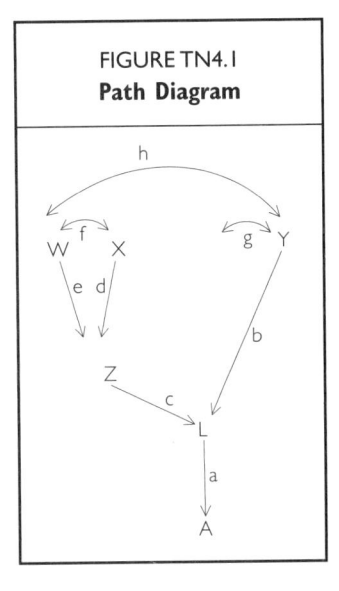

**FIGURE TN4.1
Path Diagram**

- A compound path must not go twice through the same variable.
    - A path cannot go forward then backward.
    - A maximum of one curved arrow can be used in any given path.

To illustrate, the correlation between variables W and Z is a combination of the direct path from W to Z and the indirect path from W to X to Z. To compute the strength of a compound path, one multiplies the path coefficients involved. The strength of a direct path is the path coefficient itself. Thus, the correlation between W and Z can be computed using the following formula:

$$r_{WZ} = e + fd$$

Using the values presented above, the computation is as follows:

$$r_{WZ} = .13 + (.41)(.21)$$
$$= .22$$

2. Factor Analytic Studies

The purpose of factor analytic studies is to identify the underlying, or "latent," traits within a set of variables. Like path analytic studies, factor analytic studies employ correlations (see Fruchter, 1954; Mulaik, 1972). The basic mathematical equation employed in factor analysis is

$$r_{jk} = a_{j1} a_{k1} + a_{j2} a_{k2} + a_{j3} a_{k3} + \ldots + a_{jm} a_{km}$$

where

r_{jk} = the correlation between variable j and variable k,
a_{j1} = the factor loading of variable j on factor 1,
a_{k1} = the factor loading of variable k on factor 1,
a_{j2} = the factor loading of variable j on factor 2,
a_{k2} = the factor loading of variable k on factor 2,
a_{j3} = the factor loading of variable j on factor 3,
a_{k3} = the factor loading of variable k on factor 3,
a_{jm} = the factor loading of variable j on factor m, and
a_{km} = the factor loading of variable k on factor m.

The primary outcome of a factor analysis is a matrix containing the factor loadings for the variables within the set. This is depicted in Figure TN4.2.

Given the basic factor analytic equation, a correlation between any two variables can be reconstructed from the factor loading matrix. To illustrate, the correlation between variables j and k can be computed as follows:

FIGURE TN4.2
Factor Loading Matrix

Variable	Factor 1	Factor 2	Factor 3
J	.42	.23	.02
K	.61	.27	.04
L	.32	.02	.42
M	.41	.01	.36

$$r_{jk} = a_{j1} a_{k1} + a_{j2} a_{k2} + a_{j3} a_{k3}$$
$$= (.42)(.61) + (.23)(.27) + (.02)(.04)$$
$$r_{jk} = .32$$

3. Studies Using High- and Low-Achieving Schools

Some studies did not use two continuous measures—one of leadership ability and one of academic achievement. Rather, they used a design in which "high-achieving" and "low-achieving" schools were identified. Principal leadership was then measured in the low- and high-achieving schools. To convert data from these designs into an estimate of a product-moment correlation, a number of techniques were employed. In all situations, the first step was to convert the data into a 2-by-2 contingency table like that depicted in Figure TN4.3.

FIGURE TN4.3
Contingency Table

		Achievement		
		High	Low	
Leadership	High	A	B	(a + b)
	Low	C	D	(c + d)
		(a + c)	(b + d)	

The following process was used to construct contingency tables:

1. The number of schools in the high-achieving and low-achieving groups on the achievement variable were identified.

2. The mean difference on the leadership variable between the high-achieving and low-achieving groups on the achievement variable was computed, along with the standard deviation (*sd*) of each group.

3. The grand mean on the leadership variable was computed and considered the "cut point" separating high versus low performance on the leadership variable.

4. The proportion of principals above and below the cut point on the leadership variable was then computed for the high- and low-achieving groups on the achievement variable.

5. The identified proportions were translated to frequencies.

To illustrate this process, consider the following situation. A study has identified 20 high-achieving and 20 low-achieving schools using some criterion such as high-achieving schools being defined as those above the mean on an achievement test and low-achieving schools being defined as those below the mean. The principals in the high-achieving and low-achieving schools have been rated by their teachers on their general leadership behavior. The mean on this general leadership factor for the 20 principals in the high-achieving schools is 65, and the mean for the 20 principals in the low-achieving schools is 55. The grand mean for all principals combined is 60. For the purposes of this illustration, let us assume that the combined variance of the two distributions is 100 with a standard deviation of 10.

To summarize, the scores on the leadership variable have a grand mean of 60; the principals in the high-achieving groups have a mean score of 65; the principals

FIGURE TN4.4
Contingency Table with Estimated Frequencies

		Achievement		
		High	Low	
Leadership	High	14 (a)	6 (b)	(a + b) 20
	Low	6 (c)	14 (d)	(c + d) 20
		(a + c) 20	(b + d) 20	

in the low-achieving groups have a mean of 55. Using the grand mean of 60 as the cut score and a standard deviation of 10, we can compute the proportion of principals in the high-achieving group on the achievement variable who are also in the high-performing group on leadership, as well as the proportion of principals in the high-achieving group who are in the low-performing group on the leadership variable. The same logic can be applied to the distribution of scores on the leadership variable for those in the low-achieving group on the achievement variable.

To illustrate using the low-achieving principals, the cut score, or grand mean, of 60 on the leadership variable is .50 standard deviations above their group mean of 55. Consulting the unit normal distribution, we find that .3085 of the unit normal distribution is above the Z score of .5 and .6915 is below the Z score of .5. Applying these proportions to the 20 principals in the low-achieving group, we find that 6.17 are in the high-performing group on the leadership variable (i.e., .3085 × 20) and 13.83 (i.e., .6915 × 20) are in the low-performing group on the leadership variable. Applying this same logic to the principals in the high-achieving group (and using rounding), the frequencies in the 2-by-2 contingency table are computed as depicted in Figure TN4.4.

When appropriate, an adjustment, or "correction," was made to the observed, standardized difference between means on the leadership variable. This occurred when the high-achieving and low-achieving groups on the achievement variable represented extremes. Specifically, given a distribution on the achievement variable dichotomized at the grand mean, the proportion of principals in the high-achieving group on the achievement variable who are in the high-performing group on the leadership variable and the proportion who are in the low-performing group on the leadership variable can be computed using the technique discussed above. The same can be done with the principals in the low-achieving group on the achievement variable.

However, in some studies the high-achieving and low-achieving schools were not defined as the top half and the bottom half of the achievement distribution. Rather, the high-achieving group might be defined as those schools whose achievement scores were one standard deviation above the grand mean and the low-achieving group as those whose achievement scores were one standard deviation below the mean. In such cases the differences between the two groups on the leadership variable will most likely be much larger than would be found if high-achieving and low-achieving groups were drawn from equal halves of the overall achievement distribution. Using the process described above to construct a contingency table will result in an overestimation of the proportion of principals in the high group on the achievement variable who are in the high group on the leadership variable and an underestimation of the proportion of principals in the high group on the achievement variable who are in the low group on the leadership variable. The same logic can be applied to the principals in the low group on the achievement variable. This results in an overestimation of the strength of relationship between leadership and achievement (see the discussion of *phi* beginning on p. 141).

To correct this situation, begin by computing the difference in performance on the leadership variable between the high and low groups *under the assumption that they had been drawn from a distribution dichotomized at the grand mean on the achievement variable*. This is accomplished by scaling the observed difference between groups on the leadership variable.

To illustrate, assume that the frequencies reported in Figure TN4.4 are drawn from groups of schools that represent extremes. Specifically, assume that the high-achieving group represents schools whose average achievement scores are at least one standard deviation above the grand mean and the low-achieving group represents schools whose average achievement scores are at least one standard deviation below the grand mean. Also assume the average achievement score of the high-achieving group is 1.25 standard deviations above the grand mean for the achievement variable and the average achievement score of the low-achieving group is 1.25 standard deviations below the grand mean (recall that plus and minus one standard deviations from the mean represent the end points of the high- and low-achieving groups, not the means of those groups.) Next, estimate the average achievement in Z score terms of the schools in the top and bottom half of a distribution dichotomized at the grand mean. An estimate of the average Z score of the top half of a distribution dichotomized at the grand mean would be the point that is in the center of the top half of the distribution. Consulting the unit normal distribution indicates that this point is approximately $Z = +.675$. Using the same logic for the mean of the bottom half of the distribution indicates that $Z = -.675$. Thus, the scaling factor (or correction factor) to estimate the difference between means on the leadership variable under the assumption that the high- and low-achieving groups are drawn from the top and bottom halves of the distribution (as opposed to one standard deviation above and below the grand mean) would be $1.35/2.50 = .54$.

This scaling factor is simply the ratio of the theoretical standardized difference between the means on the leadership variable of high- versus low-achieving groups dichotomized at the grand mean on the achievement variable over the standardized difference between the observed means of the high- and low-achieving groups, which were dichotomized at one standard deviation above and below the grand mean on the achievement variable. Stated differently, the theoretical means of the high- and low-achieving groups dichotomized at the grand mean are 1.35 standard deviations apart (i.e., the theoretical mean of the low-achieving group is $-.675$ from the grand mean, and the theoretical mean of the high-achieving group is $+.675$ from the grand mean, for a standardized difference of 1.35). However, the means of the observed high- and low-achieving groups are 2.50 standard deviations apart (i.e., the mean of the low-achieving group is -1.25 standard deviations from the grand mean, and the mean of the high-achieving group is $+1.25$ standard deviations from the grand mean).

In practice, the product of the correction factor of .54 and the observed standardized difference on the leadership variable between high- and low-achieving groups and the grand mean on the leadership variable represents an estimate of what the standardized difference would be if the groups were drawn from a distribution dichotomized at the grand mean on the achievement factor. Using the quantities employed in the construction of contingency depicted in Figure TN4.4, recall that for the low-achieving group, the standardized difference between its group mean and the grand mean on the leadership variable was .50. Scaling this by .54 yields .27 ($.50 \times .54 = .27$). We can now recompute the estimated frequencies in the contingency table. Consulting the unit normal distribution, we find that .3894 percent of the distribution is above a Z score of .27 and .6064 of the distribution is below a Z score of .27 (as opposed to .3095 and .6915, respectively, in the original calculations). Using these corrected proportions, we can compute a corrected contingency table (see Figure TN4.5).

Given the calculation of cell frequencies (corrected or uncorrected) in a contingency table, a number of different types of correlations can be computed, all of which are estimations of the product moment correlation. Four types of correlations were computed in our meta-analysis.

FIGURE TN4.5
Corrected Contingency Table

		Achievement		
		High	Low	
Leadership	High	12 (a)	8 (b)	(a + b) 20
	Low	8 (c)	12 (d)	(c + d) 20
		(a + c) 20	(b + d) 20	

Phi. *Phi* is used when both variables are dichotomous. The formula for computing *phi* (see Lipsey & Wilson, 2001, p. 194) is

$$phi = \frac{ad - bc}{((a+c)(b+d)(a+b)(c+d))^{.5}}$$

where ^.5 stands for the square root and *a*, *b*, *c*, and *d* represent the cells in the contingency table. Using this formula with the data in the contingency table depicted in Figure TN4.4, we have the following:

$$phi = \frac{(14 \times 14) - (6 \times 6)}{(20 \times 20 \times 20 \times 20)^{.5}} = .40$$

It is clear from the formula for *phi* that it has a value of +1.00 when all of the principals in the high-achieving group on the achievement variable are also in the high-performing group on the leadership variable and all of the principals in the low-achieving group on the achievement variable are in the low-performing group on the leadership variable. If the *phi* coefficient were computed on the values in the corrected contingency table depicted in Figure TN4.5, we would have the following:

$$phi = \frac{(12 \times 12) - (8 \times 8)}{(20 \times 20 \times 20 \times 20)^{.5}} = .27$$

As discussed earlier, the correction factor is critical when high and low groups on the achievement factor represent extremes. Otherwise, *phi* will overestimate the correlation between leadership and achievement.

Point Biserial. The point biserial correlation is used when one variable is a natural dichotomy and the other is continuous. In the present context, the dichotomized variable would be the high- and low-performing principals on the leadership variable. The continuous variable would be student achievement. The formula for the point biserial correlation (see Magnusson, 1966, p. 200) is

$$\text{point biserial correlation} = \left(\frac{M_p - M_q}{sd}\right)(pq^{\wedge}.5)$$

where

M_p = the mean achievement score of those in the high-performing leadership group,
M_q = the mean achievement score of those in the low-performing leadership group,
sd = the standard deviation of the achievement test,
p = the proportion of principals in the high-performing leadership group, and
q = the proportion of principals in the low-performing leadership group.

To illustrate, assume that the high- and low-achieving groups are drawn from the top and bottom halves of the overall achievement distribution (i.e., the achievement distribution has been dichotomized at the grand mean). Also assume that the high-achieving group has an average achievement score of +.675 standard deviations above the mean and the low-achieving group has an average achievement score of −.675 standard deviations below the mean. Also assume that the contingency table depicted in Figure TN4.6 is computed or imputed.

From Figure TN4.6 we see that $p = .5$ and $q = .5$. In fact, given the manner in which the proportions of high-performing and low-performing groups on the leadership variable are computed for a contingency table, when there are an equal number of principals in the high-achieving and low-achieving groups and the standard deviations of both groups are equal, p will always be .5 and q will be .5. That is, given equal numbers of principals in the high- and low-achievement groups and equal standard deviations in the groups on the leadership variable, half of the principals will be classified as being in the high-performing group on the leadership variable, and half will be classified as being in the low-performing group on the leadership variable. M_p and M_q can also be computed using the contingency table. In Figure TN4.6, 14 principals from the high-achieving group are also in the high-performing group on the leadership variable, and 6 principals from the low-achieving group are

FIGURE TN4.6
Contingency Table Used for Point Biserial Computations

		Achievement		
		High	Low	
Leadership	High	14 (a)	6 (b)	(a + b) 20
	Low	6 (c)	14 (d)	(c + d) 20
		(a + c) 20	(b + d) 20	

in the high-performing group on the leadership variable. Stated differently, of the 20 principals in the high-performing leadership group, 14 had achievement Z scores of +.675, and 6 had achievement Z scores of −.675, for an average Z score of .27 ((14 × (+.675) + 6 × (−.675)) / 20) = .27). Thus, M_p = +.27 in Z score form. Using the same logic, M_q = −.27. Therefore, $(M_p - M_q) / sd$ = .54 because sd equals 1.00 when scores are reported in Z score form. Because p = .5 and q = .5, the square root of pq = .5. Consequently, the point biserial correlation for the sample data is (.54 × .5) = .27.

The Biserial Correlation. The biserial correlation is used when both variables are continuous but one is organized as a dichotomy. The biserial correlation can be computed directly from the point biserial correlation using the following formula (see Magnusson, 1966, p. 205):

$$\text{biserial correlation} = r_{pb} \left(\frac{pq^{\wedge}.5}{h} \right)$$

where

r_{pb} = the point biserial correlation,
p and q are defined as before, and
h = the ordinate (height) of the unit normal distribution at the point on the distribution defining p and q.

Using the data in Figure TN4.6 and the assumptions underlying that data, p and q are both .50. Therefore, the point on the unit normal distribution that separates p and q is Z = .00. The ordinate at this point is .3989. Therefore, $(pq^{\wedge}.5) / h$ = 1.25. Consequently, the biserial correlation is 1.25 x .27 = .34.

The Tetrachoric Correlation. The tetrachoric correlation is used when two continuous variables are dichotomized. Computing a tetrachoric correlation is quite complex because it involves an infinite series (Cohen & Cohen, 1975; Downie & Heath, 1965). However, approximations are commonly employed. One approximation is to compute the following quantity:

$$\frac{ad}{bc}$$

where

a, d, b, and c represent the cells in the contingency table.

Tables are then consulted that translate this quantity into a tetrachoric correlation. Using the sample data in the contingency table depicted in Figure TN4.5, ad/bc = ((12 x 12) / (8 x 8)) = 2.25. Consulting the table provided by Downie & Heath (1965), this quantity translated to a tetrachoric correlation of .31.

Reconciling the Various Correlations. As evidenced from these various examples, the different approaches to computing correlations produce different estimates of the product-moment correlation. In all cases, we made a judgment as to the approach that best represented the data in the study under consideration.

4. Studies Employing High-, Medium-, and Low-Achieving Schools

In some studies, three groups of schools were identified—high-, medium-, and low-achieving. One approach to computing a correlation coefficient in a situation involving three groups is to compute the linear trend. In a traditional ANOVA (analysis of variance) approach, the F-ratio for the linear trend (Winer, Brown, & Michels, 1991, p. 205) is

$$F = \frac{\text{SS linear trend}}{\text{MS error}}$$

where

SS linear trend is the sum of squares for the linear trend among the means, and

MS error is the mean square error.

It should be noted that the sum of squares for the linear trend is equal to the mean square for the linear trend because only one degree of freedom is involved with this sum of squares. To compute SS linear, one must use a set of coefficients that are applied to the means of the groups involved in the analysis. The coefficients when three groups are involved are −1, 0, +1. The formula for SS linear is

$$\text{SS linear} = \frac{C^2 \text{ linear}}{\text{Summation}\left(\frac{c^2}{n}\right)}$$

where

C^2 linear is the square of the summation of the coefficients times the means for each group, and
summation (c^2/n) is the summation of the square of each coefficient divided by the number of subjects in each group.

To illustrate, assume that three groups of 10 subjects each have the following means: 55, 50, 65. The quantity C^2 linear would be

$$C^2 \text{ linear} = [55(-1) + 60(0) + 65(+1)]^2$$
$$= (-55 + 65)^2 = 100$$

The quantity summation (c^2/n) would be

$$\text{Summation}(c^2/n) = [(-1^2/10) + (0^2/10) + (1^2/10)]$$
$$= (.1 + 0 + .1) = .2$$

Therefore,

$$\text{SS linear} = \frac{C^2 \text{ linear}}{\text{summation}(c^2/n)} = \frac{100}{.2} = 500$$

With the SS linear computed, a ratio can be formed that represents the proportion of variance accounted for by the linear trend. That ratio is

$$\frac{\text{SS linear}}{\text{SS total}}$$

where SS total is the sum of squares of all subjects defined in the traditional ANOVA sense. When raw data are available, SS total can be computed using the traditional ANOVA formula (see Winer, Brown, & Michels, 1991, p. 81).

The ratio *SS linear/SS total* is referred to as the correlation ratio squared, or *eta squared*, and represents the proportion of the total variance attributable to the hypothesis about the treatment means—in this case, the linear trend of those means. When the linear trend among means is being tested, the square root of the correlation ratio, or *eta,* is analogous to a product-moment correlation. To illustrate using the example above, assume that the total sum of squares is computed to be 2000:

$$eta^2 = \frac{500}{2000} = .25$$

Therefore,

$$eta = .50$$

In this case, *eta* can be interpreted as the Z score increase in the dependent variable associated with a 1.00 Z score increase in the independent variable.

An alternative to computing the linear trend when three groups are involved is to compute the triserial correlation, the formula (see Downie & Heath, 1965, p. 194) for which is the following:

$$\text{triserial correlation} = \frac{Y_h (M_h) + (Y_c - Y_h) M_c - Y_c (M_l)}{sd \, [(Y_h^2/p_h) + ((Y_c - Y_h)^2/p_c) + (Y_c^2/p_l)]}$$

where

M_h is the mean achievement score of the subjects in the high group,
M_c is the mean achievement score of the subjects in the center group,
M_l is the mean achievement score of the subjects in the low group,
sd is the pooled standard deviation,
p_h is the proportion of subjects in the high group,
p_c is the proportion of subjects in the center group,
p_l is the proportion of subjects in the low group,
Y_h is the ordinate (height) of the unit normal distribution at the point on the distribution defining p_h,
Y_c is the ordinate (height) of the unit normal distribution at the point on the distribution defining p_c, and
Y_l is the ordinate (height) of the unit normal distribution at the point on the distribution defining p_l.

To illustrate, assume that a study identifies three groups of schools—high-achieving, low-achieving, and a group in the center. The means for M_h, M_c, and M_l, respectively, are 55, 60, and 65. The pooled standard deviation is 10. There are 10 schools in each group. Therefore, p_h, p_c, and p_l are all .33. The ordinate on the unit normal distribution corresponding to .33 on the smaller end of the distribution is .36. Therefore, Y_h, Y_c, and Y_l are all .3621. Given these quantities, the triserial correlation can be computed.

$$\text{triserial correlation} = \frac{(.3621)(65) + (.3621 - .3621)(60) - (.3621)(55)}{10\,[(.3621^2/.33) + ((.3621 - .3621)^2/.33) + (-.3621^2/.33)]}$$
$$= .46$$

Technical Note 5: *BESD* Applied to Students Versus Schools

The *BESD* in Figure 1.1 (p. 4) is based on the correlation between school effectiveness and student academic achievement reported by Marzano (2000b, 2003). Figure 1.1 reports the expected passing rates of individual students in effective schools versus ineffective schools where effective schools are defined as the top half of the effectiveness distribution and ineffective schools are defined as the bottom half of the effectiveness distribution. The unit of analysis is the individual student. In contrast, Figure 3.2 (p. 31) is based on the correlation between principal leadership and the average achievement of students in a school. The unit of analysis is the school. Thus, the figures reported are in terms of the percentage of schools for which the average achievement of students would be above a given cut score.

Technical Note 6: Distinguishing Features of Our Meta-Analysis

Our meta-analysis employed some techniques that distinguish it from other similar efforts. The reader should note that in this technical note we use the terms *effect size* and *correlation* interchangeably. As described in Technical Note 7, we computed average effect sizes within and between studies using homogeneous sets of items. Lipsey and Wilson (2001) explain the importance of using homogeneous sets of data:

> An important question to ask is whether the various effect sizes that are averaged into a mean value all estimate the same population effect size. This is a question of the homogeneity of the effect size distribution. In a homogeneous distribution, the dispersion of the effect sizes around their mean is no greater than that expected from sampling error alone (the sampling error associated with the subject samples upon which the individual effect sizes are based). In other words, in a homogeneous distribution an individual effect size differs from the population mean only by sampling error. (p. 115)

In other words, Lipsey and Wilson caution that a set of correlations that are not homogeneous most probably includes effect sizes that measure different constructs than do other members of the set. As described in Technical Note 7, in our meta-analysis we computed average effect sizes using homogeneous sets in four situations: (1) when computing the effect sizes for the 21 responsibilities within studies, (2) when computing the average effect sizes for the 21 responsibilities across studies, (3) when computing the effect size for general leadership behavior within studies, and (4) when computing the average effect size for general leadership behavior across studies. To review briefly, when computing the effect sizes for the 21 responsibilities within studies (situation 1), we first excluded conceptual outliers from a set and then excluded statistical outliers using the Q statistic and graphing methods to arrive at a homogeneous set. When computing the average effect sizes for the 21 responsibilities across studies (situation 2), we excluded statistical outliers using the Q statistic and graphing methods to arrive at a homogeneous set. We employed these same two processes for situations 3 and 4, respectively.

When considering how the average effect size for general leadership within a single study was computed, it becomes clear that we excluded outliers at three points: (1) conceptual outliers were excluded from the overall set, (2) statistical outliers were excluded when computing the effect sizes for the 21 responsibilities, and (3) statistical outliers were excluded when combining the effect sizes within a study to compute the effect size for general leadership behavior. This process produced findings for general leadership behavior that differed from other efforts. To illustrate, consider the study by Witziers, Bosker, and Kruger (2003), which reports an overall correlation between general leadership behavior and student achievement of .02. This, of course, is dramatically lower than our average correlation of .25. As described in Chapter 3, the Witziers study is heavily influenced by studies outside of the United States. Relative to the United States, Witziers and his coauthors report a correlation of .11 between general leadership behavior and student achievement (p. 409). However, this is still considerably smaller than our average correlation of .25.

A comparison of how we approached one of the studies included in the Witziers study helps explain these differences. One of the studies used in both the Witziers' meta-analysis and ours was that by Krug (1992). It involved correlations between 12 leadership behaviors and student achievement in reading and mathematics at grades 3, 6, and 8. Within our meta-analysis, these three grade levels were categorized as elementary (grade 3) and middle school/junior high (grades 6 and 8). The overall effect size for general leadership behavior at the elementary level (using the procedures described above) was .23; for middle school/junior high, it was .17. When these are combined into a weighted average across grade levels, the effect size is .19. However, if outliers are not excluded at any point in the aggregations process, the effect size for the elementary grades is .19 and the effect size for middle school/junior high is .013. When these are combined into a weighted average across grade levels, the effect size is .07. Thus our process produced an effect size estimate that is .12 units higher. Assuming that this study (Krug, 1992) exemplifies the pattern of differences between our meta-analysis and that by Witziers and his colleagues, it is understandable why they report an average effect size of .11 for general leadership behavior in U.S. schools and we report an average effect size of .25.

Another difference between our meta-analysis and other similar efforts is that we corrected correlations for attenuation. We describe this in Technical Note 8.

Technical Note 7: Computing Average Correlations Within and Between Studies

We computed average correlations in a variety of situations for general leadership and for the 21 leadership responsibilities.

Computing the Correlation for General Leadership Behavior Within Individual Studies

For each study, the correlation between general leadership behavior and student academic achievement was either directly recorded or computed. That is, in some cases, a correlation between general leadership behavior and student academic achievement was explicit in the study. In studies in which no correlation for general leadership and student achievement was reported, we computed a correction using the following protocol.

1. We transformed the computed correlations for the 21 responsibilities represented in the study using the Fisher Z transformation.

2. We computed the weighted average for the set of Z-transformed correlations and computed a Q statistic to test the homogeneity of the set. The Q statistic is used to test for homogeneity (Hedges & Olkin, 1985). As described by Lipsey and Wilson (2001, p. 115), the generic formula for the Q statistic is

$$Q = \text{Summation } w_i \, (ES_i - MES)^2$$

where

> w_i is the individual weight applied to effect size i (in this case the weight was the inverse variance);
>
> ES_i is a specific effect size (in this case the correlation between leadership and student achievement transformed via the Fisher Z transformation; and
>
> MES   is the mean of the effect sizes in a set.

3. When we found a Q statistic to be significant—indicating heterogeneity within a set—we identified outliers using the graphic procedures described by Hedges and Olkin (1985, pp. 251–253). Specifically, we used the software program *Comprehensive Meta-analysis* (Borenstein & Rothstein, 1999) to generate the graphic representations of effect sizes with their associated 95 percent confidence interval. We deleted visually identified outliers until the Q statistic was nonsignificant. Then we recomputed the average weighted correlation for the homogeneous set.

4. We converted the Z-transformed correlations to their original metric.

Computing the Average Correlation for General Leadership Behavior Between Studies

Using the correlations for general leadership behavior reported in or computed from each of the studies as described above, we computed the overall effect size for general leadership behavior using the process described by Hunter and Schmidt (1990a). This approach is similar to that described above except that the correlations were not transformed using the Fisher Z transformation, and weights applied to correlations were different. In the example above, the inverse variance was used as the weight. When an average correlation was computed across studies, the weight employed was as follows:

$$w_i = (N_i - 1)A_i^2$$

where

> N_i is the number of schools used to compute correlation i, and
>
> A_i is the square of the artifact multiplier for correlation i.

The artifact multiplier is the product of the individual artifact multipliers. In this case, there were two artifact multipliers representing corrections for attenuation in the independent and dependent variables. (See Technical Note 8 and Hunter & Schmidt, 1990a, for discussions.)

Computing the Correlations for the 21 Responsibilities Within Studies

Within each study, correlations for specific leadership behaviors that were considered to be components of a specific responsibility were aggregated to compute an effect size for a given responsibility using the following process.

1. We dropped conceptual outliers from the set of effect sizes that were considered to be components of the responsibility. A conceptual outlier was defined as a data point or a set of data that the researcher identified as an outlier for one reason or another. To illustrate, consider the Krug (1986) study that reported correlations between 11 specific principal leadership behaviors and student achievement in mathematics, written language, and reading at grades 3 and 6. Of the 33 correlations at the 6th grade level, 25 were negative. The average of this set of negative correlations was −.25, and the most extreme score was −.67. The researcher remarked that these findings were thought to be an artifact of a sampling anomaly in two of the schools with large populations of students with specific socioeconomic characteristics (see Krug, 1986, p. 135).

2. We transformed all remaining correlations using the Fisher Z transformation.

3. We computed the average for the set of Z-transformed correlations and computed a Q statistic to test the homogeneity of the set using the procedure specified by Hedges and Olkin (1985).

4. When we found a Q statistic to be significant—indicating heterogeneity within a set—we identified outliers using the graphic procedures described by Hedges and Olkin (1985, pp. 251–253).

5. We converted the Z-transformed correlations to their original metric.

Computing the Average Correlations for the 21 Responsibilities Across Studies

For each of the 21 responsibilities, we computed an average effect size across studies using the approach described by Hunter and Schmidt (1990a). This approach is similar to that described above except that we did not transform correlations using the Fisher Z transformation, and the weights we applied to the correlations were different. In the example above, the inverse variance was used as the weight. When we computed an average correlation across studies, the weight employed was as follows:

$$w_i = (N_i - 1)A_i^2$$

where

> N is the number of schools used to compute correlation i, and
> A_i is the square of the artifact multiplier for correlation i as defined above.

Finally, conceptual outliers were not an issue because we eliminated them when computing correlations for the responsibilities within studies.

Technical Note 8: Correcting for Attenuation

A factor distinguishing our meta-analysis from others involves the correction of correlations for attenuation due to unreliability of the independent measure (in this case, general and specific leadership behaviors) and the dependent measure (in this case, student achievement). Hunter and Schmidt have detailed the rationale and importance of correcting for artifacts (1990a, 1990b, 1994). Hunter and Schmidt (1994) list 10 attenuation artifacts—2 of which are random error associated with measurement of the independent variable and random error associated with measurement of the dependent variable (1994, pp. 325–326). To illustrate, assume that the population correlation between general leadership behavior and student academic achievement is .50. A given study attempts to estimate that correlation but employs a measure of general leadership that has a reliability of .81. According to attenuation theory, this observed correlation will be reduced by a factor of .90. That is, the observed correlation will be .45 (.50 × .90) even if there is no attenuation due to the other nine attenuation artifacts listed by Hunter and Schmidt. To correct an observed correlation for attenuation due to measurement error, one divides the observed correlation by the square root of the reliability. In this case the observed correlation of .45 would be divided by .90 (.45/.90 = .50).

If the study also employs a measure of the dependent variable (in this case, student achievement) that involves measurement error, then the observed correlation is even further from the true population correlation. Again, assume that the reliability of the dependent measure is .81. The observed correlation will be a function of both artifact attenuation factors, or .90 × .90 × .50 = .405. Again, to correct the observed correlation of .405 for measurement error in the independent and dependent variables, one divides by the product of the square roots of the reliabilities, or .81 (.90 × .90). Thus, .405/.81 = .50.

The consequences of not correcting for attenuation can be quite profound, as the example above illustrates. Fan (2003) explains:

> . . . the attenuation on sample correlation coefficients caused by measurement error may be more severe than many researchers realize. In many situations, it is not uncommon to have measurement reliabilities in the range of .60 to .80. Under such

conditions, even the upper confidence interval limit itself may fail to capture the true correlation between two composites. (p. 923)

Reliabilities in the social sciences are typically rather low. Osborne (2003) found that the average reliability reported in psychology journals is .83. Lou and colleagues (1996) report a typical reliability on standardized achievement tests of .85 and a reliability of .75 for unstandardized tests of academic achievement. Within our meta-analysis, reliabilities for measures of leadership and student achievement that were reported in studies were used to correct the correlations in those studies for attenuation. When reliabilities were not reported in a study, we used estimates based on the observed distribution of reliabilities (see Hunter & Schmidt, 1990b). Finally, it should be noted that Baugh (2002) cautions against the overuse of correction techniques. He states:

> Correction of effect sizes for unreliability of scores has obvious benefits and yet requires considerable caution—the correction itself can yield an adjusted effect size correlation greater than 1.00. . . . Attenuation adjustments to effect sizes are not the norm; therefore, presentation of both adjusted and unadjusted estimates allows ready comparisons of effect sizes across studies. (p. 260)

Technical Note 9: Confidence Intervals

The correlations reported in Figure 4.1 (p. 42) are averages computed from the correlations found in a number of studies (see Technical Note 7 for a discussion). Each average can be considered an estimate of the true correlation between achievement and the various leadership responsibilities. The level of certainty that the average correlation accurately represents the true correlation is reported in the 95 percent confidence interval for each of the average correlations. This interval includes the range of correlations in which one can be 95 percent sure that the true correlation falls. For example, assume that average correlation is reported to be .19 and the 95 percent confidence interval is reported to be .08 to .29. This indicates that we are 95 percent sure that the true correlation is between the values of .08 and .29. If a 95 percent confidence interval does not include the value .00, it is tantamount to saying that the correlation is significant at the .05 level, which is a commonly accepted level of significance in the social sciences.

Technical Note 10: Moderator Variables

We examined eight moderator variables for their relationship to the effect sizes (i.e., correlation sizes) computed in our meta-analysis using the fixed effects, analysis of variance technique described by Hedges and Olkin (1985). In all cases, outliers (as described in Technical Note 7) were excluded from the analysis. The moderators were (1) Study Quality, (2) School Level, (3) Subject Area, (4) Inference Level for Effect Size, (5) Achievement Metric, (6) Ethnicity, (7) Community Type, and (8) Socioeconomic Status.

1. Study Quality refers to the methodological quality of the studies involved. Because all studies were descriptive in nature (i.e., there was no assignment of subjects to experimental and control groups), we could not use factors such as random assignment and use of covariates to judge methodological quality. However, we did use the following factors to analyze the quality of the studies:

- Manner in which the sample was identified
- Appropriateness of the measure used for the independent variable
- Appropriateness of the measure used for the dependent variable
- Return rate for surveys
- Appropriateness of the method used to analyze the data

We rated each study high (H), medium (M), or low (L) in each of these factors. The overall quality of a study was considered high if the majority of factors were rated high and no factor was rated low. The overall quality of a study was considered low if the majority of factors were rated low and no factor was rated high. The overall quality of a study was considered medium if the study did not fall into the high or low categories. Findings for this moderator variable are reported in Figures TN10.1 and TN10.2.

As indicated in Figure TN10.2, the test of the null hypothesis between classes was not significant ($p \leq .05$). However, it approached significance, indicating that study quality might possibly be related to effect sizes within our study. Figure TN10.1 illustrates that the highest correlation was found in studies that were rated as having the highest methodological quality.

2. School Level refers to the level of the schools involved in the studies. We used five categories to classify the studies in our meta-analysis: elementary (ELEM),

FIGURE TN10.1 Point Estimation for Quality				
Group	Point Estimation	95% Confidence Interval	No. of Studies	No. of Schools
H	.31	.25 to .37	22	820
L	.17	.09 to .25	14	567
M	.23	.18 to .28	28	1,212

FIGURE TN10.2
Analysis of Variance for Quality

Source	Q–Value	df	PValue
Between Classes	5.06	2	.08
Within Classes	20.33	61	1.00
H	5.94	21	.99
L	1.83	13	.99
M	12.57	27	.99

FIGURE TN10.3
Point Estimation for School Level

Group	Point Estimation	95% Confidence Interval	No. of Studies	No. of Schools
ELEM	.29	.24 to .34	36	1,175
HS	.26	.16 to .36	9	325
K12	.16	.07 to .24	6	499
K8	.15	.03 to .26	7	277
MSJH	.24	.13 to .34	6	323

high school (HS), kindergarten through grade 12 (K12), kindergarten through grade 8 (K8), and middle school and junior high (MSJH). Figures TN10.3 and TN10.4 report the results of the analysis for this moderator variable. As indicated in Figure TN10.4, no contrasts were significant ($p \leq .05$).

3. Subject Area refers to the academic subject area used as the dependent measure in a study. We organized subject areas into seven categories: general (G), language arts (LA), mathematics (M), combined mathematics and language arts (MLA), combined mathematics and reading (MR), reading (R), and science (S). Figures TN10.5 and TN10.6 report the results of the analysis for this moderator variable. As Figure TN10.6 indicates, no contrasts were significant ($p \leq .05$).

4. Inference Level refers to the extent to which effect sizes had to be imputed. We classified studies into three categories for this moderator variable: studies were classified as low inference (L) when correlations were reported in the study and

FIGURE TN10.4
Analysis of Variance for School Level

Source	Q–Value	df	PValue
Between Classes	5.31	4	.26
Within Classes	20.08	59	1.00
ELEM	11.68	35	.99
HS	.87	8	.99
K12	2.06	5	.84
K8	2.09	6	.91
MSJH	3.37	5	.64

FIGURE TN10.5
Point Estimation for Subject Area

Group	Point Estimation	95% Confidence Interval	No. of Studies	No. of Schools
G	.21	.15 to .27	23	1,125
LA	.31	–.08 to .61	1	27
M	.34	–.12 to .68	1	20
MLA	.28	.05 to .48	5	70
MR	.25	.19 to .31	18	833
R	.25	.17 to .33	15	512
S	.26	–.37 to .73	1	12

could simply be recorded; studies were classified as medium inference (M) when correlations were computed from factor analytic or path analytic studies, as described in Technical Note 4; studies were classified as high inference (H) when a phi, point biserial, biserial, tetrachoric, or eta coefficient was computed, as described in Technical Note 4. The results of the analysis for this moderator variable are reported in Figures TN10.7 and TN10.8. As Figure TN10.8 indicates, no contrasts were significant ($p \leq .05$).

FIGURE TN10.6
Analysis of Variance for Subject Area

Source	Q–Value	df	PValue
Between Classes	.89	6	.99
Within Classes	24.49	57	1.00
G	10.12	22	.98
LA	.00	0	1.00
M	.00	0	1.00
MLA	.07	4	.99
MR	8.44	17	.96
R	5.87	14	.97
S	.00	0	1.00

FIGURE TN10.7
Point Estimation for Inference Level

Group	Point Estimation	95% Confidence Interval	No. of Studies	No. of Schools
H	.23	.17 to .29	21	951
L	.23	.18 to .28	34	1,369
M	.34	.23 to .44	9	279

FIGURE TN10.8
Analysis of Variance for Inference Level

Source	Q–Value	df	PValue
Between Classes	2.52	2	.28
Within Classes	22.83	61	1.00
H	6.28	20	.99
L	13.17	33	.99
M	3.37	8	.91

FIGURE TN10.9
Point Estimation for Achievement Metric

Group	Point Estimation	95% Confidence Interval	No. of Studies	No. of Schools
PTILES	.25	.20 to .29	44	1,656
COMPOSITE	.24	.10 to .37	3	184
GAIN	.16	.02 to .29	6	199
PASSING	.22	.12 to .31	4	370
RESID	.16	.02 to .30	7	190

FIGURE TN10.10
Analysis of Variance for Achievement Metric

Source	Q–Value	df	PValue
Between Classes	1.86	4	.76
Within Classes	23.53	59	1.00
PTILES	16.78	43	.99
COMPOSITE	.54	2	.76
GAIN	2.66	5	.75
PASSING	1.66	3	.64
RESID	1.89	6	.93

5. Achievement Metric refers to the manner in which achievement scores were computed for schools in a study. We used five categories to classify studies for this moderator variable: studies that employed percentiles, NCEs, and the like were classified as PTILES; studies that employed an index that combined scores on standardized or state tests with other indicators were classified as COMPOSITE; studies that used gain scores from one administration of a test to another were classified as GAIN; studies that used the proportion of students meeting or exceeding a given level of achievement were classified as PASSING; studies that used deviation scores from a regression equation were classified as RESID. Figures TN10.9 and TN10.10 report the results of the analysis for this moderator variable. As indicated in Figure TN10.10, no contrasts were significant ($p \leq .05$).

FIGURE TN10.11
Point Estimation for Ethnicity

Group	Point Estimation	95% Confidence Interval	No. of Studies	No. of Schools
OTHER	.24	.20 to .28	62	2,583
AFAM	.36	−.46 to .85	1	8
HISP	.22	−.57 to .80	1	8

FIGURE TN10.12
Analysis of Variance for Ethnicity

Source	Q–Value	df	PValue
Between Classes	.05	2	.97
Within Classes	25.34	61	1.00
OTHER	25.34	61	1.00
AFAM	.00	0	1.00
HISP	.00	0	1.00

6. Ethnicity refers to the ethnic makeup of the schools in a study. We used five categories to classify studies for this moderator variable: Anglo-American (ANGLO), Hispanic (HISP), African-American (AFAM), Asian (ASIA), and OTHER if ethnicity could not be determined. Figures TN10.11 and TN10.12 report the results for this moderator variable. As the figures indicate, we found data on two categories of ethnicity only—AFAM and HISP. Additionally, we found only one study that provided data in each of these categories. Even though Figure TN10.12 indicates that no contrasts were significant (p ≤ .05) for this moderator variable, no conclusion should be inferred because of the lack of data.

7. Community Type refers to the size of the community in which schools were located. We used four categories for this moderator variable: schools in urban areas were classified as URB; schools in suburban areas were classified as SUBURB; schools in rural areas were classified as RURAL; and schools for which community type could not be identified were classified as OTHER. Figures TN10.13 and TN10.14 report the findings for this moderator variable. As the figures indicate, no

FIGURE TN10.13
Point Estimation for Community Type

Group	Point Estimation	95% Confidence Interval	No. of Studies	No. of Schools
OTHER	.25	.21 to .29	56	2,174
SUBURB	.23	−.01 to .44	2	72
URBAN	.22	.12 to .32	6	353

FIGURE TN10.14
Analysis of Variance for Community Type

Source	Q-Value	df	PValue
Between Classes	.15	2	.93
Within Classes	25.24	61	1.00
OTHER	23.76	55	.99
SUBURB	.06	1	.81
URBAN	1.42	5	.92

data were found for RURAL. Additionally, we found only one study for SUBURB and five for URBAN. Even though Figure TN10.14 indicates that no contrasts were significant ($p \leq .05$) for this moderator variable, no conclusions should be inferred because of the lack of data.

8. Socioeconomic Status (SES) refers to the economic and social status of schools within studies. We used four categories for this moderator variable: those studies describing schools as high SES were classified as H; those studies describing schools as medium SES were classified as M; those studies describing schools as low SES were classified as L; and those studies that did not identify the SES of schools were classified as OTHER. Figures TN10.15 and TN10.16 report the findings for this moderator variable. As the figures indicate, no data were found for H or M. Additionally, we found only three studies for L. Even though Figure TN10.16 indicates that no contrasts were significant ($p \leq .05$) for this moderator variable, no conclusions should be inferred because of lack of data.

FIGURE TN10.15
Point Estimation for SES

Group	Point Estimation	95% Confidence Interval	No. of Studies	No. of Schools
OTHER	.24	.20 to .28	61	2,517
L	.27	.05 to .46	3	82

FIGURE TN10.16
Analysis of Variance for SES

Source	Q–Value	df	PValue
Between Classes	.06	1	.81
Within Classes	25.33	62	1.00
OTHER	23.75	60	1.00
L	1.59	2	.45

Technical Note 11: The Factor Analysis

To determine how the 21 responsibilities are interrelated, we constructed a 92-item questionnaire for building principals, with multiple items for each responsibility. The questionnaire used a four-point response format for each item. Here's an example of an item designed to measure one of the behaviors associated with the responsibility of Communication:

Teachers in my school have ready and easy access to me:
4   This characterizes me or my school to a great extent.
3
2
1   This does not characterize me or my school.

In addition to items that addressed the 21 responsibilities, the questionnaire included items designed to determine the extent to which a school was involved in first-order change or second-order change. Figure TN11.1 presents the 92 items.

The questionnaire was posted on a Web page managed by Mid-continent Research for Education and Learning (McREL) in Aurora, Colorado, from September 2003 to February 2004. Through a variety of informal venues, principals from schools across the country were invited to complete the online questionnaire.

FIGURE TN11.1
Questionnaire Used for the Factor Analysis

1. The changes I am trying to make in my school will represent a significant challenge to the status quo when they are implemented.
2. Teachers in my school regularly share ideas.
3. In my school, the instructional time of teachers is well protected.
4. There are well-established procedures in my school regarding how to bring up problems and concerns.
5. I have been successful in protecting teachers from undue distractions and interruptions to their teaching.
6. In my school, I have been successful at ensuring that teachers have the necessary resources and professional opportunities to maintain a high standard of teaching.
7. I am directly involved in helping teachers design curricular activities for their classes.
8. Concrete goals for achievement have been established for each student in my school.
9. I am very knowledgeable about effective instructional practices.
10. I make systematic and frequent visits to classrooms.
11. Individuals who excel in my school are recognized and rewarded.
12. Teachers in my school have ready and easy access to me.
13. I make sure that my school complies with all district and state mandates.
14. In my school, teachers have direct input into all important decisions.
15. The accomplishments of individual teachers in my school are recognized and celebrated.
16. I am aware of the personal needs of the teachers in my school.
17. I consciously try to challenge the status quo to get people thinking.
18. I try to inspire my teachers to accomplish things that might seem beyond their grasp.
19. The teachers in my school are aware of my beliefs regarding schools, teaching, and learning.
20. I continually monitor the effectiveness of our curriculum.
21. I am comfortable making major changes in how things are done.
22. I am aware of the informal groups and relationships among the teachers in my school.
23. I stay informed about the current research and theory regarding effective schooling.
24. In my school, we systematically consider new and better ways of doing things.
25. I am directly involved in helping teachers address instructional issues in their classrooms.
26. I have successfully developed a sense of cooperation in my school.
27. I have successfully created a strong sense of order among teachers about the efficient running of the school.
28. One of the biggest priorities in my school is to keep the staff's energy level up and maintain the progress we have already made.
29. The changes we are trying to make in our school require the people making the changes to learn new concepts and skills.
30. We have made good progress, but we need another "shot in the arm" to keep us moving forward on our improvement efforts.

FIGURE TN11.1 (continued)
Questionnaire Used for the Factor Analysis

31. In my school, we have designed concrete goals for our curriculum.
32. I am very knowledgeable about classroom curricular issues.
33. I have frequent contact with the students in my school.
34. In my school, seniority is not the primary method of reward and advancement.
35. Effective ways for teachers to communicate with one another have been established in my school.
36. I am a strong advocate for my school to the community at large.
37. Teachers are directly involved in establishing policy in my school.
38. The accomplishments of the students and the school in general are recognized and celebrated.
39. I have a personal relationship with the teachers in my school.
40. I am comfortable initiating change without being sure where it might lead us.
41. I always portray a positive attitude about our ability to accomplish substantive things.
42. I continually monitor the effectiveness of the instructional practices used in our school.
43. I encourage people to express opinions that are contrary to my own.
44. I am aware of the issues in my school that have not formally come to the surface but might cause discord.
45. I continually expose teachers in my school to cutting-edge ideas about how to be effective.
46. There are deeply ingrained practices in my school that must be ended or changed if we are to make any significant progress.
47. I can be highly directive or nondirective as the situation warrants.
48. There is a strong team spirit in my school.
49. There are well-established routines regarding the running of the school that staff understand and follow.
50. I am directly involved in helping teachers address assessment issues in their classrooms.
51. Teachers in my school are regularly involved in professional development activities that directly enhance their teaching.
52. The changes I am trying to make in my school will challenge the existing norms.
53. We have specific goals for specific instructional practices in my school.
54. I am very knowledgeable about effective classroom assessment practices.
55. I am highly visible to the teachers and students in my school.
56. In my school, we have a common language that is used by administrators and teachers.
57. Lines of communication are strong between teachers and myself.
58. I am a strong advocate for my school to the parents of our students.
59. In my school, decisions are made using a team approach.
60. In my school, we systematically acknowledge our failures and celebrate our accomplishments.
61. I stay informed about significant personal issues in the lives of the teachers.
62. Unless we make significant changes in my school, student achievement is not going to improve much.

(continued on next page)

FIGURE TN11.1 *(continued)*
Questionnaire Used for the Factor Analysis

63. I try to be the driving force behind major initiatives.
64. I have well-defined beliefs about schools, teaching, and learning.
65. I continually monitor the effectiveness of the assessment practices used in my school.
66. I adapt my leadership style to the specific needs of a given situation.
67. In my school, we have a shared understanding of our purpose.
68. In my school, we systematically have discussions about current research and theory.
69. The most important changes we need to make in my school are the ones the staff most strongly resists.
70. In my school, teachers are not brought into issues external to the school that would detract from their emphasis on teaching.
71. In my school, controversies or disagreements involving only one or a few staff members do not escalate into schoolwide issues.
72. We have established specific goals for the assessment practices in my school.
73. I provide conceptual guidance for the teachers in my school regarding effective classroom practice.
74. In my school, advancement and reward are not automatically given for simply "putting in your time."
75. I make sure that the central office is aware of the accomplishments of my school.
76. I make sure that significant events in the lives of the teachers in my school are acknowledged.
77. In my school, we consistently ask ourselves, "Are we operating at the edge versus the center of our competence?"
78. I believe that we can accomplish just about anything if we are willing to work hard enough and if we believe in ourselves.
79. I have explicitly communicated my strong beliefs and ideals to teachers.
80. At any given time, I can accurately determine how effective our school is in terms of enhancing student learning.
81. In my school, we are currently experiencing a period during which things are going fairly well.
82. I can accurately predict things that may go wrong in my school on a day-to-day basis.
83. In my school, we systematically read articles and books about effective practices.
84. Our schoolwide goals are understood by all teachers.
85. I am aware of what is running smoothly and what is not running smoothly in my school.
86. Our schoolwide goals are a prominent part of our day-to-day lives.
87. My behavior is consistent with my ideals and beliefs regarding schools, teachers, and learning.
88. In my school, it would be useful to have a period of time during which we do not undertake any new, big initiatives.
89. In my school, the materials and resources teachers request are procured and delivered in a timely fashion.
90. Individuals who work hard and produce results are identified and rewarded in my school.
91. I am aware of the details regarding the day-to-day running of the school.
92. In my school, we share a vision of what we could be like.

Immediately upon completion of the questionnaire, respondents received an analysis of their responses in the form of a report on the 21 responsibilities and their perceived involvement in first- and second-order change.

In all, 652 principals completed the questionnaire. The responses to the questionnaire had a reliability of .92 (Cronbach's Coefficient Alpha).

We subjected the 652 responses to a principal component factor analysis. Two fairly clear factors emerged that were ranked first and second in terms of their eigen values. Together they accounted for 50 percent of the variance in responses. Figure TN11.2 presents the factor loadings for the 92 items on these two factors.

The figure reports positive and negative factor loadings that exceed the absolute value of .10 (and in the case of item 83, a factor loading as low as .031). This is a departure from the typical convention of reporting only those factor loadings that have an absolute value of .30. Bryant and Yarnold (1995) explain this convention as follows:

> Typically, researchers consider variables with factor loading coefficients of at least .30 in absolute value as "loading on the eigenvector" and thus as worthy of consideration in the interpretation of the meaning of the eigenvector. Variables with negative factor loading coefficients are negatively correlated with the eigenvector; eigenvectors that have variables with positive factor loadings as well as variables with negative factor loadings are called *bipolar eigenvectors*. Note that a factor loading coefficient of .30 implies that the variable and the eigenvector share $(.30)^2 \times 100\%$, or 9% of their variance. (p. 106)

However, Stevens (1986) has noted that this practice ignores the number of observations in the sample—in this case, the number of principals who completed the questionnaire. Specifically, Stevens explains that because the statistical significance between a factor loading and an eigenvector (i.e., factor) depends on the sample size, the criterion for classifying a variable as an element of a factor should be based on the value of the factor loading (i.e., correlation) needed to achieve an acceptable error rate.

In this factor analysis, any loading with an absolute value of .15 or greater was considered indicative of a relationship. (Figure TN11.2 reports factor loadings with absolute values lower than .15 in cases in which the items for a responsibility exhibited a pattern indicating that the responsibility might be related to one or both factors.) Given that 652 principals took the questionnaire, the one-tailed probability of a .15 correlation under the null hypothesis is as follows:

$$\frac{r_z}{\text{standard error of } r_z} = \frac{.15}{.039} = \text{Z score of } 3.846 < .0005 \text{ (approximately)}$$

FIGURE TN11.2
Factor Loadings on the First Two Factors

Category	Item	Factor I	Factor II	Category	Item	Factor I	Factor II
First-Order Change	28	.495		Involvement in CIA	7	.496	.144
	*30	.090	.269		25	.620	
	81	.479			50	.596	.134
	88	.228			8	.511	
Second-Order Change	1	.183	.555		31	.570	
	62	−.218	.569		53	.509	
	46	−.242	.598	Focus	72	.573	
	69	−.255	.550		84	.604	−.206
	52	.187	.641		86	.639	−.124
	29	.343	.422		9	.574	.284
Culture	26	.597	−.407	Knowledge of CIA	32	.585	.306
	2	.535	−.172		54	.571	.262
	48	.582	−.431		73	.597	.237
	56	.597	−.241	Visibility	10	.442	
	67	.681	−.220		33	.372	
	92	.651	−.254		55	.414	−.126
Order	4	.537	−.236	Contingent Rewards	11	.450	
	27	.587	−.201		34	.413	
	49	.549	−.254		90	.493	
Discipline	5	.405	−.130		74	.403	
	3	.428	−.172	Outreach	13	.368	
	70	.200	.170		36	.440	
	71	.416			58	.532	
Resources	6	.432	−.133		75	.324	
	89	.385		Input	14	.497	−.159
	51	.552			37	.431	−.201
					59	.561	−.202

*Given the pattern of loadings exhibited by this item as well as the item's content, it is probably best classified as addressing second-order change.

FIGURE TN11.2 (continued)
Factor Loadings on the First Two Factors

	Item	Factor I	Factor II		Item	Factor I	Factor II
Affirmation	15	.516		Situational Awareness	22	.415	
	38	.513			44	.477	.260
	60	.619			91	.443	
Relationships	16	.529		Intellectual Stimulation	82	.302	
	39	.419	−.144		85	.556	
	61	.481			23	.511	.341
	76	.520			45	.589	.315
Change Agent	17	.471	.424		68	.592	.222
	40	.178	.237		83	.502	.031
	24	.658	.100	Communication	12	.369	−.113
	77	.519	.150		35	.569	−.283
Optimizer	18	.600	.360		57	.552	−.342
	41	.572	.061				
	63	.332	.368				
	78	.367	.251				
Ideals/ Beliefs	19	.601	.201				
	64	.553	.232				
	79	.629	.119				
	87	.596	.016				
Monitoring/ Evaluating	20	.633	.237				
	42	.642	.201				
	65	.624	.240				
	80	.616	.072				
Flexibility	21	.485	.267				
	43	.444	.130				
	66	.434	.104				
	47	.463	.202				

where

r_z = the Fisher Z transformation of the correlation

standard error of r_z = the standard error of the Z transformed correlation or

$$\frac{1}{(N-3)^{.5}}$$

In this case N is 652.

Stated differently, given the sample size of 652, a correlation of .15 is significant at $p < .0005$. However, there are 92 items on the questionnaire. According to Winer, Brown, and Michels (1991, pp. 154–155), the joint level of significance or alpha (joint) confidence for all 92 items, given an individual error rate of .0005, is as follows:

alpha (joint) = $1 - (1 - \text{alpha (individual)})^m$ where m is the number of variables in the set—in this case, 92.

Thus, alpha (joint) = $1 - (1 - .0005)^{92}$ = .045. Stated differently, considering any factor loading with an absolute value of .15 or greater as a viable constituent of a factor produces a joint level of significance of $p < .05$, the typically accepted criterion in the social sciences.

Technical Note 12: How We Computed Rank Orders for Responsibilities

We computed the rank order for each responsibility for each of the two primary factors reported in Figure TN11.2 (pp. 166–167). This was done by computing the average of the factor loadings for the items related to each responsibility. Given that factor loadings are analogous to correlations between an item and a factor, we first transformed the loadings using the Fisher Z transformation, computed the average, and then transformed back to the original metric.

Technical Note 13: The Standardized Mean Differences

One of the most commonly used indices of the impact of an independent variable (e.g., principal leadership) on a dependent variable (e.g., student academic achievement) is the standardized mean difference effect size, or *ES*. Actually, the generic term *effect size* applies to a variety of indices including *r*, *R,* and *PV*. However, as used in this book, *ES* means the standardized mean difference effect size. Glass (1976) first popularized this index, which is the difference between experimental and control means divided by an estimate of the population standard deviation—hence, the name, standardized mean difference.

$$\text{standardized mean difference effect size} = \frac{\text{mean of experimental group} - \text{mean of group control group}}{\text{estimate of population standard deviation}}$$

To illustrate the use of ES, assume that the achievement mean of a school with a given characteristic is 90 on a standardized test and the mean of a school that does not possess this characteristic is 80. Also assume that the population standard deviation is 10. The effect size would be as follows:

$$ES = \frac{90 - 80}{10} = 1.0$$

This effect size can be interpreted in the following way: The mean of the experimental group is 1.0 standard deviation larger than the mean of the control group. We might infer, then, that the characteristic possessed by the experimental school raises achievement test scores by one standard deviation. Thus, the effect size (ES) expresses the differences between means in standardized, or "Z score," form. It is this characteristic that gives rise to another index commonly used in the research on school effects—percentile gain.

Percentile gain, or *Pgain*, is the expected gain (or loss) in percentile points of the average student in the experimental group compared to the average student in the control group. To illustrate, consider the same example. Given an effect size (ES) of 1.0, we can conclude that the average score in the experimental group is about 34 percentile points higher than the average score in the control group. This is necessarily so because the ES translates the difference between experimental and control group means into Z score form. Distribution theory tells us that a Z score of 1.0 is at the 84.134 percentile point of the standard normal distribution. To compute the *Pgain*, then, ES is transformed into percentile points above or below the 50th percentile point on the unit normal distribution.

Technical Note 14: The Impact of Staff Development on Effect Sizes for CSR Programs

The study by Borman and colleagues (2003) conducted a regression analysis using effect size as the dependent variable and a number of study features and program features as independent variables. One program feature included in the analysis was the extent to which programs offer staff development in support of the programs.

The weight (i.e., unstandardized partial regression weight) for this factor was –.09, which was the largest among the independent variables in this category. Given that the dependent variable was the standardized mean difference effect size (see Technical Note 13), this indicates that an increase of one standard deviation in staff development is associated with a .09 decrease in the effect size for a given CSR model after controlling for the other independent variables in the model. The probability for this independent variable was .088. Given that this value is greater than the traditionally accepted significance level of .05, Borman and his coauthors did not discuss it. However, given that current statistical theory supports the notion that absolute cut scores in probability levels should not be used as the sole criterion for considering a variable significant in a practical sense to the interpretation of a model (see Cohen, 1988; Harlow, Mulaik, & Steiger, 1997) and the importance of this factor to the discussion in Chapter 6, it is worthy of consideration. Specifically, a probability of .088 is not significant at the .05 level when a nondirectional null hypothesis is employed, but it is significant at the .05 level if a directional null hypothesis is used. Additionally, if the relationship reported in the Borman model represents a true relationship between CSR program characteristics and the effect size for a given CSR program, the implications are important. These implications are discussed in Chapter 6.

Appendix A: Reports Used in the Meta-Analysis

In all, we found 70 reports that met the criteria specified in Chapter 3. Two reports basically addressed the same study. Therefore, discussions of the meta-analysis in Chapters 1 through 7 refer to 69 studies. The 70 reports are listed here.

Andrews, R. L., & Soder, R. (1987, March). Principal leadership and student achievement. *Educational Leadership, 44*(6), 9–11.

Ayres, R. E. (1984). *The relationship between principal effectiveness and student achievement.* Unpublished doctoral dissertation, University of Missouri, Columbia.

Balcerek, E. B. (2000, May). *Principals' effective leadership practice in high performing and inadequately performing schools.* Unpublished doctoral dissertation, University of Tennessee, Knoxville.

Bamburg, J. D., & Andrews, R. (1991). School goals, principals and achievement. *School Effectiveness and School Improvement, 2*(3), 175–191.

Bedford, W. P., Jr. (1987). *Components of school climate and student achievement in Georgia middle schools.* Unpublished doctoral dissertation, University of Georgia.

Benoit, J. D. (1990). *Relationships between principal and teacher perceptions of principal instructional management and student achievement in selected Texas school districts with an emphasis on an index of effectiveness (school effectiveness).* Unpublished doctoral dissertation, New Mexico State University.

Berry, F. A. (1983). *Perceived leadership behavior of school principals in selected California public elementary schools with a high Hispanic student population and high or low sixth grade reading achievement scores.* Unpublished doctoral dissertation, University of the Pacific, Stockton, CA.

Blank, R. K. (1987). The role of principal as leader: Analysis of variation in leadership of urban high schools. *Journal of Educational Research, 81*(2), 69–80.

Braughton, R. D., & Riley, J. D. (1991, May). *The relationship between principals' knowledge of reading process and elementary school reading achievement.* (ERIC Document Reproduction Service No. ED341952)

Brookover, W. B., Schweitzer, J. H., Schneider, J. M., Beady, C. H., Flood, P. K., & Wisenbaker, J. M. (1978, Spring). Elementary school social climate and school achievement. *American Educational Research Journal, 15*(2), 301–318.

Brooks, F. K. (1986). *Relationships between school effectiveness and the perceptions of teachers on leadership effectiveness and school climate.* Unpublished doctoral dissertation, Memphis State University.

Cantu, M. M. I. (1994, May). *A study of principal instructional leadership behaviors manifested in successful and nonsuccessful urban elementary schools.* Unpublished doctoral dissertation, University of Texas at Austin.

Combs, M. W. (1982). *Perceptions of principal leadership behaviors related to the reading program in elementary schools with high and low student achievement.* Unpublished doctoral dissertation, University of Florida.

Crawford, J., Kimball, G., & Watson, P. (1985, March). *Causal modeling of school effects on achievement.* Paper presented at the annual meeting of the American Educational Research Association, Chicago, IL.

Crawford, J., & Watson, P. J. (1985, February). Schools make a difference: Within and between-school effects. *Journal of Research and Evaluation of the Oklahoma City Public Schools, 15*(8), 1–98.

Czaja, M. D. (1985). *The relationship of selected principals' motive patterns to school climate and school climate to effectiveness.* Unpublished doctoral dissertation, University of Texas at Austin.

Dixon, A. E., Jr. (1981). *The relationship of elementary principal leadership performance to reading achievement of students in two counties in California.* Unpublished doctoral dissertation, University of San Francisco.

Duggan, J. P. (1984). *The impact of differing principal supervisory communication styles on teacher and student outcomes (consensus, achievement, leadership).* Unpublished doctoral dissertation, Rutgers, The State University of New Jersey, New Brunswick.

Durr, M. T. (1986). *The effects of teachers' perceptions of principal performance on student cognitive gains.* Unpublished doctoral dissertation, Indiana University.

Edwards, P. I., Jr. (1984). *Perceived leadership behaviors and demographic characteristics of principals as they relate to student reading achievement in elementary schools.* Unpublished doctoral dissertation, University of South Florida.

Erpelding, C. J. (1999). *School vision, teacher autonomy, school climate, and student achievement in elementary schools.* Unpublished doctoral dissertation, University of Northern Iowa.

Ewing, T. M. (2001, December). *Accountable leadership: The relationship of principal leadership style and student achievement in urban elementary schools.* Unpublished doctoral dissertation, Northern Illinois University, DeKalb.

Finklea, C. W. (1997). *Principal leadership style and the effective school (secondary school principals).* Unpublished doctoral dissertation, University of South Carolina.

Floyd, J. E. (1999). *An investigation of the leadership style of principals and its relation to teachers' perceptions of school mission and student achievement.* Unpublished doctoral dissertation, North Carolina State University, Raleigh.

Friedkin, N. E., & Slater, M. R. (1994, April). School leadership and performance: A social network approach. *Sociology of Education, 67,* 139–157.

Gentile, M. (1997). *The relationship between middle school teachers' perceptions of school climate and reading and mathematics achievement.* Unpublished doctoral dissertation, Widener University, Chester, PA.

Griffin, G. D. (1996). *An examination of factors contributing to exemplary schools in an urban public school district in the Midwest (urban education).* Unpublished doctoral dissertation, Western Michigan University.

Hallinger, P., Bickman, L., & Davis, K. (1996, May). School context, principal leadership, and student reading achievement. *The Elementary School Journal, 96*(5), 527–549.

Hauser, B. B. (2001). *A comparison of principal perceiver themes between highly successful and less successful principals in a selection of public elementary schools in Kentucky.* Unpublished doctoral dissertation, University of Kentucky, Lexington.

Heck, R. H. (1992). Principals' instructional leadership and school performance: Implications for policy development. *Educational Evaluation and Policy Analysis, 14*(1), 21–34.

Heck, R. H., Larsen, T. J., & Marcoulides, G. A. (1990, May). Instructional leadership and school achievement validation of a causal model. *Educational Administration Quarterly, 26*(2), 94–125.

Heck, R. H., & Marcoulides, G. A. (1990). Examining contextual differences in the development of instructional leadership and school achievement. *The Urban Review, 22*(4), 247–265.

Hedges, B. J. (1998). *Transformational and transactional leadership and the school principal: An analysis of Catholic K–8 school principals (Catholic schools).* Unpublished doctoral dissertation, University of Maryland, College Park.

Hopkins-Layton, J. K. (1980). *The relationships between student achievement and the characteristics of perceived leadership behavior and teacher morale in minority, low socio-economic, and urban schools.* Unpublished doctoral dissertation, University of Houston.

Hurwitz, N. F. (2001). *The effects of elementary school principal instructional leadership on reading achievement in effective versus ineffective schools.* Unpublished doctoral dissertation, St. John's University, Jamaica, NY.

Jackson, S. A. C. (1982). *Instructional leadership behaviors that characterize schools that are effective for low socioeconomic urban black students.* Unpublished doctoral dissertation, Catholic University of America, Washington, DC.

Jones, P. A. (1987, May). *The relationship between principal behavior and student achievement in Canadian secondary schools.* Unpublished doctoral dissertation, Stanford University.

Knab, D. K. (1998). *Comparison of the leadership practices of principals of blue ribbon schools with principals of randomly selected schools.* Unpublished doctoral dissertation, American University.

Kolakowski, R. E. L. (2000). *Instructional leadership and home-school relations in high- and low-performing schools—SBM team perceptions.* Unpublished doctoral dissertation, University of Maryland, College Park.

Krug, F. S. (1986, May). *The relationship between the instructional management behavior of elementary school principals and student achievement.* Unpublished doctoral dissertation, University of San Francisco.

Krug, S. E. (1992, June). *Instructional leadership, school instructional climate, and student learning outcomes.* Project Report. Urbana, IL: National Center for School Leadership. (ERIC Document Reproduction Service No. ED359668)

LaFontaine, V. T. C. (1995). *Implementation of effective schools correlates by Bureau of Indian Affairs Elementary Pilot Schools: Staff perceptions and achievement scores (Native Americans).* Unpublished doctoral dissertation, University of North Dakota.

Larsen, T. J. (1984). *Identification of instructional leadership behaviors and the impact of their implementation on academic achievement (Effective Schools, High Achieving Schools; Los Angeles County, California)*. Unpublished doctoral dissertation, University of Colorado at Boulder.

Lee, C. M. (2001). *Teacher perceptions of factors impacting on student achievement in effective and less effective urban elementary schools*. Unpublished doctoral dissertation, Wayne State University, Detroit, MI.

Lewis, L. W., Jr. (1983). *Relationship between principals' leadership style and achievement scores of third-grade students from low-income families*. Unpublished doctoral dissertation, Duke University, Durham, NC.

Madison, T., Jr. (1988). *A correlational study of the leadership behavior of school principals and the reading achievement of sixth grade students from the low and upper social classes*. Unpublished doctoral dissertation, Georgia State University.

McCord, H. C. (1982). *Title I school principals' characteristics and behaviors and their relationship to student reading achievement*. Unpublished doctoral dissertation, Northern Illinois University, DeKalb.

McMahon-Dumas, C. E. (1981). *An investigation of the leadership styles and effectiveness dimensions of principals, and their relationship with reading gain scores of students in the Washington, D.C., public schools*. Unpublished doctoral dissertation, George Washington University, Washington, DC.

Meek, J. P. (1999). *Relationship between principal instructional leadership and student achievement outcomes in North Carolina public elementary schools*. Unpublished doctoral dissertation, North Carolina State University, Raleigh.

Morey, M. K. (1996). *The relationships among student science achievement, elementary science teaching efficacy, and school climate*. Unpublished doctoral dissertation, Illinois State University.

Norvell, C. A. (1984). *Characteristics of perceived leadership, job satisfaction, and central life interests in high-achieving, low-achieving, and improving Chapter I schools (Los Angeles, California)*. Unpublished doctoral dissertation, University of California, Los Angeles.

O'Day, K. A. (1984). *The relationship between principal and teacher perceptions of principal instructional management behavior and student achievement*. Unpublished doctoral dissertation, Northern Illinois University, DeKalb.

Pounder, D. G., & Ogawa, R. T. (1995, November). Leadership as an organization-wide phenomenon: Its impact on school performance. *Educational Administration Quarterly, 31*(4), 564–588.

Reed, D. E. (1987). *Organizational characteristics, principal leadership behavior and teacher job satisfaction: An investigation of the effects on student achievement.* Unpublished doctoral dissertation, University of Rochester.

Rigell, C. D. (1999, May). *Leadership behaviors of principals and student achievement.* Unpublished doctoral dissertation, University of Tennessee, Knoxville.

Ruzicska, J. K. (1989). *The relationships among principals' sense of efficacy, instructional leadership, and student achievement.* Unpublished doctoral dissertation, University of San Francisco.

Skilling, W. C. (1992). *A study of the relationship between middle school principal leadership behavior and seventh-grade student reading achievement.* Unpublished doctoral dissertation, Michigan State University.

Skrapits, V. A. (1986). *School leadership, interpersonal communication, teacher satisfaction, and student achievement.* Unpublished doctoral dissertation, Fordham University, Bronx, NY.

Smith, C. L. (1995). *Secondary principals: A study of relationships, leadership styles, and student achievement.* Unpublished doctoral dissertation, Wayne State University, Detroit, MI.

Smith, W. F., & Andrews, R. L. (1989). *Instructional leadership: How principals make a difference.* Alexandria, VA: Association of Supervision and Curriculum Development.

Soltis, G. J. (1987). *The relationship of a principal's leadership style in decision patterns to teacher perception of building leadership and to student learning.* Unpublished doctoral dissertation, Temple University, Philadelphia, PA.

Spirito, J. P. (1990). *The instructional leadership behaviors of principals in middle schools in California and the impact of their implementation on academic achievement (effective schools).* Unpublished doctoral dissertation, University of La Verne, Bakersfield, CA.

Standley, N. L. (1985). *Administrative style and student achievement: A correlational study.* Unpublished doctoral dissertation, Washington State University, Pullman, WA.

Thomas, M. D. (1997). *The relationship of teachers' perceptions of instructional leadership behaviors of principals in Virginia to student achievement levels.* Unpublished doctoral dissertation, Wilmington College, Delaware.

Traufler, V. J. (1992). *The relationship between student achievement and individual correlates of effective schools in selected schools of South Carolina.* Unpublished doctoral dissertation, University of South Carolina.

Van Zanten, R. C. (1988). *Leadership style of principals in effective urban elementary schools.* Unpublished doctoral dissertation, Seton Hall University, South Orange, NJ.

Vernotica, G. J. (1988). *Principal goal clarity and interaction behaviors on teacher and student outcomes in the elementary public schools of Newark, New Jersey.* Unpublished doctoral dissertation, Seton Hall University, South Orange, NJ.

Verona, G. S. (2001, May). *The influence of principal transformational leadership style on high school proficiency test results in New Jersey comprehensive and vocational-technical high schools.* Unpublished doctoral dissertation, Rutgers University, New Brunswick, NJ.

Walton, L. E. (1990). *The relationship of teachers' perceptions of school climate and principal competencies with the third-grade Georgia Criterion Referenced Test scores in rural Georgia elementary schools (rural schools).* Unpublished doctoral dissertation, Georgia State University.

Wolfson, E. (1980). *An investigation of the relationship between elementary principals' leadership styles and reading achievement of third and sixth grade students.* Unpublished doctoral dissertation, Hofstra University, Hempstead, NY.

Appendix B: Cotton's 25 Leadership Practices and the 21 Responsibilities

As described in Chapters 2 and 4, Cotton (2003) identified 25 leadership practices that were similar to our 21 responsibilities. This table compares Cotton's 25 practices with our 21 responsibilities.

Cotton's 25 Practices	21 Responsibilities
1. Safe and Orderly School Environment	• Order
2. Vision and Goals Focused on High Levels of Student Learning	• Focus • Optimizer
3. High Expectations for Student Learning	• Focus
4. Self-Confidence, Responsibility, and Perseverance	• Ideals/Beliefs • Optimizer
5. Visibility and Accessibility	• Input • Visibility
6. Positive and Supportive School Climate	• Culture
7. Communication and Interaction	• Communication • Relationship
8. Emotional and Interpersonal Support	• Relationship • Visibility
9. Parent and Community Outreach and Involvement	• Outreach

Cotton's 25 Practices	21 Responsibilities
10. Rituals, Ceremonies, and Other Symbolic Actions	• Contingent Rewards • Affirmation
11. Shared Leadership, Decision Making, and Staff Empowerment	• Input • Communication
12. Collaboration	• Culture
13. Instructional Leadership	• Knowledge of Curriculum, Instruction, & Assessment • Involvement in Curriculum, Instruction, & Assessment
14. Ongoing Pursuit of High Levels of Student Learning	• Focus • Optimizer
15. Norm of Continuous Improvement	• Focus • Intellectual Stimulation
16. Discussion of Instructional Issues	• Intellectual Stimulation
17. Classroom Observation and Feedback to Teachers	• Monitoring/Evaluating • Involvement in Curriculum, Instruction, & Assessment
18. Support of Teacher Autonomy	• Flexibility
19. Support of Risk Taking	• Change Agent
20. Professional Development Opportunities and Resources	• Resources
21. Protecting Instructional Time	• Discipline
22. Monitoring Student Progress and Sharing Findings	• Monitoring/Evaluating • Focus
23. Use of Student Progress Data for Program Improvement	• Monitoring/Evaluating
24. Recognition of Student and Staff Achievement	• Contingent Rewards • Affirmation
25. Role Modeling	• Knowledge of Curriculum, Instruction, & Assessment • Involvement in Curriculum, Instruction, & Assessment

References

Abelson, R. P. (1985). A variance explained paradox: When a little is a lot. *Psychological Bulletin, 97,* 166–169.

Anderson, J. R. (1983). *The architecture of cognition.* Cambridge, MA: Harvard University Press.

Argyris, C., & Schön, D. (1974). *Theory in practice. Increasing professional effectiveness.* San Francisco: Jossey-Bass.

Argyris, C., & Schön, D. (1978). *Organizational learning: A theory of action perspective.* Reading, MA: Addison-Wesley.

Bamburg, J., & Andrews, R. (1990). School goals, principals and achievement. *School Effectiveness and School Improvement, 2,* 175–191.

Bandura, A. (1997). *Self-efficacy: The exercise of control.* New York: W. H. Freeman.

Bass, B. M. (1981). *Stogdill's handbook of leadership: A survey of theory and research.* New York: Free Press.

Bass, B. M. (1985). *Leadership and performance beyond expectations.* New York: Free Press.

Bass, B. M. (1990). *Bass and Stogdill's handbook of leadership.* New York: Free Press.

Bass, B. M., & Avolio, B. J. (1994). *Improving organizational effectiveness through transformational leadership.* Thousand Oaks, CA: Sage.

Baugh, F. (2002). Correcting effect sizes for score reliability: A reminder that measurement and substantive issues are linked inextricably. *Educational and Psychological Measurement, 62*(2), 254–263.

Benecivenga, A. S., & Elias, M. J. (2003). Leading schools of excellence in academics, character, social-emotional development. *Bulletin 87*(637), 60–72.

Bennis, W. (2003). *On becoming a leader.* New York: Basic Books.

Bennis, W., & Nanus, B. (2003). *Leaders: Strategies for taking charge.* New York: Harper & Row.

Blanchard, K., Zigarmi, D., & Zigarmi, P. (1985). *Leadership and the one minute manager: Increasing effectiveness through situational leadership.* New York: William Morrow.

Blanchard, K. H., Carew, D., & Parisi-Carew, E. (1991). *The one minute manager builds high performing teams.* New York: William Morrow.

Blanchard, K. H., & Hersey, P. (1996, January). Great ideas revisited. *Training and Development, 50*(1), 42–47.

Blase, J., & Blase, J. (1999). Principals' instructional leadership and teacher development: Teachers' perspectives. *Educational Administration Quarterly, 35*(3), 349–380.

Blase, J., & Kirby, P. C. (2000). *Bringing out the best in teachers: What effective principals do* (2nd ed.). Thousand Oaks, CA: Corwin Press.

Block, P. (2003). *The answer to how is yes: Acting on what matters.* San Francisco: Berrett-Koehler.

Bloom, B. S. (1976). *Human characteristics and school learning.* New York: McGraw-Hill.

Borenstein, M., & Rothstein, H. (1999). *Comprehensive meta-analysis program.* Englewood, NJ: Brostat.

Borman, G. D., Hewes, G. M., Overman, L. T., & Brown, S. (2003). Comprehensive school reform and achievement: A meta-analysis. *Review of Educational Research, 73*(2), 125–230.

Bossert, S., Dwyer, D., Rowan, B., & Lee, G. (1982). The instructional management role of the principal. *Educational Administration Quarterly, 18,* 34–64.

Brookover, W. B., Beady, C., Flood, P., Schweitzer, J., & Wisenbaker, J. (1979a). *School social systems and student achievement: Schools can make a difference.* New York: Praeger.

Brookover, W. B., & Lezotte, L. W. (1979b). *Changes in school characteristics coincident with changes in student achievement.* East Lansing: Institute for Research on Teaching, Michigan State University. (ERIC Document Reproduction Service No. ED181005)

Brookover, W. B., Schweitzer, J. G., Schneider, J. M., Beady, C. H., Flood, P. K., & Wisenbaker, J. M. (1978). Elementary school social climate and school achievement. *American Educational Research Journal, 15,* 301–318.

Bryant, F. B., & Yarnold, P. R. (1995). Principal-component analysis and explanatory and confirmatory factor analysis. In L. G. Grimm & P. R. Yarnold (Eds.), *Reading and understanding multivariate statistics* (pp. 99–136). Washington, DC: American Psychological Association.

Buckingham, M., & Clifton, D. (2001). *Now, discover your strengths.* New York: Free Press.

Burns, J. M. (1978). *Leadership.* New York: Harper & Row.

Chubb, J. E., & Moe, T. M. (1990). *Politics, markets, and America's schools.* Washington, DC: Brookings Institute.

Clarke, P. (2000). *Learning schools, learning systems.* London: Continuum International Publishing Group.

Cohen, E., & Miller, R. (1980). Coordination and control of instruction in schools. *Pacific Sociological Review, 4,* 446–473.

Cohen, J. (1988). *Statistical power for the behavioral sciences.* Hillsdale, NJ: Erlbaum.

Cohen, J., & Cohen, P. (1975). *Applied multiple regression/correlation analysis for the behavioral sciences.* New York: John Wiley & Sons.

Collins, J. (2001). *Good to great.* New York: Harper Collins.

Comer, J. P. (1984). Home–school relationships as they affect the academic success of children. *Education and Urban Society, 16*(3), 323–337.

Comer, J. P. (1988). Educating poor minority children. *Scientific American, 259*(5), 42–48.

Comer, J. P. (2003). Transforming the lives of children. In M. J. Elias, H. Arnold, & C. S. Hussey (Eds.), *EQ + IQ = Best leadership practices for caring and successful schools* (pp. 11–22). Thousand Oaks, CA: Corwin Press.

Cooper, H. M., & Rosenthal, R. (1980). Statistical versus traditional procedures for summarizing research findings. *Psychological Bulletin, 87,* 442–449.

Cotton, K. (2003). *Principals and student achievement: What the research says.* Alexandria, VA: Association for Supervision and Curriculum Development.

Cottrell, D. (2002). *Monday morning leadership.* Dallas, TX: Cornerstone Leadership Institute.

Covey, S. (1991). The taproot of trust. *Executive Excellence, 8*(12), 3–4.

Covey, S. R. (1989). *The 7 habits of highly effective people: Powerful lessons in personal change.* New York: Simon & Schuster.

Covey, S. R. (1992). *Principle-centered leadership.* New York: Simon & Schuster.

Covey, S. R., Merrill, A. R., & Merrill, R. R. (1994). *First things first.* New York: Simon & Schuster.

Covington, M. V. (1992). *Making the grade: A self-worth perspective on motivation and school reform.* New York: Cambridge University Press.

Csikszentmihalyi, M. (1990). *Flow: The psychology of optimal experience.* New York: Harper & Row.

Cuban, L. (1987, July). *Constancy and change in schools (1880s to the present).* Paper presented at the conference on Restructuring Education, Keystone, CO.

Datnow, A., Borman, G. D., Stringfield, S., Overman, L. T., & Costellano, M. (2003). Comprehensive school reform in culturally diverse contexts: Implementation and outcomes from a four-year study. *Educational Evaluation and Policy Analysis, 25*(2), 142–170.

Deal, T. E., & Kennedy, A. A. (1983). Culture and school performance. *Educational Leadership, 40*(5), 14–15.

Deering, A., Dilts, R., & Russell, J. (2003). Leadership cults and culture. *Leader to Leader, 28,* 31–38.
Deming, W. E. (1986). *Out of crisis.* Cambridge, MA: MIT Center for Advanced Engineering.
De Pree, M. (1989). *Leadership is an art.* New York: Bantam Doubleday Dell.
Dochy, F., Segers, M., & Buehl, M. M. (1999). The relationship between assessment practices and outcomes of studies: The case of research on prior knowledge. *Review of Educational Research, 69*(2), 145–186.
Donmoyer, R. (1985). Cognitive anthropology and research on effective principals. *Educational Administration Quarterly, 22,* 31–57.
Downie, N. M., & Heath, R. U. (1965). *Basic statistical methods* (2nd ed.). New York: Harper & Row.
Drucker, P. (1974). *Management.* New York: Harper & Row.
DuFour, R. (1998). *Professional learning communities at work.* Alexandria, VA: Association for Supervision and Curriculum Development.
DuFour, R. (2004). What is a "professional learning community"? *Educational Leadership, 61*(8), 6–11.
Duke, D. (1982). Leadership functions and instructional effectiveness. *NASSP Bulletin, 66,* 5-9.
Duke, D., & Canady, L. (1991). *School policy.* New York: McGraw Hill.
Dwyer, D. (1986). Understanding the principal's contribution to instruction. *Peabody Journal of Education, 63,* 3–18.
Eberts, R., & Stone, J. (1988). Student achievement in public schools: Do principals make a difference? *Economics of Education Review, 7,* 291–299.
Ebmeier, H. (1991, April). *The development of an instrument for client-based principal formative evaluation.* Paper presented at the annual meeting of the American Educational Research Association, Chicago.
Edmonds, R. R. (1979a). *A discussion of the literature and issues related to effective schooling.* Cambridge, MA: Center for Urban Studies, Harvard Graduate School of Education.
Edmonds, R. R. (1979b, October). Effective schools for the urban poor. *Educational Leadership, 37,* 15–27.
Elmore, R. (2003). *Knowing the right thing to do: School improvement and performance-based accountability.* Washington, DC: NGA Center for Best Practices.
Elmore, R. F. (2000). *Building a new structure for school leadership.* New York: Albert Shanker Institute.
Elmore, R. F. (2002, January/February). The limits of change. *Harvard Educational Letter: Online Research.* Retrieved September 8, 2004, from http://www.edletter.org/past/issues/2002-jf/limitsofchange.shtml
Evans, L., & Teddlie, C. (1995). Facilitating change in schools. Is there one best style? *School Effectiveness and School Improvement, 6*(1), 1–22.
Fan, X. (2003). Two approaches for correcting correlation attenuation caused by measurement error: Implications for research practice. *Educational and Psychological Measurement, 63*(6), 915–930.
Fink, E., & Resnick, L. B. (2001). Developing principals as instructional leaders. *Phi Delta Kappan, 82*(8), 598–626.
Fraser, B. J., Walberg, H. J., Welch, W. W., & Hattie, J. A. (1987). Synthesis of educational productivity research [Special issue]. *International Journal of Educational Research, 11*(2), 145–252.
Friedkin, N. E., & Slater, M. R. (1994). School leadership and performance: A social network approach. *Sociology of Education, 67,* 139–157.
Fritz, R. (1984). *The path of least resistance: Learning to become the creative force in your own life.* New York: Fawcett Columbine.
Fruchter, B. (1954). *Introduction to factor analysis.* Princeton, NJ: D. Van Nostrand.
Fullan, M. (1993). *Change forces: Probing the depths of educational reform.* London: Falmer Press.
Fullan, M. (2001). *Leading in a culture of change.* San Francisco: Jossey-Bass.
Glasman, N., & Binianimov, I. (1981). Input-output analyses of schools. *Review of Educational Research, 51,* 509–539.
Glass, G. V. (1976). Primary, secondary, and meta-analyses of research. *Educational Researcher, 5,* 3–8.
Glass, G. V. (2000, January). *Meta-analysis at 25.* [Online]. Retrieved July 1, 2004, from http://glass.ed.asu.edu/gene/papers/meta25.html
Glass, G. V., McGaw, B., & Smith, M. L. (1981). *Meta-analysis in social research.* Beverly Hills, CA: Sage.
Glass, G. V., Willson, V. L., & Gottman, J. M. (1975). *Design and analysis of time-series experiments.* Boulder, CO: Colorado Associated University Press.

Glickman, C. D., Gordon, S. P., & Ross-Gordon, J. M. (1995). *Supervision of instruction: A developmental approach* (3rd ed.). Boston: Allyn & Bacon.

Goddard, R. D., Hoy, W. K., & Hoy, A. W. (2004). Collective efficacy beliefs: Theoretical developments, empirical evidence, and future directions. *Educational Researcher, 33*(3), 3–13.

Goleman, D., Boyatzis, R., & McKee, A. (2002). *Principal leadership: Realizing the power of emotional intelligence.* Boston: Harvard Business School Press.

Goodwin, B., Arens, S., Barley, Z. A., & Williams, J. (2002). *Understanding no child left behind: A report on the No Child Left Behind Act of 2001 & its implications for schools, communities & public support for education.* Aurora, CO: Mid-continent Research for Education and Learning.

Greenleaf, R. (1970). *The servant as leader.* Indianapolis: Robert K. Greenleaf Center for Servant-Leadership.

Greenleaf, R. (1977). *Servant leadership: A journey into the nature of legitimate power and greatness.* New York: Paulist Press.

Griffith, J. (2000). School climate as group evaluation and group consensus: Student and parent perceptions of the elementary school environment. *The Elementary School Journal, 101*(1), 35–61.

Hall, G. E., & Hord, S. M. (1987). *Change in schools: Facilitating the process.* Albany, NY: State University of New York Press.

Hall, G. E., & Loucks, S. F. (1978). A developmental model for determining whether the treatment is actually implemented. *American Educational Research Journal, 14*(3), 263–270.

Hall, G. E., Loucks, S. F., Rutherford, W. L., & Newlove, B. W. (1975). Levels of use of the innovation: A framework for analyzing innovation adoption. *Journal of Teacher Education, 26*(1), 52–56.

Hallinger, P., & Heck, R. H. (1998). Exploring the principal's contribution to school effectiveness: 1980–1995. *School Effectiveness and School Improvement, 9*(2), 157–191.

Hallinger, P., Murphy, M., Weil, M., Mesa, R. P., & Mitman, A. (1983). Identifying the specific practices, behaviors for principals. *NASSP Bulletin, 67*(463), 83–91.

Hallinger, P. H., & Heck, R. H. (1996). Reassessing the principal's role in school effectiveness: A review of the empirical research, 1980–1995. *Educational Administration Quarterly, 32*(1), 5–44.

Hanson, M. (2001). Institutional theory and educational change. *Educational Administration Quarterly, 37*(5), 637–661.

Harlow, L. L., Mulaik, S. A., & Steiger, J. H. C. (1997). *What if there were no significant tests?* Mahwah, NJ: Erlbaum.

Harter, S. (1999). *The construction of the self: A developmental perspective.* New York: Guilford Press.

Hattie, J. A. (1992). Measuring the effects of schooling. *Australian Journal of Education, 36*(1), 5–13.

Heck, R., Larsen, T., & Marcoulides, G. (1990, April). *Principal leadership and school achievement. Validation of a causal model.* Paper presented at the annual meeting of the American Educational Research Association, Boston.

Heck, R. H. (1992). Principals' instructional leadership and school performance: Implications for policy development. *Educational Evaluation and Policy Analysis, 14*(1), 22–34.

Heck, R. H., & Hallinger, P. (1999). Next generation methods for the study of leadership and school improvement. In J. Murphy & K. S. Louis (Eds.), *Handbook of research on educational administration* (2nd ed., pp. 141–162). San Francisco: Jossey-Bass.

Hedges, L. V., & Olkin, I. (1985). *Statistical methods for meta-analysis.* Orlando, FL: Academic Press.

Heifetz, R. A. (1994). *Leadership without easy answers.* Cambridge, MA: Belknap Press of Harvard University Press.

Heifetz, R. A., & Laurie, D. L. (2001). The work of leadership. *Harvard Business Review, 79*(11), 131–140.

Heifetz, R. A., & Linsky, M. (2002a). *Leadership on the line: Staying alive through the dangers of leading.* Boston: Harvard Business School Press.

Heifetz, R. A., & Linsky, M. (2002b). Leadership with an open heart. [Online]. Available: http://leadertoleader.org/leaderbooks/L2L/fall2002/heifetz.html

Herman, R., Aladjem, D., McMahon, P., Masem, E., Mulligan, I., O'Malley, A., et al. (1999). *An educator's guide to schoolwide reform.* Washington, DC: American Institutes for Research.

Hersey, P., Blanchard, K. H., & Johnson, D. E. (2001). *Management of organizational behavior: Leading human resources* (8th ed.). Englewood Cliffs, NJ: Prentice Hall.

High, R. M., & Achilles, C. M. (1986, April). *Principal influence in instructionally effective schools*. Paper presented at the 67th annual meeting of the American Educational Research Association, San Francisco.

Hill, P. T., & Guthrie, J. W. (1999). A new research paradigm for understanding (and improving) twenty-first century schooling. In J. Murphy & K. S. Louis (Eds.), *Handbook of research on educational administration* (2nd ed., pp. 511–524). San Francisco: Jossey-Bass.

Hirsch, E. D., Jr. (1996). *The schools we need and why we don't have them*. New York: Doubleday.

Hord, S. M., Rutherford, W. L., Huling-Austin, L., & Hall, G. E. (1987). *Taking charge of change*. Alexandria, VA: Association for Supervision and Curriculum Development.

Hunt, M. (1997). *How science takes stock: The story of meta-analysis*. New York: Russell Sage Foundation.

Hunter, J. E., & Schmidt, F. L. (1990a). Dichotomization of continuous variables: The implications for meta-analysis. *Journal of Applied Psychology, 73*(3), 334–349.

Hunter, J. E., & Schmidt, F. L. (1990b). *Methods of meta-analysis: Correcting error and bias in research findings*. Beverly Hills, CA: Sage.

Hunter, J. E., & Schmidt, F. L. (1994). Correcting for sources of artificial variation across studies. In H. Cooper & L. V. Hedges (Eds.), *The handbook of research synthesis* (pp. 323–336). New York: Russell Sage Foundation.

Hunter, M. (1984). Knowing, teaching, and supervising. In P. Hosford (Ed.), *Using what we know about teaching* (pp. 169–192). Alexandria, VA: Association for Supervision and Curriculum Development.

Jackson, G. B. (1978, April). *Methods for reviewing and integrating research in the social sciences*. (Final report to the National Science Foundation for Grant No. DIS 76-20309). Washington, DC: Research Group, George Washington University.

Jackson, G. B. (1980). Methods for integrative reviews. *Review of Educational Research, 50,* 438–460.

Jensen, A. R. (1980). *Bias in mental testing*. New York: Free Press.

Kaagan, S. S., & Markle, B. W. (1993). Leadership for learning. *Perspective, 5*(1), 1–16.

Kaplan, R., & Norton, D. (2004). Measuring the strategic readiness of intangible assets. *Harvard Business Review, 82*(2), 52–53.

Kelehear, Z. (2003). Mentoring the organization: Helping principals bring schools to higher levels of effectiveness. *Bulletin, 87*(637), 35–47.

Kouzes, J. M., & Posner, B. Z. (1999). *Encouraging the heart: A leaders' guide to rewarding and recognizing others*. San Francisco, CA: Jossey-Bass.

Krug, F. S. (1986, May). *The relationship between the instructional management behavior of elementary school principals and student achievement*. Unpublished doctoral dissertation, University of San Francisco.

Krug, S. E. (1992, June). *Instructional leadership, school instructional climate, and student learning outcomes*. Project Report. Urbana, IL: National Center for School Leadership. (ERIC Document Reproduction Service No. ED359668)

Lashway, L. (2001). Leadership for accountability. *Research Roundup, 17*(3), 1–14. Eugene, OR: Clearinghouse on Education Policy & Management.

Leithwood, K. (1994). Leadership for school restructuring. *Educational Administration Quarterly, 30*(4), 498–518.

Leithwood, K., Jantzi, D., & Steinbach, R. (1999). *Changing leadership for changing times*. Philadelphia: Open University Press.

Leithwood, K., Louis, K. S., Andersen, S., & Wahlstrom, K. (2004). *How leadership influences student learning: Review of research*. Minneapolis, MN: Center for Applied Research, University of Minnesota.

Leithwood, K. A., Begley, P. T., & Cousins, J. B. (1990). The nature, causes and consequences of principals' practices: An agenda for future research. *Journal of Educational Administration, 28*(4), 5–31.

Leithwood, K. A., & Riehl, C. (2003). *What do we already know about successful school leadership?* Paper presented at the annual meeting of the American Educational Research Association, Chicago.

Levine, D. U., & Lezotte, L. W. (1990). *Unusually effective schools: A review and analysis of research and practice*. Madison, WI: National Center for Effective Schools Research and Development.

Lipsey, M. W., & Wilson, D. B. (2001). *Practical meta-analysis*. Thousand Oaks, CA: Sage.

Loehlin, J. C. (1992). *Latent variable models: An introduction to factor, path and structural analysis* (2nd ed.). Hillsdale, NJ: Lawrence Erlbaum Associates, Inc.

Lou, Y., Abrami, P. C., Spence, J. C., Poulsen, C., Chambers, B., & d'Apollonia, S. (1996). Within-class grouping: A meta-analysis. *Review of Educational Research, 66*(4), 423–458.

Magnusson, D. (1966). *Test theory.* Reading, MA: Addison-Wesley.

Markus, H., & Ruvulo, A. (1990). Possible selves. Personalized representations of goals. In L. Pervin (Ed.), *Goal concepts in psychology* (pp. 211–241). Hillsdale, NJ: Lawrence Erlbaum.

Marzano, R. J. (1998). *A theory-based meta-analysis of research on instruction.* Aurora, CO: Mid-continent Research for Education and Learning. (ERIC Document Reproduction No. ED 427 087)

Marzano, R. J. (2000a). *A new era of school reform: Going where the research takes us.* Aurora, CO: Mid-continent Research for Education and Learning. (ERIC Document Reproduction Service No. ED454255)

Marzano, R. J. (2000b). *Transforming classroom grading.* Alexandria, VA: Association for Supervision and Curriculum Development.

Marzano, R. J. (2003). *What works in schools: Translating research into action.* Alexandria, VA: Association for Supervision and Curriculum Development.

Marzano, R. J. (2005). A tool for selecting the "right work" in your school. [Online]. http://www.marzanoandassociates.com/pdf/schooleffect_09.pdf.

Marzano, R. J., Gaddy, B. B., & Dean, C. (2000). *What works in classroom instruction?* Aurora, CO: Mid-continent Research for Education and Learning.

Marzano, R. J., Kendall, J. S., & Gaddy, B. B. (1999). *Essential knowledge: The debate over what American students should know.* Aurora, CO: Mid-continent Research for Education and Learning.

Marzano, R. J., Marzano, J. S., & Pickering, D. J. (2003). *Classroom management that works: Research-based strategies for every teacher.* Alexandria, VA: Association for Supervision and Curriculum Development.

Marzano, R. J., Paynter, D. E., & Doty, J. (2004). *The pathfinder project: Exploring the power of one.* Conifer, CO: Pathfinder Education.

Marzano, R. J., Pickering, D. J., & Pollock, J. E. (2001). *Classroom instruction that works: Research-based strategies for increasing student achievement.* Alexandria, VA: Association for Supervision and Curriculum Development.

Masaaki, I. (1986). *Kaizen: The key to Japan's competitive success.* New York: Random House.

Mayer, D. P., Mullens, J. E., Moore, M. T., & Ralph, J. (2000). *Monitoring school quality: An indicator's report.* Washington, DC: U.S. Department of Education, National Center for Education Statistics.

McDill, E., Rigsby, L., & Meyers, E. (1969). Educational climates of high schools: Their effects and sources. *American Journal of Sociology, 74,* 567–586.

Meehl, P. E. (1978). Theoretical risks and tabular asterisks: Sir Karl, Sir Ronald, and the slow progress of soft psychology. *Journal of Consulting and Clinical Psychology, 46,* 806–834.

Miller, S., & Sayre, K. (1986, April). *Case studies of affluent effective schools.* Paper presented at the annual meeting of the American Educational Research Association, San Francisco.

Mulaik, S. A. (1972). *The foundations of factor analysis.* New York: McGraw-Hill.

Murphy, J., & Hallinger, P. (1989). Equity as access to learning: Curricular and instructional differences. *Journal of Curriculum Studies, 21,* 129–149.

National Center for Education Statistics. (2002a). *Common core of data. Overview of public elementary and secondary schools and districts: School year 2001–02.* [Online]. Retrieved September 1, 2004, from http://nces.ed.gov/ccd

National Center for Education Statistics. (2002b). *Table 1: Projected number of participants in educational institutions, by level and control of institution.* Fall 2002. [Online]. Retrieved September 1, 2004, from http://www.nces.ed.gov/programs/digest/d02/tables/dt001.asp

National Education Goals Panel. (1994, August). *Data volume for the national education goals report, Vol. 1: National data.* Washington, DC: Author.

National Institute on Educational Governance, Finance, Policymaking, & Management. (1999). *Effective leaders for today's schools: Synthesis of a policy forum for educational leadership.* Washington, DC: United States Department of Education Office of Educational Research & Improvement.

Northwest Regional Educational Laboratory. (2000). *Catalog of school reform models* (2nd ed.). Portland, OR: Author.

Nunnelley, J. C., Whaley, J., Mull, R., & Hott, G. (2003). Brain compatible secondary schools: The visionary principal's role. *Bulletin, 87*(637), 48–59.

Oakes, J. (1989). Detracking schools: Early lessons from the field. *Phi Delta Kappan, 73,* 448–454.

Osborne, J. W. (2003). Effect sizes and disattenuation of correlation and regression coefficients: Lessons from educational psychology. *Practical Assessment, Research and Evaluation, 8*(11). [Online]. Retrieved December 29, 2003, from http://PAREonline.net/getvn.asp?v=8&n=11

Postlethwaite, N., & Ross, K. (1993). *Effective schools in reading: Implications for educational planners.* Den Haag, the Netherlands: International Association for the Evaluation of Educational Achievement.

Prestine, N. (1992). *Benchmarks of change: Assessing essential school restructuring efforts.* Paper presented at the annual meeting of the American Educational Research Association, San Francisco.

Purkey, S. C., & Smith, M. S. (1983). Effective schools: A review. *The Elementary School Journal, 83*(4), 427–452.

Reeves, D. B. (2004). *Assessing educational leaders.* Thousand Oaks, CA: Corwin Press.

Robinson, D. H. (2004). An interview with Gene V. Glass. *Educational Researcher, 33*(3), 26–30.

Rosenthal, R. (1991). *Meta-analytic procedures for social research* (Rev. ed.). Newbury Park, CA: Sage.

Rosenthal, R., & Rubin, D. B. (1982). A simple general purpose display of magnitude of experimental effects. *Journal of Educational Psychology, 74*(2), 166–169.

Rutter, M., Maughan, B., Mortimore, P., Ouston, J., & Smith, A. (1979). *Fifteen thousand hours: Secondary schools and their effects on children.* Cambridge, MA: Harvard University Press.

Sammons, P. (1999). *School effectiveness: Coming of age in the twenty-first century.* Lisse, the Netherlands: Swets and Zeitlinger.

Scheerens, J., & Bosker, R. (1997). *The foundations of educational effectiveness.* New York: Elsevier.

Schmoker, M. (2001). *The results handbook: Practical strategies from dramatically improved schools.* Alexandria, VA: Association for Supervision and Curriulum Development.

Scribner, J. P., Cockrell, K. S., Cockrell, D. H., & Valentine, J. W. (1999). Creating professional learning communities in schools through organizational learning: An evaluation of the school improvement process. *Educational Administration Quarterly, 35*(1), pp. 130–160.

Sergiovanni, T. J. (2004). Building a community of hope. *Educational Leadership, 61*(8), 33–38.

Silins, H. C., Mulford, W. R., & Zarins, S. (2002). Organizational learning and school change. *Educational Administration Quarterly, 38*(5), 613–642.

Smith, W. F., & Andrews, R. L. (1989). *Instructional leadership: How principals make a difference.* Alexandria, VA: Association for Supervision and Curriculum Development.

Sosik, J. J., & Dionne, S. D. (1997). Leadership styles and Deming's behavior factors. *Journal of Business and Psychology, 11*(4), 447–462.

Spillane, J. P., Halverson, R., & Diamond, J. B. (2001). Investigating school leadership practice: A distributed perspective. *Educational Researcher, 30*(3), 23–28.

Spillane, J. P., Halverson, R., & Diamond, J. B. (2003). *Distributed leadership: Towards a theory of school leadership practice.* The Distributed Leadership Study: Northwestern University.

Spillane, J. P., & Sherer, J. Z. (2004). *A distributed perspective on school leadership: Leadership practices as stretched over people and place.* The Distributed Leadership Study: Northwestern University.

Stein, M. K., & D'Amico, L. (2000). *How subjects matter in school leadership.* A paper presented at the annual meeting of the American Educational Research Association, New Orleans.

Stevens, J. P. (1986). *Applied multivariate statistics for the social sciences.* Hillsdale, NJ: Erlbaum.

Stevenson, H. W., & Stigler, J. W. (1992). *The learning gap: Why our schools are failing and what we can learn from Japanese and Chinese education.* New York: Simon & Schuster.

Supovitz, J. A. (2002). Developing communities of instructional practice. *Teachers College Record, 104*(8), 1591–1626.

Tangri, S., & Moles, O. (1987). Parents and the community. In V. Richardson-Koehler (Ed.), *Educators' handbook: A research perspective* (2nd ed., pp. 519–550). New York: Longman.

U.S. Census Bureau. (2002, March). *Income in 2001 by educational attainment for people 18 years old and over, by age, sex, and Hispanic origin.* [Online]. Retrieved September 1, 2004, from http://www.census.gov/population/socdemo/education/pp1-169/tab08.pdf

References

U.S. Congress, Senate Committee on Equal Educational Opportunity. (1970). *Toward equal educational opportunity.* Washington, DC: Government Printing Office.

U.S. Department of Education. (2002). *Comprehensive school reform program overview: (CSR) program guidance.* [Online]. Retrieved June 20, 2003. To find, go to http:/www.ed.gov/offices/chiefltr/html and search for comprehensive school reform.

Villani, C. J. (1996). *The interaction of leadership and climate in four suburban schools: Limits and possibilities.* Doctoral dissertation, Fordham University, New York. (UMI No. 9729612)

Wagner, T. (2002). *Making the grade: Reinventing America's schools.* New York: Routledge-Falmer.

Waldman, M. (1993). A theoretical consideration of leadership and TQM. *Leadership Quarterly, 4*(1), 65–79.

Wang, M. C., Haertel, G. D., & Walberg, H. J. (1993). Toward a knowledge base for school learning. *Review of Educational Research, 63*(3), 249–294.

Waters, J. T., Marzano, R. J., & McNulty, B. (2004a). Developing the science of educational leadership. *Spectrum: Journal of Research and Information, 22*(1), 4–13.

Waters, J. T., Marzano, R. J., & McNulty, B. (2004b). Leadership that sparks learning. *Educational Leadership, 81*(7), 48–51.

Whitaker, B. (1997). Instructional leadership and principal visibility. *The Clearing House, 70*(3), 155–156.

White, K. R. (1982). The relationship between socioeconomic status and academic achievement. *Psychological Bulletin, 91*(3), 461–481.

Wimpleberg, R., Teddlie, C., & Stringfield, S. (1989). Sensitivity to context: The past and future of effective schools research. *Educational Administration Quarterly, 25*(1), 82–107.

Winer, B. J., Brown, D. R., & Michels, K. M. (1991). *Statistical principles in experimental design* (3rd ed.). Boston, MA: McGraw-Hill.

Witziers, B., Bosker, R. J., & Kruger, M. L. (2003). Educational leadership and student achievement: The illusive search for an association. *Educational Administration Quarterly, 39*(3), 398–425.

Wright, S. (1960). Path coefficients and path regressions: Alternative or complementary concepts? *Biometrics, 16,* 189–202.

Youngs, P., & King, M. B. (2002). Principal leadership for professional development to build school capacity. *Educational Administration Quarterly, 38*(5), 643–670.

Index

Page references for figures are indicated with an *f* after the page number.

accomplishment recognition, 14, 45–46
accountability, 44
Achilles, C. M., 28
affirmation, responsibility of, 41–44, 101
Anderson, J. R., 11
Anderson, Stephen, 26–27
Andrews, Richard, 18
The Answer to How is Yes (Block), 19
anticipatory leadership, 60
Argyris, C., 66, 67, 73
assessment, responsibility of, 52–55, 106, 116, 118
assets, development and use of, 100, 102
Avolio, B. J., 14, 15

background knowledge, 95–96
the balcony view, 106–107
Bass, B. M., 4, 14, 15
On Becoming a Leader (Bennis), 19
beliefs/ideals, responsibility of, 51, 102, 119
Bennis, Warren, 19, 51
Blanchard, Kenneth, 17

Blase, J., 18, 56, 61
Block, Peter, 19–20
Borman, G. D., 78–80
Bosker, R. J., 6, 25–26, 32
Boyatzis, R., 102
Brookover, W. B., 88–89
Brown, S., 78–80
Buckingham, Marcus, 20, 46
buffering, responsibility of, 48
Burns, James, 13–14

change
    deep, 66
    first- and second-order, 65–75
    first-order, management of, 112–115, 113*f*
    incremental, 66
    second-order, management of, 120*f*, 122*f*
change agency, 15, 44–45, 73, 118
Change Forces (Fullan), 22
Clarke, P., 45, 67–68
classroom curriculum design, 92–94
classroom management, 90, 92
Clifton, Donald, 20, 46

climate, 88–89. *See also* environment, safe and orderly
Cockrell, D. H., 46, 48
Cockrell, K. S., 46, 48
college graduates, earning potential, 3
collegiality, 88–89
Collins, James, 20, 43, 101
Comer, J. P., 58, 77
communication
    in first- vs. second-order change management, 119
    principal leaders and, 46–47, 52, 58
    What Works in Schools model, 87
community, purposeful, 99–104
community involvement, 58, 87–88
Comprehensive School Reform (CSR) model, 77–81, 79*f*, 97
constructional transactional leadership, 14
contingent rewards, responsibility of, 45–46

continuous improvement, 16
Cooper, H. M., 9
correlation coefficients, interpreting, 124–129, 127f
Costellano, M., 80
Cotton, Kathleen, 24, 58
Cottrell, D., 43–44, 51–52
Covey, Stephen, 20–21
Cuban, L., 65–66, 68
culture
    of collegiality and professionalism, 88–89
    in first- vs. second-order change management, 119
    principal leaders and, 47–48, 73–74, 103
curriculum
    classroom design, 92–94
    first- vs. second-order change management, 116, 118
    leadership team involvement, 106
    principal leaders involvement, 52–55
    What Works in Schools model, 83–84

D'Amico, L., 53
Datnow, A., 80
Deal, T. E., 89
Deering, A., 49, 59, 60
delegating style of leadership, 18
Deming, Edward, 15–16
De Pree, M., 51, 52, 56
Dilts, R., 49, 59, 60
Dionne, S. D., 14, 15–16
Direct Instruction, 77
discipline, responsibility of, 48–49
Donmoyer, R., 6
Drucker, Peter, 16

earning potential, high school vs. college graduates, 3

"Educational Leadership and Student Achievement" (Witziers, Bosker and Kruger), 25–26, 32
efficacy, collective, 99, 101
Elias, M. J., 58
Elmore, Richard, 21–22, 48, 50, 54, 55, 58–59, 60, 76, 98
Engelmann, Siegfried, 77
environment, safe and orderly, 57–58, 88
evaluating and monitoring, responsibility of, 55–56, 118
Evans, L., 28
"Exploring the Principal's Contribution to School Effectiveness" (Hallinger and Heck), 24

feedback, 84–87. *See also* recognition of accomplishment
Fink, E., 61
First Things First (Covey), 21
flexibility, responsibility of, 49–50, 73, 106–107, 118
focus, responsibility of, 50–51
Fritz, R., 57, 67, 72
Fullan, M., 22, 44–45, 49, 50, 53, 54–55, 59, 67, 74

Gaddy, B. B., 83
Glass, Gene, 7, 9, 10, 11, 34, 35–36
Glickman, C. D., 18–19
goal eradication, 16
goal setting, 16, 50–51, 84–87, 100, 102
Goddard, R. D., 99
Goleman, D., 102
Good to Great (Collins), 101
Gordon, S. P., 18–19
governance, 87
Greenleaf, Robert, 16

Hallinger, P., 6, 19, 24
Hanson, M., 47

Hattie, J. A., 55, 84
Heck, R. H., 6, 24
Hedges, L. V., 68
Heifetz, Ronald, 22–23, 66, 67, 74, 106–107
Hersey, Paul, 17
Hewes, G. M., 78–80
High, R. M., 28
high school graduates, earning potential, 3
Hirsch, E. D., Jr., 83
home environment, 94–95
Hott, G., 46, 57, 60
How Science Takes Stock (Hunt), 7, 36
Hoy, A. W., 99
Hunt, M., 7
Hunter, J. E., 90

ideals/beliefs, responsibility of, 51, 102, 119
individual consideration, 14, 45–46
influence, idealized, 14
input, responsibility of, 51–52, 103–104, 121
instruction
    in first- vs. second-order change management, 116, 118
    leadership team involvement, 106
    principal leaders involvement, 52–55
    What Works in Schools model, 89–90, 91f
instructional leadership theory, 18–19
intellectual stimulation responsibility, 14, 52–53, 118

Jantzi, D., 18, 19

Kaagan, S. S., 53, 56
Kelehear, Z., 56
Kendall, J. S., 83

Kennedy, A. A., 89
King, M. B., 48, 51
Kirby, P. C., 56
Kouzes, J. M., 46
Kruger, M. L., 6, 25–26, 32

Lashway, L., 44, 49, 53, 57, 60
Leaders (Bennis and Nanus), 19
leadership. *See also* school leadership
  beliefs regarding, 4–6
  defined, 13
  effective, theories of, 19–23
  school effectiveness correlation, 5–6, 10–12, 11*f*
  synthesis of the research on, 23–27
Leadership Profile 360, Web site, vi
leadership styles
  anticipatory, 60
  delegating, 18
  instructional, 18–19
  participating, 17, 52
  selling, 17
  servant, 16–17
  situational, 17–18
  telling, 17
  total quality management, 15–16
  transformational/transactional, 13–15
leadership team, the
  distributed responsibilities, 106–107, 108–109*f*
  principal's responsibilities, support function, 117*f*
  second-order change management, 120f, 122f
  selection and development, 99–105
Leading in a Culture of Change (Fullan), 22
learned intelligence, 95–96

learning, single- and double-loop, 66–67
Leithwood, Kenneth, 15, 18, 19, 26–27, 47, 50
Linsky, Marty, 22–23, 106–107
Louis, Karen Seashore, 26–27

Madden, Nancy, 78
Making the Grade (Wagner), 100
management-by-exception, 14
Markle, B. W., 53, 56
Marzano, J. S., 90
Marzano, R. J., 82, 83, 84, 90
McGaw, B., 9
McKee, A., 102
McRel's Balanced Leadership Profile 360, Web site, vi
Meehl, P. E., 11
mental maps, 67
Mesa, R. P., 19
meta-analysis. *See also* principal leadership practices-student achievement meta-analysis
  correlation coefficients, interpreting, 124–129, 127*f*
  correlation computation methods, 133–147
  CSR models, 78
  general features, 7–9, 130–133, 132*f*
Mitman, A., 19
modeling, 14
Moles, O., 87
monitoring and evaluating, 55–56, 118
motivation, 14, 96–97
Mulford, W. R., 45, 51–52
Mull, R., 46, 57, 60
Murphy, M., 19

Nanus, B., 19
narrative reviews, 9

No Child Left Behind Act, 8
Nunnelley, J. C., 46, 57, 60

Olkin, I., 68
open education, 68
optimizer, responsibility of, 56–57, 73, 101, 118
order
  first- vs. second-order change management, 120
  principal leaders and, 57–58
  What Works in Schools model, 88
outreach, responsibility of, 58
Overman, L. T., 78–80

parent involvement, 87–88, 94–95
participating style of leadership, 17
participation, 87
participative style of leadership, 52
Pickering, D. J., 90
Posner, B. Z., 46
Prestine, N., 68
principal leaders,
  responsibilities of. *See also* school leadership
  affirmation, 41–44, 101
  assessment, involvement with and knowledge of, 52–55, 116, 118
  beliefs/ideals, 51, 102, 119
  categories resulting in positive affect, 24–25
  change agent, 44–45, 73, 118
  communication, 46–47
  contingent rewards, 45–46
  culture, 47–48, 73–74, 103
  curriculum, involvement with and knowledge of, 52–55, 116, 118

discipline, 48–49
evaluating and monitoring, 55–56, 118
first-order change management, 115–116
for first- vs. second-order change, 68–75
flexibility, 49–50, 73, 118
focus, 50–51
ideals/beliefs, 51, 102, 119
input, 51–52, 103–104
instruction, involvement with and knowledge of, 52–55, 116, 118
intellectual stimulation, 52–53, 118
listed, 71*f*
monitoring and evaluating, 55–56, 118
observable characteristics, 71*f*
optimizer, 56–57, 73, 101, 118
order, 57–58
outreach, 58
purposeful communities, establishing, 100–101, 115
relationships, 58–59, 103
resources, 59–60
in second-order change management, 116, 118–121
situational awareness, 60–61, 63–64, 103
student achievement correlation data, 42–43*f*, 61–64, 63*f*
visibility, 61, 102–103
principal leadership practices-student achievement meta-analysis. *See also* meta-analysis; school leadership-student achievement correlation

attenuation, correcting for, 33–34, 152–153
average correlation computation, 33, 149–152
characteristics of studies used, 29–30, 29*f*
conclusions, 38
confidence intervals, 153
correlation computation methods, 133–147
correlation distribution, 34–36, 35*f*
distinguishing features, 32–34, 147–149
leadership impact overall (correlation interpretation), 30–32, 31–32*f*, 147
meta-analysis criteria, 28–29
moderator variables, 36–37*f*, 36–38, 153–161, 154–159*f*
potential impact, 133–147
questionnaire, 162–164*f*
questionnaire factor analysis, 65, 161–168
studies used in meta-analysis, 171–177
Witziers meta-analysis compared, 32–34
Principals and Student Achievement (Cotton), 24
Principle-Centered Leadership (Covey), 21
principles, defined, 11–12
process in purposeful communities, 100, 103
professional development, 59–60, 80, 89, 169–170
professionalism, 88–89
protection, responsibility of, 48

recognition of accomplishment, 14, 45–46
Reeves, D. B., 54–55
Reglection-Growth (RG) model, 18
relationships, responsibility of, 58–59, 103
the research base, 1–12
research-based practices. *See* meta-analysis
Resnick, L. B., 61
resources, responsibility of, 59–60
Riehl, C., 47, 50
Rosenthal, R., 9
Ross-Gordon, J. M., 18–19
Russell, J., 49, 59, 60

safety, 88
Schön, D., 66, 67, 73
School Development Program, 77–78
school improvement plans. *See also* What Works in Schools model components
Comprehensive School Reform (CSR) model, 77–81, 79*f*, 97
professional development and, 80, 169–170
site-specific approaches, 81–82
school leadership, a plan for effective. *See also* principal leaders, responsibilities of
change-level determination, 112–114
conclusions, 121–122
the leadership team, 99–107, 108–109*f*, 117*f*, 120*f*, 122*f*
management of change initiative, 115–121
overview of process, 98
responsibilities distribution, 106–107, 108–109*f*
right work identification, 107, 109–112, 110–111*f*

school leadership-student achievement correlation. *See also* principal leadership practices-student achievement meta-analysis; student achievement
- Cotton's conclusion on, 25
- countries outside the U.S., 32–33
- by responsibility characteristic, 42–43f, 61–64, 63f
- synthesis of the research on, 6, 25–27

schools, effective vs. ineffective, 3–4, 4f, 129–130
Scribner, J. P., 46, 47
self-system theory, 96
selling style of leadership, 17
Sergiovanni, T. J., 101
servant leadership, 16–17
The 7 Habits of Highly Effective People (Covey), 21
Silins, H. C., 45, 51–52
situational awareness, responsibility of, 60–61, 63–64, 103
situational leadership theory, 17–18
Sizer, T., 68
Slavin, Robert, 78
Smith, M. L., 9
Smith, Wilma, 18
Sosik, J. J., 14, 15–16
Spillane, James, 23
standardized mean differences, 78–79, 168–169
standards movement, 83
Stein, M. K., 53
Steinbach, R., 18, 19
Stevenson, H. W., 83
Stigler, J. W., 83
Stringfield, S., 41, 80
student achievement. *See also* school leadership-student achievement correlation
- Comprehensive School Reform (CSR) model, 77–81, 79f
- effective vs. ineffective schools, 3–4, 4f
- estimating performance, 129–130

Success for All, 78
Supovitz, J. A., 52, 57

Tangri, S., 87
teams/teamwork, 15–16
Teddlie, C., 28, 41
telling style of leadership, 17
theory, defined, 11
total quality management (TQM), 15–16
transformational/transactional leadership, 13–15
trust building, 16

Valentine, J. W., 46, 48
visibility, responsibility of, 61, 102–103

Wagner, T., 100
Wahlstrom, Kyla, 26–27
Waldman, M., 15
Weil, M., 19
Whaley, J., 46, 57, 60
What Works in Schools (Marzano), 82
What Works in Schools model components
- background knowledge, 95–96
- classroom curriculum design, 92–94
- classroom management, 90, 92
- collegiality, 88–89
- community involvement, 87–88
- conclusions, 97
- curriculum, guaranteed and viable, 83–84
- environment, safe and orderly, 88
- factors, categories of, 82f, 110–111f
- feedback, effective, 84–86f, 84–87
- goals, challenging, 84–86f, 84–87
- home environment, 94–95
- instructional strategies, 89–90, 91f
- learned intelligence, 95–96
- motivation, 96–97
- parent involvement, 87–88, 94–95
- professionalism, 88–89
- report cards, standards-based, 84–86f
- safety, 88
- school-level factors, 82, 82f
- student-level factors, 82, 82f
- teacher-level factors, 82, 82f

What Works in Schools online survey, 109, 112, 114
Whitaker, B., 61
Wimpleberg, R., 41
Witziers, B., 6, 25–26, 32

Youngs, P., 48, 51

Zarins, S., 45, 51–52

About the Authors

Robert J. Marzano is a Senior Scholar at Mid-Continent Research for Education and Learning in Aurora, Colorado; an Associate Professor at Cardinal Stritch University in Milwaukee, Wisconsin; Vice President of Pathfinder Education, Inc.; and President of Marzano & Associates consulting firm in Centennial, Colorado. He has developed programs and practices used in K–12 classrooms that translate current research and theory in cognition into instructional methods. An internationally known trainer and speaker, Marzano has authored more than 20 books and 150 articles and chapters on topics such as reading and writing instruction, thinking skills, school effectiveness, restructuring, assessment, cognition, and standards implementation. Recent ASCD titles include *Building Background Knowledge for Academic Achievement* (2004); *Classroom Management That Works: Research Based Strategies for Every Teacher* (Marzano, Marzano, & Pickering, 2003); *What Works in Schools: Translating Research into Action* (2003); *A Handbook for Classroom Instruction That Works* (Marzano, Paynter, Pickering, & Gaddy, 2001); and *Classroom Instruction That Works: Research-Based Strategies for Increasing Student Achievement* (Marzano, Pickering, & Pollack, 2001). Additionally, Marzano headed a team of authors who developed *Dimensions of Learning* (ASCD, 1992). Another recent work is *The Pathfinder Project: Exploring the Power of One* (Pathfinder Education, 2003). Marzano received his B.A. in English from Iona College in New York, a M.Ed. in Reading/Language Arts from Seattle University, and a Ph.D. in Curriculum and

Instruction from the University of Washington. He can be contacted at 7127 South Danube Court, Centennial, CO 80016 USA. Phone: 303-796-7683. E-mail: robertjmarzano@aol.com.

Timothy Waters has served as CEO for Mid-continent Research for Education and Learning (McREL) since 1995; before that he worked for 23 years in public education, the last seven of which were as the superintendent of the Greeley, Colorado, school system. Waters serves on the Board of Directors of the National Education Knowledge Industry Association and is a past Commissioner of the Colorado Commission on Higher Education. He received his B.A. from the University of Denver, and his M.A. and Ed.D. from Arizona State University. Waters may be contacted at McREL, Suite 500, 2550 S. Parker Road, Aurora, CO 80014-1678. Phone: 303-632-5562. E-mail: twaters@mcrel.org.

Brian A. McNulty is Vice President of Field Services at McREL (Mid-continent Research for Education and Learning), responsible for coordinating McREL's consulting, training, and technical assistance and developing new programs and services to implement McREL's applied research and development. Prior to joining McREL, McNulty served as the Assistant Superintendent for Educational Services, Adams County School District 14, Commerce City, Colorado. He is a former Assistant Commissioner of Education at the Colorado Department of Education. McNulty has more than 30 years of experience in education; his areas of expertise include leadership development, school effectiveness and improvement, early childhood education, and special education. McNulty has published and lectured extensively in these areas. He received a Ph.D. in Special Education Administration and Public Administration from University of Denver. McNulty may be contacted at McREL, Suite 500, 2550 S. Parker Road, Aurora, CO 80014-1678. Phone: 303-632-5557. E-mail: bmcnulty@mcrel.org.

Related ASCD Resources

At the time of publication, the following ASCD resources were available; for the most up-to-date information about ASCD resources, go to www.ascd.org. ASCD stock numbers are noted in parentheses.

Networks
Visit the ASCD Web site (www.ascd.org) and search for "networks" for information about professional educators who have formed groups around topics like "Arts in Education," "Authentic Assessment," and "Brain-Based Compatible Learning." Look in the "Network Directory" for current facilitators' addresses and phone numbers.

Online Course
What Works in Schools: An Introduction by John Brown (#PD04OC36)

Print Products
Classroom Instruction That Works: Research-Based Strategies for Increasing Student Achievement Robert J. Marzano, Debra J. Pickering, Jane E. Pollock (#101010)

Classroom Management That Works: Research Based Strategies for Every Teacher Robert J. Marzano, Jana S. Marzano, Debra J. Pickering (#103027)

Doc: The Story of Dennis Littky and His Fight for a Better School Susan Kammeraad-Campbell (#105056)

From Standards to Success: A Guide for School Leaders Mark O'Shea (#105017)

Grading and Reporting Student Learning Robert J. Marzano and Tom Guskey (Professional Inquiry Kit; (#901061)

A Handbook for Classroom Instruction That Works Robert J. Marzano, Jennifer S. Norford, Diane E. Paynter, Debra J. Pickering, Barbara B. Gaddy (#101041)

How to Thrive as a Teacher Leader John Gabriel (#104150)

The New Principal's Fieldbook: Strategies for Success Pam Robbins and Harvey Alvy (#103019)

Promises Kept: Sustaining School and District Leadership in a Turbulent Era Steven Jay Gross (#101078)

What Works in Schools: Translating Research into Practice by Robert J. Marzano (#102271)

Videotapes
Classroom Management That Works: Sharing Rules and Procedures (Tape 1, #404039)
Classroom Management That Works: Developing Relationships (Tape 2; #404040)
Classroom Management That Works: Fostering Student Self-Management (Tape 3; #404041)
What Works in Schools: School-Level Factors with Robert J. Marzano (Tape 1; # 403048)
What Works in Schools: Teacher-Level Factors with Robert J. Marzano (Tape 2; #403049)
What Works in Schools: Student-Level Factors with Robert J. Marzano (Tape 3; #403050)

For more information, visit us on the World Wide Web (http://www.ascd.org), send an e-mail message to member@ascd.org, call the ASCD Service Center (1-800-933-ASCD or 703-578-9600, then press 2), send a fax to 703-575-5400, or write to Information Services, ASCD, 1703 N. Beauregard St., Alexandria, VA 22311-1714 USA.